THE MAN
BEHIND
THE CURTAIN

Also by Matt Palumbo

Debunk This!: Shattering Liberal Lies

Spygate: The Attempted Sabotage of Donald J. Trump

Dumb and Dumber: How Cuomo and de Blasio Ruined New York

INSIDE THE SECRET NETWORK
OF GEORGE SOROS

THE MAN
BEHIND
THE CURTAIN

Liberatio
Protocol

MATT PALUMBO

A LIBERATIO PROTOCOL BOOK
An Imprint of Post Hill Press
ISBN: 978-1-63758-332-6
ISBN (eBook): 978-1-63758-333-3

The Man Behind the Curtain:
Inside the Secret Network of George Soros
© 2022 by Matt Palumbo

Cover Design by Cody Corcoran

Post Hill Press
New York • Nashville
posthillpress.com

Published in the United States of America
1 2 3 4 5 6 7 8 9 10

For my parents

Table of Contents

Acknowledgments

What initially began as a single chapter expanding on George Soros' influence in Ukraine as outlined in Dan Bongino's book "Follow the Money" quickly ended up becoming an overview of every sphere of influence that Soros boasts. I had two goals when writing this book; to provide a biography of Soros that documents his lifetime of political meddling, and also to provide a reference guide to help anyone immediately identify Soros-backed organizations wherever they pop up.

First and foremost, I'm grateful to Dan for choosing me to write this book as the first for his new imprint. And as always, thanks to Post Hill Press' Anthony Ziccardi for always being immensely supportive of my writing projects.

As is the case with any book I have written recently, none of this would've been possible without help.

The Post Millennial's Mia Cathell was enormously helpful in reading and extensively editing early drafts of this book. Beth Baumann provided a good deal of help in assembling the book's appendix, which gives a comprehensive list of every significant organization Soros has ever touched. And lastly, thanks to my highly regarded friend Samuel Gautsch for accommodating some mild laziness and helping with formatting my footnotes.

The Origin of George Soros

"My goal is to become the conscience of the world"
—George Soros

There is quite simply no man in politics more influential than George Soros in terms of his wealth, his direct global sphere of influence, and his indirect influence from the political infrastructure he's built over his lifetime.

He boasts a net worth of $8.6 billion—which is what's left over after he donated more than $32 billion during his lifetime to his Open Society Foundations (OSF), the vehicle he uses to fuel his political influence. (Of note, when I make references to "Soros funding" any-thing, it's through his OSF.) No other billionaire has "donated" such a large percentage of their net worth according to *Forbes*, though such donations are largely for his own ideological benefit.

Without even knowing a single thing about Soros, a surface-level understanding of his circle can be gleaned simply by reading the list of guests at his third wedding ceremony back in 2013. They included World Bank President Jim Yong Kim, Estonian President Toomas Hendrick Ilves, Liberian President Ellen Johnson Sirleaf, Albanian Prime Minister Edi Rama, International Monetary Fund (IMF) Man-aging Director Christine Lagarde, California Governor Gavin New-som, and Nancy Pelosi, among others. Even Bono made an appear-ance—and that's not mentioning the other five hundred guests.[1]

Although most of the politically inclined are aware of Soros and his activities, he is at times Schrodinger's meddler, denying his in-fluence to some and boasting about it to others. One such case comes

---

1   Ablan, Jennifer, "Billionaire Soros Weds Consultant in Third Marriage," *Reuters*, September 21, 2013. https://www.reuters.com/article/us-soros-wedding/billionaire-soros-weds-consultant-in-third-marriage-idUSBRE-98J0XZ20130922

regarding Soros facilitating coups in the name of "democratization." In a 1995 profile in the *New Yorker*, Soros admits to the "subversive" mission of his network, and that it has required him to wear a "variety of masks." "I would say one thing in one country and another thing in another country," he said, laughing.[2]

When Georgia's President Eduard Shevardnadze was toppled Soros denied having anything to do with it, telling reporters on March 31, 2004: "Everything in Georgia was done by its people, not by me. I had nothing to do with it." He'd later tell the *Los Angeles Times* in July that "I'm delighted by what happened in Georgia, and I take great pride in having contributed to it."[3]

Elsewhere, it's common to see publications (especially those that have received funding from Soros) simply deny any accusations of Soros' influence and claim they're examples of "anti-Semitism" without paying any attention to whether the allegations against him are true (because they are).

Whether he wants us to know about it or not, his massive influence and seemingly omnipotent nature of Soros is something that took him a lifetime to achieve. Here is his story.

EARLY LIFE

An ethnic Jew, Soros was born in Budapest in 1930 and survived the Nazi occupation of Hungary before moving to the U.K. in 1947. The Nazi occupation of Hungary began on March 19, 1944, forcing Soros into hiding until being liberated by the Russians on January 12, 1945.[4]

In spring 1944, the Nazis ordered the creation of the Central Council of Hungarian Jews, which was tasked with communicating the wishes of the Nazis and local collaborating authorities to the Jewish community. The council included Jews who were aware of the Nazis' atrocities but believed that they would be exempted from them. And they were exempted from persecution—initially.

Soros was part of the Council before assuming a new identity. He recalled the experience in an interview with the *New Yorker*: "This was a profoundly important experience for me. My father said, 'You should go ahead and deliver [the summonses], but tell the people that

2   Bruck, Connie, "The World According to George Soros," *The New Yorker*, January 23, 1995. https://www.newyorker.com/magazine/1995/01/23/the-world-according-to-soros
3   Horowitz, David, and Richard Poe, *Shadow Party: How George Soros, Hillary Clinton, and Sixties Radicals Seized Control of the Democratic Party*. Nelson Incorporated, Thomas, 2007, page 21.
4   Soros, Tivadar, *Masquerade: The Incredible True Story of How George Soros' Father Outsmarted the Gestapo*. Arcade Books, New York, 2011, page viiii.

if they report they will be deported.' The reply from one man was 'I am a law-abiding citizen. They can't do anything to me.' I told my father, and that was an occasion for a lecture that there are times when you have laws that are immoral, and if you obey them you perish."[5]

George's father Tivadar recalled that after George's second day on the job, he returned home with a summons, to which Tivadar asked if George knew what it meant. George replied, "I can guess. They'll be interned." Tivadar then told him the Jewish Council has no right to give people orders like that, recalling in his memoir:

> "I tried to tell the people I called on not to obey" he [George] said, clearly disappointed that I wouldn't let him work anymore. He was beginning to enjoy his career as a courier: it was all a big adventure.[6]

Soros' biographer echoed similar sentiments, noting that "George had liked the excitement of being a courier but he obeyed his father without complaint." Soros would later cite this experience as a reason for disliking fellow Jews (for being collaborators), while exempting himself.[7]

During the Nazi occupation, Tivadar obtained papers giving his immediate family Christian identities. He decided to split up the family so that if one of them were outed as Jewish, the rest of the family had a chance of surviving.

After the family was split up for their own safety, Soros went to live as Sandor Kiss with a man named Baumbach, as arranged by his father. Baumbach was a friend of Tivadar, an official at the Ministry of Agriculture, and a Nazi collaborator. Baumbach played the role of Soros' godfather. Soros would never acknowledge the role that Baumbach played in likely saving his life, and he died anonymously in 1999. His identity was later revealed in 2018 as Miklós Prohászka.[8]

The "godfather" had the job of taking inventory of possessions seized from Jewish families—trips that Soros accompanied him on. During an interview Soros gave with *60 Minutes*,[9] host Steve Kroft asked, "My understanding is that you went...went out, in fact, and

5   Mead, Rebecca, "A Soros Survivor's Guide," *The New Yorker*, October 7, 2001. https://www.newyorker.com/magazine/2001/10/15/a-soros-survivors-guide
6   Soros, Tivadar, *Masquerade*, pages 12–13.
7   Horowitz and Poe, *The Shadow Party*, page 79.
8   Simons, Jake Wallace, "Revealed: The Hungarian 'Schindler' Who Saved George Soros from Nazi Death Squads During the Occupation by Hiding Him Behind a Cupboard," *Daily Mail*, November 26, 2018. https://www.dailymail.co.uk/news/article-6415189/Revealed-Hungarian-Schindler-hid-George-Soros-Gestapo-death-squads.html
9   "Charlton Heston/50,000 White Farmers/George Soros," *60 Minutes*, December 20, 1998.

helped in the confiscation of property from the Jews." A number of fact-checkers have attempted to debunk the implications of this interview by stating that Soros merely tagged along instead of actively participated in persecution—but Soros has no remorse even for doing that.

"I mean, that's—that sounds like an experience that would send lots of people to the psychiatric couch for many, many years. Was it difficult?" Kroft asked.

"Not, not at all. Not at all. Maybe as a child you don't...you don't see the connection. But it was—it created no—no problem at all," Soros said emotionlessly.

"No feeling of guilt," Kroft replied.

"No."

When asked how he couldn't sympathize with other Jews being persecuted, Soros sociopathically replied by noting the "humor" in how his behavior then is similar to his behavior now in finance, and then employed the old "just following orders" defense.

"Well, of course...I could be on the other side or I could be the one from whom the thing is being taken away. But there was no sense that I shouldn't be there, because that was—well, actually, in a funny way, it's just like in the markets—that if I weren't there—of course, I wasn't doing it, but somebody else would—would—would be taking it away anyhow. And it was the—whether I was there or not, I was only a spectator, the property was being taken away. So the—I had no role in taking away that property. So I had no sense of guilt."

A lack of conscience would later prove lucrative in the business world.

SOROS THE PHILOSOPHER

Soros has said that communism repelled him, but also told his father in 1946: "I'd like to go to Moscow and find out about communism. I mean that's where the power is. I'd like to learn more about it." His father advised him to go to London instead.[10]

Soros arrived in England in 1947 and became a student at the London School of Economics (LSE) where he would become acquainted with the philosophy of Karl Popper, who would have a profound influence on his own ideological development.

---

10   Horowitz and Poe, *The Shadow Party*, page 81.

It's Popper's 1945 book *The Open Society and Its Enemies* that Soros described as a "revelation"—and that his "Open Society Foundations" takes its name after. Soros said of the work: "It showed that fascism and communism have a lot in common, and they both stand in opposition to a different principle of social organization, the principle of open society."[11]

The book criticizes the ideologies that Popper believed led to both fascism and communism. Popper argued that totalitarianism came from those who favored what he called the "closed society"—a tribal world where social institutions are based on taboos. Claims to knowledge in the closed society are merely the presentation of one's version of reality. The contrasting "open society" encourages free thought, individualism, democracy, equality. One where individuals are, in Popper's words, "confronted with personal decisions" as opposed to tribal or collectivist ones.

Soros defines the open society as one where "nobody has a monopoly on truth; a society which is not dominated by the state or by any particular ideology, where minorities and minority opinions are respected."[12] He's also defined it in his book *Open Society: Reforming Global Capitalism* as: "stand[ing] for freedom, democracy, rule of law, human rights, social justice, and social responsibility as a universal idea."

Above all else, Soros is a globalist who believes that the world should be a "global community" as opposed to individual sovereign states. As early as 1998, Soros would name the U.S. as the primary opponent of "global institutions."[13]

According to *Philanthropy Daily*'s Eduardo Andino:

> For Soros, one of the most important takeaways from Popper's ideas is that no single philosophy or worldview is in possession of the truth. Groups need to let go of "their truth" and work for an open society. But then it follows that the open society becomes, by default, the regnant paradigm, the overarching "truth" by which members of the society must live. If that's the case, there is ultimately no room for diversity of thought and ways of life. Acceptance of individualism and a casting off

11   Soros, George, *Soros on Soros: Ahead of the Curve*, J. Wiley, New York, 1995, page 33.
12   Soros, George, *The Alchemy of Finance*, John Wiley & Sons, New York, 2003, page 381.
13   Bessner, Daniel, "The George Soros Philosophy—and Its Fatal Flaw," *The Guardian*, July 6, 2018. https://www.theguardian.com/news/2018/jul/06/the-george-soros-philosophy-and-its-fatal-flaw

of traditional customs becomes a prerequisite for membership, because everything else is "totalitarian." Thus, what presents itself as the best type of society for embracing different ways of life is in reality the beginning of the greatest uniformity.[14]

This is one of many ironies that you'll see in the contrast between Soros' claimed philosophy, and his actions. As I aim to make evident to the reader by the end of this book, Soros' efforts are not to uncover truth, but rather to disseminate his own narrative through his realm of influence to create the false reality needed to justify his political vision.

Soros acknowledges the optional nature of reality in his book *The Alchemy of Finance* (first published in 1987) when it comes to financial markets, and his observations there are applicable to the world of media manipulation. "We live in the real world, but our view of the world does not correspond to the real world," Soros wrote. "…Our view of the world is part of the real world—we are participants. And the gap between reality and our interpretation of it introduces an element of uncertainty into the real world."[15] He notes pages later "people base their actions not on reality but on their view of the world, and the two are not identical." [16]

He reiterated that point in his later book *In Defense of Open Society*: "There is only one objective reality, but there are as many different subjective views as there are thinking participants."[17]

The Soros conceptual framework is built upon what he calls the principle of fallibility and principle of reflexivity, both of which shine insight into the mind of a master propagandist.

Soros explains of the former term, "in situations that have thinking participants, their views of the world never perfectly correspond to the actual state of affairs. People can gain knowledge of individual facts, but when it comes to formulating theories or forming an overall view, their perspective is bound to be either biased or both."[18]

This is what makes propaganda so powerful. Because "The complexity of the world we live in exceeds our capacity to understand it," Soros explains. "Confronted by a reality of extreme com-

---

14   Andino, Eduardo, "George Soros, Karl Popper, and Ironies of the 'Open Society,'" *Philanthropy Daily*, March 7, 2017. https://www.philanthropydaily.com/george-soros-karl-popper-and-the-ironies-of-the-open-society/
15   Soros, George, *Alchemy of Finance*, page 6.
16   Ibid., page 8.
17   Soros, George, *In Defense of Open Society*, PublicAffairs, 2019, page 174.
18   Ibid., page 168–69.

plexity, we are obligated to resort to various methods of simplifica-
tion: generalizations, dichotomies, metaphors, decision rules, and
moral precepts, just to mention a few."[19] Has there been a single
leftist propaganda campaign in the past two decades that isn't predicated on this framework?

Soros calls the relationship between the mind and reality reflexivity. "I envision reflexivity as a feedback loop between the participants' understanding and the situation in which they participate and
I contend that the concept of reflexivity is crucial to understanding
situations that have thinking participants."[20] Soros was influenced by
Popper's work *The Logic of Scientific Discovery*, which argued that
empirical truth cannot be known with absolute certainty.[21]

Soros identifies three forms that reflexive interactions can take;
dynamic near-equilibrium, static far-from-equilibrium, and dynamic
far-from-equilibrium.[22]

In dynamic near-equilibrium, perception is close to reality and
critical thinking is encouraged. This is what Soros defines as open
societies. In static far-from equilibrium, perception and reality diverge wildly and depend on "tribal magic." Totalitarian states re-
side in this condition and can remain there for long periods of time,
Soros argues. In dynamic far-from-equilibrium, the gap between
reality and perception grows to a breaking point in which change
is forced to occur and reality undergoes a transformation. Soros
argues that societies in this state are susceptible to undergoing sudden radical transformations.

Soros lumps both these concepts together into what he calls the
"human uncertainty principle," a point where subjective and objective reality can meet through a change in subjective reality, or by a
change in objective reality triggered through the manipulative function (outside influence).[23]

These concepts made Soros a fortune in financial markets and
also influenced his political donations. "The trick for the investor, or
for the philanthropic backer of social revolutions," Duke University's
Barry Varela notes, "was to recognize when reflexivity had led perception and reality to diverge to the breaking point."[24]

---

19   Ibid., page 172.
20   Ibid., page 2.
21   Ibid., page 169.
22   Soros, George, *Alchemy of Finance*, page 382.
23   Dhakappa, Bhargav, "Soros's Theory of Fallibility, Reflexivity, and Human Uncertainty Principle," Indian Folk,
      April 8, 2018. https://indianfolk.com/soros-theory-fallibility-reflexivity-human-uncertainty-principle-academic/
24   "George Soros and the Founding of Central European University," Duke Stanford School of Public Policy, April
      9, 2007. https://cspcs.sanford.duke.edu/sites/default/files/SorosCEUOriginsfinal.pdf

Despite leading to the foundation of the philosophy that would guide him in business and politics, Soros described life in London as a "big letdown," recalling that at age seventeen, he was lonely and miserable with "very little money and very few connections."[25]

That would all change soon.

MOVE TO AMERICA

After earning a bachelor's (1951), master's (1954), and PhD (year unknown) from the London School of Economics, Soros worked at various merchant banks before heading to America in 1956.

Soros and his mentor Popper differed greatly in their views of America. Three years before his death in 1991, Popper reflected on his time in America with optimism; "It was my first trip to the United States in 1950 that made an optimist of me again. That first trip tore me forever out of a depression caused by the overwhelming influence of Marxism in postwar Europe. Since then I have been to America twenty or twenty-five times, and each time I have been more deeply impressed." Soros took a bleak view that has remained unchanged.

Soros arrived in New York after nine years in London with the sole goal of making money. He initially set himself a five-year deadline to save $500,000 (over $5 million in 2021 dollars), after which he planned to return to Europe. He told his biographer Michael T. Kaufman: "At the time I did not particularly care for the United States. I had acquired some British prejudices; you know, the States were, well, commercial, crass, and so on."[26]

He ended up becoming a U.S. Citizen instead in 1961,[27] but not because he warmed on the States. Soros wrote in his 2003 book *The Bubble of American Supremacy*: "Who would have thought sixty years ago, when Karl Popper wrote *Open Society and Its Enemies*, that the United States itself could pose a threat to open society? Yet that is exactly what is happening, both internally and externally."[28]

Soros' criticisms of America go back to our Declaration of Independence. In the same book, Soros argues that the principles contained within the Declaration "are not self-evident truths but arrangements necessitated by our inherently imperfect understanding."[29]

---

25 Soros, George, *In Defense of Open Society*, page 43.
26 Kaufman, Michael T., *George Soros: The Life and Times of a Messianic Billionaire*, Knopf, 2002, page 83.
27 Horowitz and Poe, *The Shadow Party*, page 72.
28 Ibid., page 73.
29 Ibid., page 69.

In 1959, Soros moved to Greenwich Village on Christopher Street. In 1961, he married and moved to a different part of the village and had a son in 1963.

Not much is known about the five years Soros spent there, or how intwined he was with the other intelligentsia there. The socialist Michael Harrington, whose book *The Other America* greatly influenced LBJ's Great Society, frequented the White House Tavern less than a half-block from Soros' apartment. Harrington served on the board of the League of Industrial Democracy in the early '60s, along with Aryeh Neier, whom Soros would later hire to lead his foundations network in 1993.[30]

Poet Allen Ginsberg, a radical whose activities got him placed on the FBI's "Dangerous Subversives" list in 1965, also frequented events in the village while Soros lived there. There's no proof that the two met during that time period, but by the mid-1980s, Ginsberg was a frequent guest at Soros' Fifth Avenue apartment and El Mirador estate on Long Island.[31]

SOROS THE HEDGE FUND MANAGER

Soros began a career in banking, eventually forming the offshore fund Double Eagle in 1969 with $4 million in investment, including $250,000 of his own money. Soros and his assistant Jim Rogers left that venture in 1973 to start Quantum Fund, which was managed by Soros Fund Management (established in 1970). While all the early shareholders are not publicly known, we do know that the extremely wealthy Rothschild family were among the investors.[32]

The fund would prove to be an immediate success and be responsible for Soros' massive fortune.

By 1981 the June issue of *Institutional Investor* called Soros the "world's greatest money manager," after he had doubled the size of his fund in a single year the year prior, leaving Soros with an estimated $100 million net worth. That ironically turned out to be the fund's worst-performing year (1981) since inception, though it wasn't until 1996 that the fund had another down year.

It was in 1992 that Soros would make his most infamous trade, breaking the Bank of England and making him £1 billion in the

---

30 Ibid., pages 84–85.
31 Ibid., page 86.
32 "Quantum Funds Plan," page archived on April 19, 2009. https://web.archive.org/web/20090419230308/http://www.quantumfundsonline.com:80/plan.asp

process (or £20 for every Englishperson). It was from this trade alone that Soros would become internationally famous (and infamous) in the financial world.

The stage for the trade was set by Britain joining the European Exchange Rate Mechanism (ERM) after its creation in March 1979, which was created to reduce variation in exchange rates among European countries by establishing fixed-exchange rates. This system was eventually succeeded by the euro.

Because Germany had the strongest economy in Europe, each country set its currency's value in terms of Deutschmarks, and exchange rates were set between the various countries' currencies and the Deutschmark within a range of plus or minus 6 percent of the agreed rate.

Maintaining that rate required central bankers to monitor currencies closely to intervene if necessary. People trade currencies every day, and they're exchanged for imports and exports, creating a supply and demand for various currencies. As a result, banks need to intervene to maintain the rate in light of this by using their foreign currency reserves to buy their own currency on the open market, by selling their own currency, or by increasing or decreasing interest rates.

Britain joined the ERM with an exchange rate of 2.95 marks per pound, allowing them a range of exchange rates between 2.78 and 3.13 marks to the pound. At this time, inflation was high and the country was also in a period of unsustainable economic growth, and there Soros saw an opportunity as the pound traded at the lower end of what is allowed. [33]

In 1992 Quantum Fund borrowed pounds and sold them for German marks (effectively shorting the pound, aiming to benefit on the difference when converting the marks back into pounds if/when they fall in value). By the end of the day, now known in the financial world as Black Wednesday, Soros had sold short £10 billion worth of pounds, putting extreme pressure on its value. The bet was that the British government wouldn't be able to maintain their commitment to value the pound without rising interest rates high enough to trigger a recession. The British government spent £27 billion in a day to support the pound, but gave up, conceding victory to Soros, who netted over a billion pounds in the process. [34]

33   Dhar, Rohin. "The Trade of the Century: When George Soros Broke the British Pound," Priceonomics, June 17, 2017. https://priceonomics.com/the-trade-of-the-century-when-george-soros-broke/

34   Ibid.

Such a trade isn't reflective of genius, but manipulation, and it came at a high cost. Britain, having exhausted its foreign currency reserves, increased interest rates from 10 percent to 12 percent—and the pound continued plummeting regardless. Britain left the ERM later that night.

The economic damage far exceeded Soros' gain, with U.K. export and import prices in pounds increasing by roughly 20 percent.[35] The economic turmoil Soros caused on Black Wednesday would also have an added political bonus for him in that it was a major contributing factor to U.K.'s Conservative Party losing to Labour in the 1997 general election in what would be Labour's largest victory in history.[36]

In almost an instant, Soros' Quantum Fund increased from $15 billion to $19 billion in value (of which Soros and his partners pocketed at least 20 percent, hence the profit of a billion pounds) when the pound was reintroduced on the open market, and only a few months later the fund would be worth $22 billion.[37]

Soros admits that when he bet against the sterling: "I was in effect taking money out of the pockets of British taxpayers. But if I had tried to take social consequences into account, it would have thrown off my risk-reward calculation, and my profits would've been refused."[38]

Soros isn't happy with being known as "the man who broke the bank of England," and blames it on his lack of denial to the press of what we know he did. He's also complained that the media exaggerated his role.[39] Regardless, that didn't stop him from repeating the strategy over and over.

Quantum was the leading offshore hedge fund the year of the infamous pound trade, and four of the six best-performing funds were those under the Soros Management umbrella.[40]

And he didn't stop there.

He wreaked similar havoc with the penning of a letter on June 9, 1993, which he sent to the *Times of London* arguing that

35   Bustos, Sebastian, and Martin Rotemberg, "Elasticity Pessimism: Economic Consequences of Black Wednesday," New York University, October 2018. https://wp.nyu.edu/mrotemberg/wp-content/uploads/sites/8049/2018/10/BR_UK_Devaluation_18_10_25.pdf
36   Elliott, Larry. "Black Wednesday, 20 Years On: A Bad Day for the Tories But Not for Britain," *The Guardian*, September 13, 2012. https://www.theguardian.com/business/2012/sep/13/black-wednesday-bad-day-conservatives
37   Devansh, Lathia, "How Soros Broke the British Pound," *The Economics Review*, October 16, 2018. https://theeconreview.com/2018/10/16/how-soros-broke-the-british-pound/
38   Horowitz and Poe, *The Shadow Party*, page 97.
39   Soros, George, *In Defense of Open Society*, page 66.
40   "Soros Fund Management LLC History," FundingUniverse, http://www.fundinguniverse.com/company-histories/soros-fund-management-llc-history/

the German mark was weak. He wrote: "I expect the mark to fall against all major currencies," which immediately triggered twenty-four hours of panic-selling, causing Soros' comment to become a self-fulfilling prophecy.[41] His theory of reflexivity had been vindicated.

He did this again on July 14, 1998, suggesting to the *Financial Times of London* that the Russian government should devalue the ruble by 15–25 percent, causing panic selling once again.[42]

Soros announced a short position against the U.S. dollar on CNN in May 2004 at a time when the dollar had already fallen to a four-year low against the euro, pushing it down even further.[43]

While it was not illegal, Soros also likely took a page out of Bobby Axelrod's playbook and shorted the markets in the aftermath of 9/11. On September 19, he spoke to a group of business leaders in Hong Kong and wouldn't divulge if his fund was short-selling U.S. assets but commented: "I don't think you can run markets on patriotic principles." Later, on CNN, Soros spoke out against military strikes on the Taliban, saying they would be bad for the markets (perhaps something he wanted to become yet another self-fulfilling prophecy).[44]

By 1993, Soros was taking in a paycheck that surpassed the GDP of forty-two member nations of the United Nations.[45]

Much of Soros' behavior thus far looks a lot like market manipulation, and it's an offense he has faced consequences for on other occasions. Soros had signed a consent decree with the SEC in 1979 after being charged with stock manipulation related to his purchase of American computer manufacturer Computer Sciences Corporation as it was about to issue new shares. The SEC alleges that Soros sold shares to push down the price of the new shares. Soros agreed to not engage in this kind of behavior in the future while admitting no wrongdoing.[46]

It wouldn't be until 2002 that Soros would run into troubles with authorities again when Soros was found guilty of insider trading following a fourteen-year investigation.

---

41   Horowitz and Poe, *The Shadow Party*, page 4.
42   Ibid., page 5.
43   Ibid.
44   Ibid., pages 10–11
45   Belec, Pierre, "Hedge Fund Managers Top Pay List," *Washington Post*, June 16, 1994. https://www.washington-post.com/archive/business/1994/06/16/hedge-fund-managers-top-pay-list/c55bf539-1cce-4dbd-9563-c976055a-5ea7/
46   Gilbert, Nick, "Soros Deal with SEC in 1979 on 'Manipulatio,'" *Financial News*, November 18, 2002. https://www.fnlondon.com/articles/soros-deal-with-sec-in-1979-on-20021118

Soros was accused of buying stakes worth $50 million in four formally state-owned French companies for his Quantum Endowment Fund in 1988. Specifically, Soros was accused of having obtained and traded on insider information before a corporate raid pushed up the stock price of Société Générale, which was privatized in 1987. He was fined €2.2 million, the amount he was accused of profiting from the trade, but that amount was later reduced to €940k on appeal, making his insider trade net profitable.

"I am astounded and dismayed by the court's ruling. I will appeal the decision to the highest level necessary," Soros said after the verdict. When it came to proving his innocence, Soros lost an appeal to France's highest court in 2006, and then took his appeal to the European Court of Human Rights (he actually claimed that fining him violated his human rights), which also shot down his appeal in 2011.[47] Given Soros' influence over the court (more on that in a later chapter), the rejection is strong evidence of his guilt.

By 2018, Soros Fund Management ranked second on the list of wealth generated for investors since inception for hedge funds (with $43.9 billion generated over that time period), beaten only by Ray Dalio's Bridgewater Associates ($57.8 billion).[48]

Someone who invested $1 million during Soros' hedge fund debut would've seen their fortune grow to an incredible $2 billion by 2011, the year he stopped managing outside money.[49]

We can all fantasize what we'd spend our fortune on if we saw such outsized gains. For Soros, the answer was what he considers "philanthropy," but everyone else can recognize as political influence, often for his own financial benefit.

SOROS THE PHILANTHROPIST

By the late 1970s, Soros' fund had reached $100 million in assets, and he amassed a personal fortune of $25 million.

Soros says it was at that point he realized he had enough money. "I determined after some reflection that I had enough money. After a great deal of thinking, I came to the conclusion that what really

---

47   Rushe, Dominic, "Soros Fails to Reverse Insider Dealing Conviction," *The Guardian*, October 6, 2011. https://www.theguardian.com/business/2011/oct/06/george-soros-insider-dealing-european-court-of-human-rights

48   Taub, Stephen, "The Best Hedge Fund Manager of All Time Is…" *Institutional Investor*, January 27, 2019. https://www.institutionalinvestor.com/article/b1cwhlb6z0963n/The-Best-Hedge-Fund-Manager-of-All-Time-Is

49   Sarwar, Siraj, "Is George Soros Still Good at Picking Stocks at the Age of 90?" *Yahoo!*, January 10, 2021. https://www.yahoo.com/now/george-soros-still-good-picking-161856536.html

mattered to me was the concept of an open society."[50] He then proceeded to grow his fortune 150-fold throughout the rest of his career.

Soros' first encounter with philanthropy was in London at the London School of Economics (LSE) when he tried to game the system and get some money from the Jewish Board of Guardians but was refused because he wasn't learning a trade. After breaking his leg during a temporary job at a railroad, Soros again tried to get some money from them, personally writing to the chairman of the board that he was sad they were "unwilling to help a young Jewish student who had broken his leg and was in need." Despite not meeting the trade school requirement, that letter got him charity. "Although I had deceived the foundation, I felt morally justified because they had investigated my case and did not find out I was lying,"[51] Soros reasoned.

Soros' first philanthropic effort was providing scholarships to black students living under apartheid at Cape Town University in 1979. In the '80s, Soros began directing his philanthropic influence toward Central and Eastern Europe, which were under the control of the Soviet Union at the time. According to one of Soros' Hungarian associates, this marked the first time that Communist authorities anywhere were met with resistance from the private sector on matters of social and cultural significance.

Soros created and named his philanthropic organization the Open Society Institute. Off to a slow start, Soros took an apprenticeship at Helsinki Watch, which later became Human Rights Watch (HRW), a group Soros would eventually donate $100 million to.[52] HRW cofounder Aryeh Neier would later serve as president of the Open Society Institute from 1993 to 2012. Soros credits Neier's tenure for the foundation, which was later renamed the Open Society Foundations, taking its modern form.[53]

In 1991, Soros wrote: "My original objective has been attained: the communist system is well and truly dead. My new objective is the establishment of an open society in its stead. That will be much harder to accomplish. Construction is always more laborious than destruction and much less fun."[54]

50   O'Mara, Richard, "Philanthropist's Ideas Rich in Irony Society: George Soros, the Capitalist's Capitalist, Says It's Time for Fairness," *Baltimore Sun*, December 16, 1998. https://www.baltimoresun.com/news/bs-xpm-1998-12-16-1998350085-story.html
51   Soros, George, *In Defense of Open Society*, page 45.
52   Ibid., page 48.
53   Ibid., page 62.
54   Soros, George, "Underwriting Democracy: Encouraging Free Enterprise and Democratic Reform Among the Soviets and in Eastern Europe," GeorgeSoros.com. https://www.georgesoros.com/wp-content/uploads/2017/10/underwriting_democracy-chap-7-2017_10_05.pdf

Many take a cynical view of the motives behind his philanthropy. In 1995, the *London Sunday Times* observed: "Soros investment funds did not pay taxes in the United States between 1969 and 1986, enjoying a 'free ride' that netted him and his investors billions of dollars. Until the American Tax Reform Act of 1986 was passed, Quantum Fund legally avoided paying a cent." The *Times* then noted that "All Soros's philanthropy began in 1987, the first year that he and his fund has to pay taxes. Charitable matters are tax deductible and Soros says his aim is to give away half his yearly income, the maximum he can deduct." While it was actually in 1979 that Soros began his philanthropy, his spike in contributions does begin in 1987. Soros' philanthropy rose from $3 million in 1987 to over $300 million a year by 1992.[55]

The *New Yorker*'s Connie Bruck said that Soros admitted to her that his philanthropy opened closed doors to political influence. Soros said when he first began giving out money in Central Europe, "People like the dictator in Romania, Iliescu, suddenly became very interested in seeing me...my influence increased."[56]

Soros is, in his own words, "both selfish and self-centered, and I have no qualms about acknowledging it."[57] He continues, "The activities of the OSF extend to every part of the globe and cover a wide range of subjects that even I am surprised by it. I am, of course, not the only one who is selfish and self-centered; most of us are. I am just more willing to admit it."

Journalist Neil Clark noted of Soros, that

> "the sad conclusion is that for all his liberal quoting of Popper, Soros deems a society 'open' not if it respects human rights and basic freedoms, but if it is 'open' for him and his associates to make money. And, indeed, Soros has made money in every country he has helped to prise 'open.' In Kosovo, for example, he has invested $50 million in an attempt to gain control of the Trepca mine complex, where there are vast reserves of gold, silver, lead and other minerals estimated to be worth in the region of $5 billion. He thus copied a pattern he has deployed to great effect over the

---

55   Horowitz and Poe, *The Shadow Party*, page 88.
56   Ibid., page 89.
57   Soros, George, *In Defense of Open Society*, page 40.

whole of eastern Europe: of advocating 'shock therapy' and 'economic reform,' then swooping in with his associates to buy valuable state assets at knock-down prices."[58]

In 2021, the left-leaning journalism nonprofit ProPublica (which receives just under 2 percent of its funding from Soros himself)[59] released a report that used fifteen years of confidential IRS records to calculate the effective tax rate that billionaires pay on their fortunes (which was low because unrealized capital gains aren't taxed). Among the billionaires named was Soros, who didn't pay a cent of income tax for three years in a row from 2016 to 2018 according to their report.

While the other billionaires listed in their report are extensively criticized, Soros only gets a brief mention, and immediate faux-rebuttal in the form of a quote from an OSF representative that "Between 2016 and 2018 George Soros lost money on his investments, therefore he did not owe federal income taxes in those years. Mr. Soros has long supported higher taxes for wealthy Americans."[60] A quick fact-check reveals that Soros Fund Management gained 5 percent in 2016,[61] 8.9 percent in 2017, and 0.8 percent in 2018.[62]

A more likely culprit for Soros' lack of tax burden (at least in 2017 and 2018) is his transfer of $18 billion of his own wealth to the OSF. That move guaranteed that those funds will be sheltered from the IRS forever in what one commentator called the "single biggest tax dodge in U.S. history, yet no one on the right or left seems to have raised an eyebrow."[63] The donation also allows Soros to deduct up to 20 percent of its market value on his personal taxes ($3.6 billion), which he can carry forward for five years, effectively giving him a double write-off (not paying taxes on future income while dodging deferred capital gains taxes on donated stock).

58 Clark, Neil, "NS Profile—George Soros," *New Statesman*, June 2, 2003. https://www.newstatesman.com/economics/economics/2014/04/ns-profile-george-soros

59 Engelberg, Stephen, "A Free Press Works for All of Us," ProPublica, August 16, 2018. https://www.propublica.org/article/a-free-press-works-for-all-of-us

60 Eisinger, Jesse, "The Secret IRS Files: Trove of Never-Before-Seen Records Reveal How the Wealthiest Avoid Income Tax," ProPublica, June 8, 2021. https://www.propublica.org/article/the-secret-irs-files-trove-of-never-before-seen-records-reveal-how-the-wealthiest-avoid-income-tax

61 Zuckerman, Gregory, and Juliet Chung, "Billionaire George Soros Lost Nearly $1 Billion in Weeks after Trump Election," *The Wall Street Journal*, January 13, 2017. https://www.wsj.com/articles/billionaire-george-soros-lost-nearly-1-billion-in-weeks-after-trump-election-1484227167

62 Chung and Dawn Lim, "Soros Fund's New Leader Upends Firm in Strategic Overhaul," *The Wall Street Journal*, April 24, 2019. https://www.wsj.com/articles/soros-funds-new-leader-upends-firm-in-strategic-overhaul-11556098200

63 Moore, Stephen, "George Soros's $18 Billion Tax Shelter," *The Wall Street Journal*, November 23, 2017. https://www.wsj.com/articles/george-soross-18-billion-tax-shelter-1511465095

Soros' initial meddling was in anticommunist activities, but he now says that he considers "market fundamentalism" and America itself to be greater threats than Marxism because Marxism has been discredited.[64] Amusingly, the only people who don't seem to agree that Marxism has been discredited are the exact kind of leftist ideologues that Soros funds.

His views evolved further from there; "Until recently, I was inveighing against market fundamentalism, which I considered a greater current threat than Marxism. Now I regard the idealogues of American supremacy as even more dangerous."[65]

Soros outlined his plans after the collapse of communism in "Underwriting Democracy," pointing to two major projects: the creation of Central European University and the creation of an international network "for the placement of East and Central European candidates as trainees in Western firms."

Soros approached the Hungarian government about setting up a foundation in 1984, which they approved. By the end of the 1980s, he'd established foundations in China, the USSR, Poland, Czechoslovakia, and Bulgaria.[66] In the 1990s, he'd direct his focus to Romania and the Ukraine.[67]

Soros' political and economic interests are intertwined more often than they're not, such as when he played a large role in shaping economic policy in Russia under Bill Clinton's administration.

Clinton dealt with Russia and former Soviet states through private back channels to circumvent State department procedures. He assembled a small team known as the "troika," which included the State Department's Strobe Talbott, Treasury's Lawrence Summers, and VP/internet inventor Al Gore. Talbott's position was elevated to chairman of a Super Committee on the former Soviet Union, earning him the de facto title of "Russian policy czar."[68]

Talbott turned to Soros for help because he was a businessman with experience in the region. Talbott would later tell the *New Yorker* in 1995 of Soros that "I would say that it [his foreign policy] is not identical to the foreign policy of the U.S. government—but it's compatible with it. It's like working with a friendly, allied, independent entity, if not a government. We try to synchronize our approach to the

64 Soros, George, *Alchemy of Finance*, page 10.
65 Ibid., page 15.
66 Ibid., page 4.
67 Soros, George, "Underwriting Democracy," page 4.
68 Horowitz and Poe, *The Shadow Party*, page 90.

former Communist countries with Germany, France, Great Britain—and with George Soros." He went on to describe Soros as "a national resource—indeed, a national treasure."[69]

Anne Williamson, who has been published widely on Soviet and Russian affairs, said,

> "The Clintons welcomed Soros with open arms. Soros performed services for the Clintons, and in return received wide latitude for his business ventures in the former Soviet bloc. Soros not only expanded his fortune under Bill and Hillary, but he also fit in with their countercultural zeitgeist. Through them, Soros found a public platform to espouse his wacky politics. With Bush in power, Soros no longer has that kind of influence. That's a big part of what's driving him crazy."[70]

Soros admitted as much in the 1995 PBS interview where he infamously showed no remorse for briefly working for the Nazis' Jewish Council in Hungary: "I like to influence policy. I was not able to get to George Bush [Senior]. But now I think I have succeeded with my influence…I do now have great access in [the Clinton] administration. There is no question about this. We actually work together as a team."[71]

Soros had begun positioning himself in 1989 when he funded Harvard economist Jeffrey Sachs to create an economic reform plan for Poland. Sachs ended up favoring economic "shock therapy"—removing all price controls, currency controls, trade restrictions, investment restrictions, and other barriers to instantly transition to capitalism. Poland implemented that plan in January 1990, causing immediate hyperinflation. Soros remarked that the transition was "very tough on the population, but people were willing to take a lot of pain in order to see real change."

After that, Soros and Sachs turned to Russia to persuade Mikhail Gorbachev to try the same policy in the Soviet Union, which he rejected. Soros would later undermine Gorbachev when he tried to secure loans from Western lenders by denouncing him in the press and arguing his reforms would fail. His attacks on Gorbachev in the West also imperiled Russia's access to foreign aid.[72]

---

69   Ibid.
70   Ibid.
71   Ibid., page 91.
72   Ibid., page 92.

Gorbachev's replacement, Boris Yeltsin, would prove to be more approving of the Soros-Sachs agenda, and he removed all price controls in January 1992, leading to inflation of 2,500 percent and an economic blowup. Corruption would also derail the needed transition to capitalism, with one scholar estimating that despite 57 percent of Russian firms being privatized, the state only received $3–5 billion in compensation for them as they were sold at a fraction of their true value to oligarchs. By 1996 a mere six Russian businessmen had controlled 60 percent of the nation's natural resources.[73]

The massive corruption was impossible to miss, as the *Washington Post*'s David Ignatius explained in a 1999 article:

> You can see the question rumbling toward Al Gore like a freight train in the night: What did the vice president know about the looting of Russia by organized crime, and why didn't he do more to stop it?
>
> That issue—what the heck, let's call it "Russiagate"—has come into sharper focus this month, thanks to some powerful reporting that has highlighted the lawlessness of modern Russia and the acquiescence of the Clinton administration in the process of decline and decay there.
>
> …..
>
> Also potentially troubling for Gore is evidence that the Russian central bank speculated with some of the roughly $20 billion the IMF has lent to Russia since 1992.
>
> ….
>
> What makes the Russian case so sad is that the Clinton administration may have squandered one of the most precious assets imaginable—which is the idealism and goodwill of the Russian people as they emerged from 70 years of Communist rule.

---

73   Ibid., page 93.

The Russia debacle may haunt us for generations.
Gore played a key role in that messy process, and
he has a lot of explaining to do.[74]

Sachs and Soros played a major role in influencing Russia in the 1990s. The U.S. Agency for International Development (US-AID) outsourced the job of overseeing Russia's economic transition to Harvard's Institute for International Development, which Sachs headed from 1995 to 1999. As such, Sachs and his team were official economic advisers to Yeltsin. They wielded so much influence over Yeltsin that he often enacted their reforms through presidential decree to avoid parliament—decrees that were sometimes drafted by Sachs and his team themselves.[75]

Sachs would later resign as director of the Institute in May 1999 amid a DOJ probe into the institute's Russia operations. Harvard shut down the Institute in January 2000, but not before it was hit with a DOJ lawsuit alleging misuse of USAID funds, which Harvard settled out of court for $26 million.[76]

While Soros insists that there was no corruption involved in his deals in Russia, he did invest in Russia's second-largest steel mill Novolipetsk Kombinat and in the Russian oil firm Sidanko as they were being privatized. He was joined in those purchases by Harvard Management Company, which invested its endowment fund. The bidding was closed to foreign investors, but Soros and Harvard Management were able to participate in the rigged auction by making their purchases through the Sputnik Fund, an investment fund tied to oligarch Vladimir Potanin.[77]

When Soros was asked in 1994 by a *New Republic* reporter to describe his power and influence in the former Soviet states, he replied, "Just write that the former Soviet Empire is now called the Soros Empire."[78]

By 1995, Soros says he completed "phase 1" of his agenda of "opening up closed societies." It was at that point that he moved on to phase two: making open societies more viable.[79] All the activities

74   Ignatius, David, "Who Robbed Russia? Did Al Gore Know About the Massive Lootings?" *The Washington Post*, August 25, 1999. https://www.washingtonpost.com/archive/opinions/1999/08/25/who-robbed-russia-did-al-gore-know-about-the-massive-lootings/8e1fc17a-19c0-48c7-93ad-873ec86e47af/
75   Ibid.
76   Horowitz and Poe, *The Shadow Party*, page 94.
77   Ibid., page 96.
78   Ibid., page 94.
79   Soros, George, *In Defense of Open Society*, page 74.

of his OSF up to that point had been concentrated internationally—it was now "time to do something at home."

Soros began reflecting on America and his perceived deficiencies of our society. He developed a strategic plan and then assembled a group of social philosophers to examine it that included Bard College President Leon Botstein and others. There were two ideas of his that came to the forefront: that market values had "penetrated into areas where they did not properly belong" and undermine professional values; and that fear has "stifled the critical process and gave rise to false dogmas characterized by prejudice and intolerance, which undermines the principles of the open society."[80]

He singles out two "problems" that are incredible to prioritize given all the problems in the modern world. They are that people aren't progressive enough on the issue of assisted suicide, and that society is too intolerant of drug use.[81]

Soros launched the Project on Death in America, which was the first project he used the media to amplify, relying on PBS's Bill Moyers, who drew heavily on work sponsored by Soros in a five-part TV series on death.[82]

Soros' own personal interests are arguably the dominant motivating factor behind everything he does. "In short, philanthropy had made me happy," Soros once wrote lines before admitting: "Clearly, I am no saint, nor do I aspire to be one."[83]

It's not until 2003 that Soros entered presidential politics, with the George W. Bush era causing him to go into overdrive in influencing both presidential elections and an array of left-wing organizations to permanently alter America's social fabric.

He claims that he has "made it a principle to pursue my self-interest in my business, subject only to legal and ethical limitations, and to serve the public interest as a public intellectual and philanthropist. If the two are in conflict, I make sure that the public interest prevails."[84]

The "self-interest" portion certainly is believable.

---

80   Ibid.
81   Ibid. page 75.
82   Ibid., pages 75–76.
83   Ibid., page 90.
84   Ibid., page 91.

George Soros, the 2020 Election, and the Biden White House

George Soros has long been involved in politics, but his foray into U.S. politics is relatively recent (in the context of the life of a nonagenarian). Rather than recede from the public eye during his twilight years, Soros has continued backing many progressive causes. "The bigger the danger, the bigger the threat, the more I feel engaged to confront it," Soros stated during the Trump presidency.

After giving over $5 billion to causes in Africa, Asia, and the former Soviet Bloc, Soros' first major interference in U.S. politics was during the administration of George W. Bush, whom he accused of being guided by a "supremacist ideology" when it came to U.S. power.

Soros contributed over $18 million toward opposing Bush in the 2004 election against John Kerry, according to the *New York Times*,[85] making him the biggest donor to 527 advocacy groups that election cycle. Soros personally estimates he spent over $27 million.[86]

Kerry and Bush were neck and neck in the polls, leaving Soros to publicly state that the presidential race was "too close for comfort," which he described at the time as "the most important election of my lifetime." In an op-ed for the *Independent*, Soros explained why he campaigned across America to put Kerry in the White House: "Under President Bush, America has lost its credibility as a champion of

---

85   Seelye, Katharine Q, "Anti-Bush Billionaire to Give More," *The New York Times*, September 24, 2004. https://www.nytimes.com/2004/09/29/politics/campaign/antibush-billionaire-to-give-more.html
86   Soros, George, "George Soros, Maintaining Political Interest," *NPR*, June 10, 2006. https://www.npr.org/templates/story/story.php?storyId=5476317

open society."[87] Soros reiterated that nobody is in possession of the "ultimate truth." "Leaders who claim to be in possession of the ultimate truth offer an escape from uncertainty," Soros wrote. "But that is a snare, because those leaders are bound to be wrong."

Bush had posited that offense was the best defense for the nation and Americans were safer at home because soldiers were fighting the terrorists abroad. The argument resonated with an electorate fearful of terrorism in the wake of the September 11 attacks, but Soros labeled Bush's call "a Siren's song" that was "exploiting the fears generated by 9/11." He urged that the country must "face reality instead of finding solace in false certainties." Soros argued that America's future as an open society depended on resisting the Siren's song.[88]

Soros asserted that "democracy cannot be imposed by military means" and terrorism cannot be fought by the use of military force alone. He believed that the war on terror was "an abstraction," arguing that the terrorists were "not all alike." Soros wrote that most of the men attacking American soldiers in Iraq "originally had nothing to do with [Al-Qaeda]" and had been "generated by the policies of the Bush administration."[89]

Soros pointed to a philosophical difference between the two contenders. He described the war on terror as "a one-dimensional presentation of reality" defined by Bush. Soros considered Bush single-minded while Kerry was nuanced. To Soros, the reelection of Bush meant the war on terror would never end. "The terrorists are invisible, therefore they can never disappear. It is our civil liberties that may disappear instead," Soros wrote.[90]

He gave $12.05 million toward Joint Victory Campaign 2004, and then $7 million to America Coming Together, $2.5 million to MoveOn.org's voter fund, $325k to the Young Voter Alliance, $325k to 21st Century Democrats, $300k to the Real Economy Group, and $250k to Democracy for America.[91]

$3 million was pledged to liberal think tank Center for American Progress, then led by John Podesta, who served as White House chief of staff during the Clinton years.

---

87   Soros, George, "Why I Have Campaigned Across America to Put John Kerry in the White House," *The Independent*, November 2, 2004. https://www.independent.co.uk/voices/commentators/george-soros-why-i-have-campaigned-across-america-to-put-john-kerry-in-the-white-house-18248.html
88   Ibid.
89   Ibid.
90   Ibid.
91   "George Soros Contributions to 527 Organizations, 2004 Cycle," OpenSecrets. https://www.opensecrets.org/527s/527indivsdetail.php?id=U0000000364&cycle=2004

Another one of the PACs he backed, America Coming Together (ACT), would later be slapped with the third-largest enforcement penalty in the history of the FEC (at the time) for using unrelated soft money to boost Kerry and other Democrats.[92]

The organizers of ACT and its executive committee members had close ties to the Democratic Party, including several prominent labor leaders such as ACT's chief executive officer Steve Rosenthal, former political director of the AFL-CIO; Andy Stern, president of the Service Employees International Union (SEIU); and Gina Glantz, assistant to the president of SEIU who also served as senior adviser to the campaign of Democrat Howard Dean. ACT's headquarters was also located in the same building in downtown Washington as the temporary headquarters of the Democratic National Committee. According to press reports, ACT was located on the fourth floor of the facility, while the DNC was located on the seventh and eighth floors.[93]

Both America Coming Together and MoveOn were 527 groups, tax-exempt organizations under Section 527 of the Internal Revenue Code that were entitled to receive unlimited contributions from individuals. Soros postured it as the wealthy financing political mobilization and grassroots discussion. In other words, what harm was done if a philanthropist tossed money to political outfits that sought to unseat Bush? In 2004, 527 groups became partisan spin-offs, a predictable consequence of placing new limitations on parties. Large donations to such groups' war chests to influence federal elections were able to buy influence with federal candidates, even if the organizations operated as independent entities.

In March 2002, Congress enacted the Bipartisan Campaign Reform Act (BCRA) to stop the injection of soft money into federal elections. Since the enactment of McCain-Feingold, as the campaign-finance law was also called, a number of political operatives and donors engaged in efforts to circumvent the act by using soft money to influence the 2004 presidential and congressional elections. The schemes involved the use of the so-called 527 groups as vehicles to raise and spend soft money.

McCain-Feingold blocked soft money from being poured into the national party committees, but it didn't stop funds from being

92   Vogel, Kenneth P., "Soros-Linked Group Hit with Large Fine," Politico, August 29, 2007. https://www.politico.com/story/2007/08/soros-linked-group-hit-with-huge-fine-005555
93   https://www.fec.gov/files/legal/murs/current/94122.pdf, page 10

sent outside the system. Party loyalists worked overtime to develop strategies to keep the soft money spigot open without also violating the complex new law.

In an op-ed column for the *Washington Post*, Soros described the BCRA as an attempt to limit the influence that special interests can gain by financing candidates and to level the playing field between the two parties, claiming that the contributions he made were "in that spirit."[94]

Soros maintained that both ACT and MoveOn were transparent and filed detailed and frequent reports with government regulators. He wrote that he contributed to independent organizations that by law, which minimized the ability to purchase influence in exchange for contributions, were forbidden to coordinate activities with political parties or candidates. Soros claimed that he was not seeking such influence. Soros maintained that his contributions were made in "the common interest," insisting that ACT was just working to register voters and MoveOn was engaging constituents in the national debate over Bush's policies.

Soros explained the "urgency" to defeat Bush during a speech before the National Press Club in October before the election. "I have never been heavily involved in partisan politics" he unironically began his speech, "but these are not normal times." The bulk of his speech was in opposition to Bush's foreign policy, particularly in Iraq.[95]

He told *USA Today* that defeating Bush is the "central focus" of his life, and that he'd spend the entirety of his fortune to remove Bush from office if his removal were a guarantee.[96] Days before the election, he commented that in the event of a Bush victory, "'I shall go into some kind of monastery to reflect...I will be asking what's wrong with us.'"[97]

Soros backed Obama back when he was running for Senate, holding a fundraiser at his New York home for his Illinois senate campaign in June 2004. Soros personally donated $60,000.[98] A spe-

94 Soros, George, "Why I Gave," GeorgeSoros.com (originally *The Washington Post*), December 5, 2003. https://www.georgesoros.com/2003/12/05/why-i-gave/
95 Soros, George, "George Soros: Why We Must Not Re-elect President Bush," CNS News, July 7, 2008. https://www.cnsnews.com/news/article/george-soros-why-we-must-not-re-elect-president-bush
96 Schweizer, Peter, *Do as I Say (Not as I Do): Profiles in Liberal Hypocrisy*, Doubleday, 2006, page 171.
97 Epstein, Edward, "Billionaire George Soros Fends Off Critics, Attacks Bush," *Rome News-Tribune*, October 29, 2004. https://www.northwestgeorgianews.com/billionaire-george-soros-fends-off-critics-attacks-bus-election/article_5af3b386-e062-5c81-ac85-0715a8838eb9.html
98 Malkin, Michelle, "A Soros Slush Fund," *New York Post*, August 20, 2008. https://nypost.com/2008/08/20/a-soros-slush-fund/

cial provision of the campaign-finance law allowed greater contributions to candidates who were running against millionaires. Four members of the Soros family had also donated to the Senate campaign, awarding Obama one of the richest Soros nods.

Two years later, Obama's campaign staff even asked to use Soros' offices on Hillary Clinton's home turf for meetings with prominent Democratic donors amid presidential musings.[99] Obama and the left-wing heavy hitters mingled one December 2006 afternoon in a midtown conference room that belonged to none other than Soros.[100]

The assembly of elites included investment banker Hassan Nemazee, Wall Street giant Blair Effron, private-equity powerhouse Mark Gallogly, and hedge-fund manager Orin Kramer. Most were considered big-time Kerry supporters in 2004, but all were uncommitted for 2008.

Robert Wolf, who would become the CEO of UBS Americas and later hold three presidential appointments under Obama, was also present and emerged as Obama's most copious cash collector, next to Soros, in the Big Apple. Known as Obama's chief Wall Street rainmaker, Wolf hosted high-dollar cocktail parties and soirées, harvested over $500,000 in the 2008 election cycle, and committed to raise the same in contributions for the reelection campaign.[101]

Obama's networking among Democratic donor circles helped to make the campaign's monstrous fundraising apparatus as daunting as Clinton's sphere of influence. The courtship of Wolf, a hungry newcomer ready to spend big bucks, was thanks to the Soros venue where Obama and Wolf met for the first time.

Soros was pictured behind Obama during a 2007 fundraiser event for his presidential campaign and would himself be a large donor.[102] White House visitor logs show that Soros paid Obama a visit during the first months of his administration on March 24 and 25.[103]

Soros waited until September 2012 to donate again to Obama, giving $1 million to PAC Priorities USA to back him and an additional $500k to two congressional super PACS, House Majority PAC and Majority PAC. The contributions were announced at a fund-

99   Healy, Patrick, "Obama Meets Party Donors in New York," *The New York Times*, December 5, 2006. https://www.nytimes.com/2006/12/05/us/politics/05obama.html

100   Ibid.

101   Williamson, Elizabeth, and Damian Paletta, "Robert Wolf, Obama Fundraiser and Adviser, Leaves UBS," *The Wall Street Journal*, July 19, 2012. https://www.wsj.com/articles/BL-WB-35257

102   Heilemann, John, "Money Chooses Sides," *New York Magazine*, April 13, 2007. https://nymag.com/news/politics/30634/

103   Javers, Eamon, "Soros, Gore among W.H. Visitors," Politico, October 30, 2009. https://www.politico.com/story/2009/10/soros-gore-among-wh-visitors-028950

raising luncheon headlined by Bill Clinton. Obama took the money despite his earlier opposition to the SCOTUS legalizing unlimited outside donations.

According to emails released by the State Department, Soros told a close Hillary Clinton ally in 2012 that he regretted backing Barack Obama over her in 2008 and praised Hillary for giving him an "open door" to discuss policy.[104]

Soros had publicly told the *New York Times* that Obama was his "greatest disappointment"—but this may not just be because Obama wasn't liberal enough for his liking. Instead, Soros complained that Obama "closed the door" on him after he secured the presidency.[105] "He made one phone call thanking me for my support, which was meant to last for five minutes, and I engaged him, and he had to spend another three minutes with me, so I dragged it out to eight minutes," Soros said.

Soros had previously complained to other financiers about Obama in 2010; "If this president can't do what we need, it is time to start looking somewhere else."[106]

Despite his criticisms, Soros still maintained influence when he could. White House visitor logs prove he met with Obama's controversial top adviser on ISIS, chief national security official Rob Malley, in October 2015.[107] Although the meeting in the Executive Office Building occurred before Malley's promotion, when he was named the ISIS czar several weeks later, the terrorist group was almost certainly the topic of discussion. At the time, Malley was Obama's "point man" leading the Middle East desk of the National Security Council before he was promoted in November to serve as the president's senior adviser for the counter-ISIS campaign.[108] Soros also sat on the International Crisis Group's board of trustees, pumping funds into the antiwar organization where Malley was the Middle East director before he was tapped by the Obama administration.

When Hillary Clinton, whose ear Soros did have, was the Democrat nominee, he ratcheted up spending once again. He donated $8

104   Cheney, Kyle, and Vogel, "Soros Regretted Supporting Obama in 2008, Clinton Emails Show," Politico, December 31, 2005. https://www.politico.com/story/2015/12/george-soros-hillary-clinton-emails-barack-obama-217272
105   O'Connor, Corrie, "Liberal Mega-Donor Soros Calls Obama His 'Greatest Disappointment,'" 710 KNUS https://710knus.com/content/all/liberal-mega-donor-soros-calls-obama-his-greatest-disappointment
106   Stein, Sam, "George Soros Tells Progressive Donors Obama Might Not Be the Best Investment," *Huffington Post*, November 17, 2010. https://www.huffpost.com/entry/george-soros-obama_n_785022
107   Scher, Brent, "George Soros Had White House Meeting with Obama's ISIS Czar," *The Washington Free Beacon*, March 1, 2016. https://freebeacon.com/national-security/george-soros-had-white-house-meeting-with-obamas-isis-czar/
108   Condon, Stephanie, "White House Appoints New ISIS Czar," *CBS News*, November 30, 2015. https://www.cbsnews.com/news/white-house-appoints-new-isis-czar/

million toward PACs backing Hillary in 2015 (most going toward Priorities USA Action),[109] and then an additional $12.6 million in 2016 to PACs backing Hillary and congressional Democrats.[110]

The 2004 Take Back America Conference in Washington, D.C. was the first time Hillary Clinton and George Soros appeared together on the same stage. Hillary introduced Soros "Now, among the many people who have stood up and said 'I cannot sit idly by and watch this happen to the country I love,' is George Soros, and I have known George Soros for a long time now, and I first came across his work in the former Soviet Union, in Eastern Europe, when I was privileged to travel there, both on my own and with my husband on behalf of our country…we need more people like George Soros, who is fearless and willing to step up when it counts."[111]

Soros began the anti-Bush speech by stating how "very, very proud" he was to be introduced by Hillary, and revealed how intwined the two are. "I have a great, great admiration for her. I've seen her deliver a speech in Davos about open society that explained the ideas better than anybody else that I've heard. I've seen her visit Central Asia, where I have foundations, and she was very effective, more effective than most of our statesmen in propagating democracy, freedom, and open society."[112]

We don't know exactly when Hillary Clinton and Soros became acquainted, but they clearly have known each other for some time. Hillary has said the first time she became aware of Soros was through his work in the former USSR.

The Clintons hosted the new president of the Ukraine Leonid Kuchma at the White House on November 22, 1994, with press reports claiming that Soros was in attendance.

In November 1997, Hillary traveled to Central Asia to visit various former Soviet Republics. During the trip, she cut the ribbon for the opening of the Soros-backed American University of Kyrgyzstan, where she received the school's first honorary degree. She praised Soros and the Open Society Institute in her acceptance speech.[113]

Regurgitating the same language he employed against Bush, in an op-ed for *The Guardian*, Soros urged voters ahead of the 2016

---

109 Vogel, "George Soros Donates $8 Million to Boost Hillary," Politico, January 31, 2016. https://www.politico.com/story/2016/01/hillary-clinton-george-soros-218494

110 "Soros, George: Donor Detail." OpenSecrets. https://www.opensecrets.org/outsidespending/donor_detail.php?cycle=2016&id=U0000000364&type=I&super=N&name=Soros%2C+George

111 Horowitz and Poe, *The Shadow Party*, page 53.

112 Ibid., page 54.

113 Ibid., pages 54–55.

presidential election to "resist the siren song" of Trump and Texas Senator Ted Cruz, the leading two candidates in nationwide polls of the GOP primary.[114] Soros chastised how Republicans have framed the fight against jihadi terrorist groups and argued that fear is the greatest threat to open society, a recapitulation of his signature "open society" rhetoric. As for what would territorially decimate jihadi terrorist groups like ISIS, one year of the Trump presidency did the trick.

Soros poured more money into the 2020 election with the goal of defeating Trump than he spent in all prior U.S. elections combined. This was an election where "dark money" spending (political contributions in which the source of funding remains anonymous) topped $1 billion—and most of it to the benefit of Democrats.[115]

Giving his own personal spin to the "this is the most important election of our lifetimes" cliché, Soros told the World Economic Forum at Davos that the fate of the world was at stake in 2020. From the sidelines at an annual private dinner set during the conference that featured business and political leaders, Soros took aim at Trump, alleging that his "narcissism" has turned into "a malignant disease." The egoist who spends billions to influence global politics then blasted Trump, a fellow billionaire, as a "con man and narcissist who wants the world to revolve around him."[116]

On the rise of Trump and populism worldwide, Soros bemoaned that "everything that could go wrong, has gone wrong"[117] (which to normal people means that everything that could go right has gone right). Soros acknowledged in an interview with *The Washington Post* that he was surprised by Trump's election victory. "Apparently, I was living in my own bubble," Soros lamented the turn of events. Trump's own America First platform ran counter to the globalist agenda that Soros continues to push. Trump, he said, "is willing to destroy the world."

Soros created Democracy PAC in 2019 to serve as his vehicle to influence the 2020 election. It raised and spent $81 million toward

114 Soros, George, "The Terrorists and Demagogues Want Us to Be Scared. We Mustn't Give In," *The Guardian*, December 28, 2015. https://www.theguardian.com/commentisfree/2015/dec/28/terrorists-demagogues-scared-charlie-hebdo

115 Massoglia, Anna, and Karl Evers-Hillstrom, "'Dark Money' topped $1 Billion in 2020, Largely Boosting Democrats," OpenSecrets, March 17, 2021. https://www.opensecrets.org/news/2021/03/one-billion-dark-money-2020-electioncycle/

116 Schwartz, Brian, "George Soros Rips Trump and Xi, Says 'Fate of the World' is at Stake in 2020," CNBC, January 23, 2020. https://www.cnbc.com/2020/01/23/davos-2020-george-soros-says-china-leader-xi-is-trying-to-exploit-trumps-weaknesses.html

117 Caruso, Justin, "George Soros Complains: 'Everything That Could Go Wrong, Has Gone Wrong,'" *The Daily Caller*, June 9, 2018. https://dailycaller.com/2018/06/09/george-soros-go-wrong/

that goal, with $70 million of the funding coming from Soros himself.[118] That represents a tripling of his presidential election spending from 2016.[119] He initially planned to "only" double 2016 spending.[120] This came after Soros ramped up lobbying spending in 2019 to levels higher than what corporate giants Amazon, Facebook, Boeing, and Alphabet (Google's parent company) spent.[121]

Among the biggest recipients of funds included the Strategic Victory Fund ($3 million), Senate Majority PAC ($1.5 million), and Working Families Organization ($1 million), among others. Soros attempted to obscure the source of his donations by donating through a PAC instead of in his own name (though he did directly donate to some funds, including the DNC-led Democratic Grassroots Victory Fund, the Nancy Pelosi Victory Fund, and the Biden Victory Fund).[122]

Although this fact is obscured by Soros mostly donating to organizations via his PAC, if his contributions were counted as personal contributions, he would've been the largest individual backer of Biden. The arrangement allowed Soros to keep his name off the top of donor lists.[123]

Democrat victors who've benefited from Soros' wallet have railed against the influence of big money in the political sector. Biden's government reform plan promised to "reduce the corrupting influence of money in politics."[124] The president's campaign website urged that we "flush big money from the system and have public financing of our elections."

"Democracy works best when a big bank account or a large donor list are not prerequisites for office, and elected representatives come from all backgrounds, regardless of resources," Biden's plan to "guarantee government works for the people" read. "But for too long, special interests and corporations have skewed the policy process in their favor with political contributions."

118 "Democracy PAC PAC Profile," OpenSecrets. https://www.opensecrets.org/political-action-committees-pacs/democracy-pac/C00693382/summary/2020

119 Schoffstall, Joe, "Soros Triples Election Spending, Pouring $70 Million Into 2020 Efforts," *The Washington Free Beacon*, October 15, 2020. https://freebeacon.com/elections/soros-triples-election-spending-pouring-70-million-into-2020-efforts/

120 Kokai, Mitch, "Soros Plans to Double 2016 Election Spending," *The Locker Room*, July 7, 2020. https://lockerroom.johnlocke.org/2020/07/07/soros-plans-to-double-2016-election-spending/

121 Wilson, Megan R., "Lobbying Spending in 2019 Reached Second Highest Point of Decade," *Bloomberg Government*, January 24, 2020. https://about.bgov.com/news/lobbying-spending-in-2019-reached-second-highest-point-of-decade

122 Schoffstall, "Soros Pours Record $50 Million into 2020 Election," *The Washington Free Beacon*, July 27, 2020. https://freebeacon.com/elections/soros-pours-record-50-million-into-2020-election/

123 Ibid.

124 "The Biden Plan to Guarantee Government Works for the People," Biden Harris Democrats, https://joebiden.com/governmentreform/

Biden's talking points parroted those of Obama's final State of the Union address: "We have to reduce the influence of money in our politics, so that a handful of families or hidden interests can't bankroll our elections."[125]

Such anti-dark money rhetoric from Soros-backed buckraking candidates underlines the Democratic Party's hypocritical dependency on large contributions from billionaires. Democrats have long understood and engaged in the battle for cash, perpetuating money's importance in signaling any candidate's plausibility—thus electability in the establishment's eyes.

Soros and failed Democratic congressional candidate Scott Wallace helped to bankroll Heartland Fund, an intricate "fiscal sponsor" network. The collaborative effort targeted Midwestern voters by building "power across the divides of the American heartland." Trump had defeated Hillary Clinton in several Midwestern states that she was expected to carry in the 2016 election. The "neglected" region has since become a honey pot for deep-pocketed megadonors and liberal activist groups alike seeking to move money there.

The Open Society Foundations contributed $200,000 to the Heartland Fund for a one-year grant in 2019;[126] however, the contribution is not mentioned in the fund's press release on the collaboration, and the total amounts given by the groups are not known.[127]

Democrats also capitalized on the coronavirus crisis to expand sought-after government control of private lives and businesses. Priorities USA Action, the Democratic Party's largest super PAC, spent millions on advertisements that criticized Trump's response to the coronavirus pandemic in the battleground states of Pennsylvania, Michigan, Florida, and Wisconsin.[128]

A thirty-second television commercial produced by Priorities USA Action called "Exponential Threat" charted the rise in coronavirus cases and was overlaid with soundbites of Trump's initial pandemic-related comments. Another fifteen-second ad visualized

---

125   "Remarks of President Barack Obama—State of the Union Address as Delivered," The White House Archives, January 13, 2016. https://obamawhitehouse.archives.gov/the-press-office/2016/01/12/remarks-president-barack-obama-%E2%80%93-prepared-delivery-state-union-address

126   Schoffstall, "Soros, Wallace Help Bankroll Dark Money Fund Aimed at Midwestern Voters," The Washington Free Beacon, May 31, 2019. https://freebeacon.com/politics/soros-wallace-help-bankroll-dark-money-fund-aimed-at-midwestern-voters/

127   Williams, Tate, "The Progressive Funders Looking to Build Power Across Divides in the American Heartland," InsidePhilanthropy, April 18, 2019. https://www.insidephilanthropy.com/home/2019/4/18/the-progressive-funders-looking-to-build-power-across-divides-in-the-american-heartland

128   Schouten, Fredreka, "Democratic Group Launches $6 Million Campaign Attacking Trump on Coronavirus Response," CNN, March 23, 2020. https://www.cnn.com/2020/03/22/politics/priorities-usa-trump-coronavirus-attack-ads/index.html

the spread of COVID-19 cases across the United States, striking a similar anti-Trump theme. Two other hits, titled "Steady Leadership" and "Better Prepared," cast Biden as the remedy to "a White House in chaos."

In February 2020, Priorities USA Action super PAC received $3 million from Soros' own Democracy PAC, according to FEC records. The seven-figure donation accounted for 77 percent of the $3.9 million Priorities USA Action reported raising during that month.[129]

While supporting organizations that backed Biden directly, Soros also moved to boost organizations looking to change the rules of the game. As the Capital Research Center uncovered from IRS filings, Soros' funding vehicles sought to boost vote-by-mail and absentee voting. The Capital Research Center's (CRC) Scott Walter writes:

> The Brennan Center for Justice, heavily funded by Soros's Open Society, is spearheading a plan that calls for a "universal vote-by-mail option for all voters," or more precisely, absentee ballot initiatives. The newest portion of the plan involves "secure drop boxes in accessible locations for voters to drop off ballots directly."
>
> ....
>
> Voting by mail expands the chain of events involved in casting a ballot and radically expands the opportunities for fraudsters to tamper with the process. In 36 states, somebody else can legally deliver voters' ballots with their permission, usually a family member or attorney. But 13 states generally allow anybody to collect absentee ballots—with serious consequences.[130]

Under the circumstances of the pandemic, the Democrat Party was also able to prey on destabilization and panic to promote the vote-by-mail scheme.

---

129   Schoffstall, "Soros Bankrolls Coronavirus Attack Ads Against Trump," *The Washington Free Beacon*, March 24, 2020. https://freebeacon.com/elections/soros-bankrolls-coronavirus-attack-ads-against-trump/

130   Walter, Scott, "Soros Groups' Vote-by-Mail Drive Aims to Expand Government Control," *The Daily Signal*, July 10, 2020. https://www.dailysignal.com/2020/07/10/soros-groups-vote-by-mail-drive-aims-to-expand-government-control/

By the middle of 2020, Democrats had already managed to pass into law some absentee ballot provisions by hiding them in the coronavirus relief bill, a monstrous $2 trillion package Congress passed in late March. Nearly half of voters would end up voting by absentee or mail-in ballot in the 2020 election. An overwhelming number of votes by mail were cast for Biden. In key swing state Pennsylvania, 75 percent of mail-in ballots went to Biden.[131]

Although the vote-by-mail system appears to make voting easier for the harried, the disabled, and the elderly, it leaves the electoral process vulnerable to fraud. For example, a seventy-nine-year-old blind Nevada woman signed an affidavit attesting that her completed ballot had already been mailed without her consent when she requested in-person assistance. Clark County election officials maintained that her signature matched and that her vote had been cast. "I said, it couldn't match, because I didn't vote," she persisted, later sharing her story at a Trump press conference.[132]

Soros backed organizations pushing vote-by-mail. The donor network Way to Win launched a $59 million effort to encourage people of color to vote by mail in November and partnered with the Ford Foundation and Soros' Open Society for that goal.[133]

The Soros-funded Center for American Progress said that voting by mail "must become the default option for the vast majority of Americans" during the pandemic.[134]

The activist group Stand Up America, which is funded by the Sixteen Thirty Fund (which the Soros-funded Democracy Alliance recommended donors invest millions into) launched a nationwide campaign to urge Americans to demand Congress to make voting changes.

Described by the left-wing *Vox* as the "closest thing that exists to a left-wing conspiracy" in the U.S., the Democracy Alliance is a network of wealthy donors that enacted a $275 million spending blitz against Trump. The alliance's leader, Gara LaMarche, worked

131 Lai, Jonathan, "Joe Biden Won 3 of Every 4 Mail Ballots in Pennsylvania. Trump Won 2 of Every 3 Votes Cast in Person. What Does That Mean for the Future," *The Philadelphia Inquirer*, November 20, 2020. https://www.inquirer.com/politics/election/mail-ballots-pennsylvania-election-trump-biden-20201119.html

132 Charns, David, "'I'm Not Going to Have This Taken Away from Me,' Blind Woman from Nevada Told She Already Voted." 8NewsNow Las Vegas, November 2, 2020, https://www.8newsnow.com/i-team/i-team-im-not-going-to-have-this-taken-away-from-me-blind-woman-from-nevada-told-she-already-voted/

133 Slodysko, Brian, "Progressive Donor Group Announces $59M Vote-by-Mail Campaign," *Associated Press*, June 18, 2020. https://apnews.com/article/george-soros-nc-state-wire-elections-az-state-wire-racial-injustice-7515f532e065d46491f96cce1c333688

134 Root, Danielle, "States Should Embrace Vote by Mail and Early Voting to Protect Higher-Risk Populations from Coronavirus," Center for American Progress, May 14, 2020. https://www.americanprogress.org/issues/democracy/news/2020/05/14/485072/states-embrace-vote-mail-early-voting-protect-higher-risk-populations-coronavirus/

for Soros as the vice president and director of U.S. programs at the Open Society Institute.

Other Soros-funded organizations that pushed for mail-in voting included Common Cause and Public Citizen. Groups indirectly funded by Soros that made the push include the National Vote at Home Institute and National Association of Non-Partisan Reformers.[135]

It's just common sense that voting by mail would damage Trump. It's simultaneously the case that young people are the most likely to oppose Trump—while also being the least likely to actually turn up to vote in presidential elections. Naturally, giving this demographic the option to vote by checking a box at home and mailing it back would boost turnout for Biden. Or to make an even simpler argument, that voting by mail would help Biden is evidenced by the fact that 100 percent of those pushing for it are Democrats.

Of course, Soros-backed groups have argued otherwise. Back in 2011, before the modern push for mail-in voting, the Soros-funded Brennan Center produced a study aimed at combating then-new laws that would reduce voter fraud and strengthen election integrity.

The Brennan Center alleged that voting law changes "could make it significantly harder for more than five million eligible voters to cast ballots in 2012." Their sixty-four-page report claimed that the negative effects "fall most heavily on young, minority, and low-income voters, as well as on voters with disabilities."[136]

The price tag for the report totaled $10 million. Open Society Foundations gave the Brennan Center for Justice over $7 million from 2000 to 2010 and New York University was tossed almost $3 million during the same time period.[137]

The Soros-funded echo chamber then pushed the story toward progressive news sites that took it to the national stage. The narrative's promotion included members of the Media Consortium (which received $425k from the Open Society Foundations), The Nation (whose foundation received $77k from the OSF), and the OSF-funded blogs Campus Progress and Think Progress.[138]

---

135 Klein, Aaron, "Soros-Funded Group: Vote-by-Mail 'Must Become the Default Option,'" Breitbart, May 16, 2020. https://www.breitbart.com/2020-election/2020/05/16/soros-funded-group-vote-by-mail-must-become-the-default-option/
136 Somberg, Iris, "Soros-Backed Voting Study Promoted by Soros-Funded Media," mrcNewsBusters, October 6, 2011. https://www.newsbusters.org/blogs/nb/iris-somberg/2011/10/06/soros-backed-voting-study-promoted-soros-funded-media
137 Ibid.
138 Ibid.

TRANSITION INTEGRITY PROJECT

Like any good investor, Soros hedged his investment in fighting Trump.

In June 2020, the Transition Integrity Project (TIP) was spawned after initially being organized in late 2019. The stated purpose was to put together thought exercises to examine "possible disruptions" in the 2020 presidential election and transition, such as if Trump refused to concede.

Members were a who's who of leftists and never-Trumpers, such as former Clinton aide John Podesta, two-time acting Democratic National Committee Chair Donna Brazile, *The Bulwark*'s editor-at-large Bill Kristol, *Washington Post* columnist Max Boot, *Trumpocalypse: Restoring American Democracy* author David Frum, and others.

Despite the roster, the project claims to "take no position on how Americans should cast their votes." And because we have a dishonest media, they presented the group as such. Every source from NPR to CNN to "insert publication here" uncritically refers to them as "nonpartisan."

The group was founded by Rosa Brooks, a former special counsel to the president at the Open Society Institute.[139] Her connection to Soros remained after she left the OSF. As we learned from emails released by WikiLeaks, she attended a Soros dinner in 2015 and emailed Podesta about it afterward.[140]

Days after the inauguration in 2017, Brooks wrote an article titled outlining varying ways to oust Trump, "3 Ways to Get Rid of President Trump before 2020," where she proposed impeaching Trump without "actual" evidence of wrongdoing because "practically anything can be considered a high crime or misdemeanor," or "a military coup" suggesting that military leaders refuse to obey the commander-in-chief's orders.[141] Brooks later doubled down on the latter proposition in an op-ed for *Foreign Policy* magazine, invoking Revolutionary War-era tales of civil disobedience, resistance to authority, and uprising against a despotic government. "After all, America was founded by men who came, slowly but surely, to believe that they could no longer obey their government," Brooks wrote. "From the perspective of American political mythology, they were heroes; from the British point of view, they were traitors."[142]

139   Vadum, Matthew, "Soros Lawyer Rosa Brooks Working in the Pentagon," *Capital Research Center*, May 12, 2009. https://capitalresearch.org/article/soros-lawyer-rosa-brooks-working-in-the-pentagon/

140   Email from Rosa Brooks to John Podesta, May 13, 2015, 12:47 p.m., *WikiLeaks*. https://wikileaks.org/podesta-emails/emailid/42288

141   Brooks, Rosa, "3 Ways to Get Rid of President Trump before 2020," *Foreign Policy*, January 30, 2017. https://foreignpolicy.com/2017/01/30/3-ways-to-get-rid-of-president-trump-before-2020-impeach-25th-amendment-coup/

142   Brooks, "And Then the Breitbart Lynch Mob Came for Me," *ForeignPolicy*, February 6, 2017. https://foreignpolicy.com/2017/02/06/and-then-the-breitbart-lynch-mob-came-for-me-bannon-trolls-trump/

Among the group's activities involved simulating potential election outcomes for the purpose of backing Biden's claim to the White House in the event of a disputed election (again, odd for a supposedly nonpartisan organization). As the *National Pulse*'s Raheem Kassam and Natalie Winters exposed:

> TIP claimed to have "war-gamed" potential outcomes of the 2020 election with a host of establishment figures such as Hillary Clinton's 2016 campaign Chair and Obama-era Counselor John Podesta, Never Trump Republican National Committee (RNC) Head Michael Steele, and acting chair of the Democratic National Committee (DNC) Donna Brazile who leaked presidential debate questions to Clinton in 2016.
>
> In one concerning iteration, Podesta, who acted as Biden, seized the presidency by "failing to concede as Mrs. Clinton had."[143]

In such a scenario, Podesta wanted Biden to allege voter suppression and persuade the governors of Wisconsin and Michigan to send pro-Biden electors to the Electoral College. If Trump were to take office, Podesta wanted California, Oregon, and Washington to secede from the union.

Any liberal complaints about Trump refusing to concede the 2020 election must be viewed in light of the Democrat establishment secretly floating secession if they didn't get the election result they wanted. Hillary Clinton herself echoed the advice of the TIP, telling Biden "Don't give an inch" and not to concede the election "under any circumstances" if it's close.[144]

Meanwhile, Fiona Hill, a Trump-impeachment witness who served on the Open Society Foundation's board and is closely linked to Rosa Brooks, was publicly demanding an "election commission."[145] The idea was first pitched in a *New York Times* article by DNI Dan Coates, who proposed creating "a supremely high-lev-

143 Kassam, Raheem, and Natalie Winters, "Soros, Gates-Linked Election 'Integrity' Group Falsifies 'Bipartisan' Claims while War-Gaming How Biden Could Seize Power Even if Trump Wins," *The National Pulse*, August 3, 2020. https://thenationalpulse.com/politics/establishment-election-interference/

144 Shabad, Rebecca, "Hillary Clinton Says Biden Should Not Concede the Election 'Under Any Circumstances,'" NBC News, August 26, 2020. https://www.nbcnews.com/politics/2020-election/hillary-clinton-says-biden-should-not-concede-2020-election-under-n1238156

145 Winters, "Soros-Linked Impeachment Witness Fiona Hill Echoes Calls for 'Electoral Commission,'" *The National Pulse*, September 22, 2020. https://thenationalpulse.com/politics/fiona-hill-election-commission/

el bipartisan and nonpartisan commission to oversee the election. This commission would not circumvent existing electoral reporting systems or those that tabulate, evaluate or certify the results. But it would monitor those mechanisms and confirm for the public that the laws and regulations governing them have been scrupulously and expeditiously followed—or that violations have been exposed and dealt with—without political prejudice and without regard to political interests of either party."[146]

In a *New York Times* article the following month, Hill echoed the Soros push for lax election laws, claiming they would somehow strengthen election integrity. "Early voting, online voting, in-person voting and paper and mail-in ballots all increase physical election security. If there is full voter turnout, and every vote is counted in every form, then it is much more difficult for anyone—domestic or foreign—to mess with the margins. If we want to restore our democracy, we need to heal our divisions and get out the vote."[147]

Hill admitted that she realized the nation's electoral system is "decentralized" while working with Homeland Security colleagues and other government agencies at the National Security Council. However, she said that since 2016, the federal government has worked with state and local officials as well as tech companies to "harden" the country's electoral infrastructure.

SOROS AND THE BIDEN WHITE HOUSE

A month after Biden's presidential victory was declared, Patrick Gaspard stepped down as president of the Open Society Foundations and began phoning labor union leaders to support his campaign to become Biden's labor secretary.[148] Gaspard, a former Obama aide, has deep ties to the labor movement, having served as vice president and chief political organizer of the potent 1199SIEU health care workers union covering New York and the Northeast. House Majority Whip James Clyburn, a Biden confidant, confirmed that Gaspard was in the running for the position.[149]

146   Coates, Dan, "What's at Stake in This Election? The American Democratic Experiment," *The New York Times*, September 17, 2020. https://www.nytimes.com/2020/09/17/opinion/2020-election-voting.html
147   Hill, Fiona, "The Biggest Risk to This Election is Not Russia. It's Us," *The New York Times*, October 7, 2020. https://www.nytimes.com/2020/10/07/opinion/trump-russia-election-interference.html
148   Penn, Ben, "Soros Official Gaspard Makes Bid for Biden Labor Secretary," Bloomberg Law, December 7, 2020. https://news.bloomberglaw.com/daily-labor-report/soros-official-gaspard-makes-bid-for-biden-labor-secretary
149   Campanile, Carl, "De Blasio Pal, Soros 'Society' Prez Patrick Gaspard in Running for Labor Lead," *The New York Post*, December 10, 2020. https://nypost.com/2020/12/10/de-blasio-pal-patrick-gaspard-in-running-for-labor-secretary/

Despite stepping down as president, he still apparently has a role within the organization. Five days after his move, he was quoted in an internal OSF memo about most program areas facing freezes on new initiatives.[150]

Biden ended up nominating Boston Mayor Marty Walsh for the head position over California Labor Secretary Julie Su and Gaspard, possibly knowing the optics of selecting someone too publicly connected to Soros.

While Gaspard didn't make it into the administration, the Soros infiltration of Team Biden began before he even took office.[151]

SOROS/TRANSITION TEAM

On the day of the 2020 election, Hungarian MP Gergely Gulyás commented: "We supported Donald Trump, whereas Joe Biden has been supported by George Soros, which is not such a great starting point."[152] Gulyás said he was "pessimistic" during the counting of votes across the United States, noting that he hoped that the foreign policy of a new Democrat government "would be better than the last one," referring to the Obama administration in which Biden was vice president. He chided the Biden campaign for accepting donations from Soros, whom Hungary's government has depicted as the financier of all the evils of liberalism.[153]

Biden's transition team was formed days later on November 7, and quickly began staffing itself with liberals connected to Soros and his network. Biden's transition team raised $20 million (much more than the $6.5 million and $4 million Donald Trump and Obama raised, respectively), of which Soros donated the maximum amount ($5,000).[154]

Biden-assembled "Agency Review Teams," which included lists of individuals "responsible for understanding the operations" of each government agency, were tapped to prepare both Biden and Kamala Harris "to hit the ground running on Day One." Soros was represented well by Biden's picks.

---

150   Kavate, Michael, "Major 'Transformation' Underway at OSF-Temporary Limits on Spending, Freeze on New Initiatives," *Inside Philanthropy*, January 19, 2021. https://www.insidephilanthropy.com/home/2021/1/19/major-transformation-underway-at-osftemporary-limits-on-spending-freeze-on-new-initiatives

151   "George Soros's People to Help Joe Biden's Transfer to Power," V4 Agency, November 15, 2020. https://v4na.com/en/george-soros-s-people-to-help-joe-biden-s-transfer-to-power

152   "Orbán Cabinet: We Supported Trump, Whereas Biden Has Been Supported by George Soros," *Daily News Hungary*, November 4, 2020. https://dailynewshungary.com/orban-cabinet-we-supported-trump-whereas-biden-has-been-supported-by-george-soros/

153   "With Donald Trump Out, EU Nationalists Are Down a US Ally," DW, November 10, 2020. https://www.dw.com/en/with-donald-trump-out-eu-nationalists-are-down-a-us-ally/a-55559084

154   De Lea, Brittany, "Biden Transition Received Donations from George Soros, Hollywood Celebrities," Fox News, February 23, 2021. https://www.foxnews.com/politics/biden-transition-donors

Sarah Cross works as advocacy director at the Soros Foundations' International Migration Initiative and worked as part of the State Department's transition team.

OSF Leadership in Government Fellow Diane Thompson was picked by Biden to head the Consumer Financial Protection Bureau's transition team.

Special adviser to the executive office of the OSF Michael Pan joined the United States Mission to the United Nations team.[155]

Sharon Burke and Vivian Graubard are members of the Soros-funded New America organization (where Soros' son Jonathan sits on the board). Burke aided the Department of Defense's transition team, while Graubard aides the Department of Labor's.

Five members of the Soros-funded Center for American progress assumed transition team roles, including Jocelyn Frye (Department of Labor), Kate Kelly (Department of the Interior), Andy Green (Department of the Treasury, Federal Reserve, Banking and Securities Regulators), Kelly Magsamen (National Security Council), and Ryan Zamarripa (Office of the U.S. Trade Representative).

Three members of the Center for Strategic and International Studies (on the board of which the former director of Soros Fund Management sits) aided with the Department of Defense's transition: Kath Hicks, Melissa Dalton, and Andrew Hunter.

Four people from the Soros-backed Center for a New American Security aided the transition team: Susanna Blume and Ely Ratner (Department of Defense), Elizabeth Rosenberg (Department of the Treasury), and Kayla Williams (Department of Veterans Affairs).

A number of individuals within the Soros sphere of influence then entered his cabinet.

Neera Tanden served as president for the Soros-funded Center for American Progress before becoming senior adviser to the president in May 2021. She had previously been nominated to head the Office of Management and Budget, but her nomination was withdrawn after Democrat Senator Joe Manchin announced he wouldn't vote in favor of her confirmation. She also made the mistake of trash-talking Senator Lisa Murkowski on twitter in the past, which came back to haunt her.

Ron Klain serves on the board of the Center for American Progress Action, the lobbying wing of the aforementioned Center for American Progress. Since day one of the Biden presidency, he's been White House chief of staff.[156]

155 Schoffstall, "George Soros Looms Large over Biden Transition," *The Washington Free Beacon*, November 11, 2020. https://freebeacon.com/elections/george-soros-looms-large-over-biden-transition/
156 "Center for American Progress Action Fund (CAP Action)," *InfluenceWatch*, https://www.influencewatch.org/

Sam Berger was a former VP for democracy and government reform at the Center for American Progress, and was made director of strategic operations and policy for the COVID-19 Response Team.

DIRECT FUNDING

Soros has been more direct in his funding of the Biden agenda, publicly pledging $20 million toward passing Biden's eight-year, multi-trillion-dollar infrastructure and social welfare agenda while seeking to raise and spend $125 million. "Every initiative proposed by President Biden has broad public support. But we've seen popular reforms get demonized before by partisans and special interests, and we are not going to let that happen," said OSF executive director Tom Perriello. "Facts don't always win without some real muscle put behind getting those facts in front of the American people."[157]

"We hope this effort on the part of organizers and donors will give the Biden administration and Congress the assurance that they need to go as big, bold and fast as possible," said progressive donor network Way to Win's cofounder Leah Hunt-Hendrix.[158]

While money talks, progressives must tread lightly with the party's prods that can slip at any moment between encouraging and antagonizing the White House. "Squad" member and progressive New York Representative Alexandria Ocasio-Cortez wants to "realistically" take it to the extreme with $10 trillion over ten years in spending, voicing "serious concerns that [Biden's number is] not enough" and calling for officials to "go way higher."

In an interview with MSNBC at the beginning of April, she said she was speaking for House Democrats by eyeing the "ideal" price tag.[159] "I know that may be an eye-popping figure for some people, but we need to understand that we are in a devastating economic moment. Millions of people in the United States are unemployed," the New York lawmaker stated. "We have a truly crippled health care system and a planetary crisis on our hands, and we're the wealthiest nation in the history of the world. So we can do $10 trillion."

---

non-profit/center-for-american-progress-cap-action/

157   Oshin, Olafimihan, "Soros Group Pledges $20M to Rally Progressives Around Biden's Infrastructure Plan," *The Hill*, April 5, 2021. https://thehill.com/policy/transportation/infrastructure/546558-soros-group-pledges-20M-to-rally-progressives

158   Ibid.

159   "Thunder on the Left: AOC Wants $10 Trillion over 10 Years for Infrastructure Plan," *Axios*, April 1, 2021. https://www.axios.com/aoc-biden-infrastructure-f2cbe0df-099e-47f6-a358-3c0938d4f642.html

Soros is also looking to invest across five "tables"; coalitions of organizations to seek the "strongest" (i.e., most liberal) jobs package. Those five coalitions, mostly funded by the Open Society Policy Center, include:

- The Care Economy: Seeking expansion of paid leave, childcare, and home and community-based care services for the elderly and people with disabilities.

- Infrastructure: Working to ensure infrastructure jobs are union jobs, ensure "racial and gender equity," and address climate change.

- Climate: Partner with key established "environmental powerhouses."

- Immigration: Protect millions of illegal immigrants.

- Real Recovery: Support messaging and communication efforts across the elements of the Biden Administration's Build Back Better package.[160]

While Soros has directly funded the Biden agenda, that arguably represents a fraction of his influence on the matter considering his existing influence in the media, at universities, and within the White House itself.

Soros is exerting indirect influence over the aforementioned proposals and even more radical leftist policies through his billionaire-financed "Poor People's Campaign."[161] Soros backed the group in 2020 when the OSF announced their $220 million investment into what they call "racial equality." The Poor People's Campaign received the OSF grant following George Floyd's death as part of the organization's "antiracist" initiative.

---

160   "Open Society Foundations Pledge $20 Million to Support Green Infrastructure, Inclusive Economic Opportunity, and Democracy Reforms," Open Society Foundations, April 7, 2021. https://www.opensocietyfoundations.org/newsroom/open-society-foundations-pledge-20-million-to-support-green-infrastructure-inclusive-economic-opportunity-and-democracy-reforms

161   Simonson, Joseph, "Soros-Backed Group Plans 'Third Reconstruction' Push," *The Washington Free Beacon*, June 9, 2021. https://freebeacon.com/democrats/soros-backed-group-plans-third-reconstruction-push/

When the grant was announced, Soros' son Alexander said, "This is the time for urgent and bold action to address racial injustice in America." In the press release announcing the grant, the OSF touted groups "fighting for an end to policing as we know it."[162]

While George Soros is openly backing Biden with his $20 million, he's afforded the ability to be invisibly "pulling the strings" with the latter group, which is arguably more dangerous because it's backed by thirty House Democrats.[163]

Under Biden, the Poor People's Campaign is unleashing a year-long campaign for a "Third Reconstruction"—which includes demands to abolish immigration enforcement, expand welfare for illegal immigrants, and remove criminal penalties for violent protesters and rioters.

Some other demands read like a progressive bingo board: automatic voter registration; single-payer health care; a reparations commission; cancellation of student, housing, utilities, and medical debt, as well as all other debt that can't be paid. They estimate the cost in the tens of trillions of dollars, which they propose funding through deficit spending and a 10 percent cut to the military. This is just an excuse to cut the military, of course. If they are funding through deficits, debt certainly isn't a concern to them in the first place, and a 10 percent cut in the military would only fund a sliver of their package of Santa Claus policies.

They justify all this with the language/word salad of the new woke paradigm, using historical injustices to justify why their credit card bills should be cancelled. They wrote in a Facebook post about the "Third Reconstruction" campaign the following word salad: "With this resolution, we (1) acknowledge the deep harms we have suffered from systemic racism, poverty, ecological devastation and the denial of health care, militarism and the false narrative of white supremacist nationalist extremism and (2) commit to heal and transform the nation by addressing these interlocking injustices, beginning with those most impacted, with moral and just laws and policies." As one ambassador sardonically put it, every societal problem to the Left nowadays is blamed on the "systemic systems of structural institutions."

---

162   "Open Society Foundations Announce $220 Million for Building Power in Black Communities," Open Society Foundations, July 13, 2020. https://www.opensocietyfoundations.org/newsroom/open-society-foundations-announce-220-million-for-building-power-in-black-communities

163   Simonson, Joseph, "Soros-Backed Group Plans 'Third Reconstruction' Push."

Intending to place pressure on Democrats to urge support of the initiative, the Poor People's Campaign is designed to climax with a march on Washington in June 2022. A previous "40 Days of Action" protest it organized in 2018 resulted in thousands of arrests. Protesters in dozens of states held sit-ins at government offices and blocked roads while demanding local legislators pass minimum wage increases and expand welfare benefits.

Among the House Democrats backing the campaign described as the "next Green New Deal" include the "Squad' Representatives Cori Bush and Rashida Tlaib, and Jamie Raskin, who was lead impeachment manager during Trump's second impeachment.

TONY BLINKEN AND ALBANIA

In May, Secretary of State Antony Blinken announced sanctions against former Albanian president (1992–1997) and prime minister (2005–2013) Sali Berisha, alleging "significant corruption," and banned him, his wife, and his children from entering the U.S. Berisha headed a center-right political party called the Democratic Party (a counterintuitive name from an American perspective) that was founded in 1990 after the ouster of the nation's Communist regime.

The seventy-six-year-old Albanian politician, an ally to both Bushes, currently serves as an opposition member of Albania's parliament, of which the Socialist Party of Albania holds a majority.

Blinken said in a statement that during his second stint in leadership, Berisha "was involved in corrupt acts, such as misappropriation of public funds and interfering with public processes, including using his power for his own benefit and to enrich his political allies and his family members."[164] No details or supporting evidence was provided. Berisha has insisted there is "zero evidence" behind the corruption allegations, asserting the U.S. ban was based on "misinformation" from outlets backed by Soros.

Even taking the allegations at face value, we're to wonder why these sanctions happened now, out of the blue. New York Republican Representative Lee Zeldin immediately flagged the move as abnormal and penned a letter to the State Department's Bureau of Legislative Affairs to request a detailed explanation of the process that the State Department followed.

---

164 Blinken, Antony J., "Public Designation of Albanian Sali Berisha Due to Involvement in Significant Corruption." U.S. Department of State, May 19, 2021. https://www.state.gov/public-designation-of-albanian-sali-berisha-due-to-involvement-in-significant-corruption/

For that, Berisha blames Soros and told the *Washington Times* that he would fight the allegations proving there is "no evidence" for a defamation suit against Blinken in a European Court. He also challenged the Biden administration to produce any evidence of corruption, stating:

> It is my deep conviction that this declaration against me has been based entirely on misinformation that Mr. Secretary of State Antony Blinken has gotten from a corrupted lobby process involving Edi Rama and George Soros, who are close friends. They have no evidence. None at all. If they announced one bit, I will be most thankful. But they have no concrete proof based on fact, not manipulation or slander."

> .....

> I have been an outspoken critic of George Soros and his close friend [Prime Minister] Edi Rama, and because of this, the State Department has made this allegation against me and blocked me. There is no other reason. There could be no other reason.

Soros and Berisha had publicly traded blows before, with Berisha saying in 2017 that Soros had turned from a "great friend" to a "great danger" to the Albanian people. "My statements on George Soros and his mafia, as a major danger for the Albanian democracy, are based on authentic documents. My statements at the Albanian Parliament against the mafia acts of Soros and his network in Albania, are based on facts which date before the current debates taking place in the United States on the activity of the chief speculator of the planet," he explained. Just nine years earlier, he had called Soros a "great friend of the Albanians."[165]

Berisha told the *Times* that Soros-backed NGOs have had vendettas against him since 2017, stemming from him publicly rejecting proposals for changes to the Serbia-Kosovo border. Berisha had opposed certain territorial swaps that Soros-backed NGOs wanted because he believed it would lead to ethnic violence, adding "chang-

---

165   "Is George Soros 'Great Friend of Albanians' or 'Great Danger'—Look at what Berisha has said in years?" TiranaEcho, February 24, 2017. http://www.tiranaecho.com/latest-news/is-george-soros-great-friend-of-albanians-or-great-danger-look-at-what-berisha-has-said-in-years/

ing borders meant cleansing and shifting of populations." He also alleged that U.S. support for the territorial swaps was engineered by Soros-backed groups working with socialist Albanian Prime Minister Edi Rama.

Rep. Zeldin made reference to the Soros connection when questioning Blinken during a House Foreign Affairs Committee meeting in June about the drastic sanctions that came "seemingly out of nowhere." "What specific information can you share with the committee at this time to justify this dramatic move?" asked Zeldin.[166]

In response to questioning, Blinken denied having any communication with Soros, but said he can't speak for anyone else at the State Department. When pressed on the evidence for corruption, Blinken said that all proper protocols were followed while providing no substantive evidence of corruption whatsoever.

Responsible for providing the facts on Berisha's alleged corruption to the Department of State is the East-West Management Institute. It's headed by a woman named Delina Fico who has the job title of director of civil society programs at East-West Management Institute. Alongside Central European University (CEU), the East-West Management Institute is one of two Soros-spawned groups that he says he would "envision as permanent institutions." She was once engaged to Edi Rama, and later married Bledi Çuçi, one of Rama's closest allies.[167]

Evidently, Blinken can't speak on behalf for anyone else at the State Department when it comes to their connections to Soros—or even his own father. Antony's father Donald Blinken and his wife Vera funded the Vera and Donald Blinken Open Society Archives at Central European University, which houses a digital collection of Hungarian historical documents. In one Soros Foundations Network report from 2002, Donald Blinken is listed on the Board of Trustees for CEU third after Soros (the chair) and Aryeh Neier, implying he's high in the pecking order.[168]

Donald Blinken was U.S. ambassador to Hungary from 1994 to 1998, right as Soros was setting up shop. He and his wife had close ties to the socialist government.

166   "Rep. Zeldin Questions Sec. Blinken on Sudden Sanctioning of Former Albanian President," July 7, 2021. https://zeldin.house.gov/media-center/press-releases/rep-zeldin-questions-sec-blinken-sudden-sanctioning-former-albanian

167   "Delina Fico sqaron lidhjen me ministrin Çuçi: S'e kam kompleks, kam që në 1994 në Shoqërinë Civile." News-Bomb, November 24, 2016. https://newsbomb.al/delina-fico-sqaron-lidhjen-me-ministrin-cuci-s-e-kam-kompleks-kam-qe-ne-1994-ne-shoqerine-civile/

168   "Building Open Societies: 2002 Report," Soros Foundations Network, 2003. https://www.opensocietyfoundations.org/uploads/569ceb5a-5a08-472e-ac5f-00b0c0595cf2/a_complete_report_0.pdf

The daily blog *Hungarian Spectrum*, which boasts Soros among its donors, celebrated Blinken as a potential Secretary of State pick after the 2020 election because "Hungary will not be forgotten in the next four or perhaps eight years in Washington."[169]

After Blinken was confirmed as Secretary of State, Hungarian newspaper *Magyar Nemzet* called it "great news for George Soros."

---

169 "After a Long Wait, the United States Has a President-Elect," *Hungarian Spectrum*, November 7, 2020. https://hungarianspectrum.org/tag/antony-blinken/

George Soros and the Ukraine

Internationally, George Soros arguably boasts more influence in Ukraine than he does in any other country.

The Russian-language Ukrainian newspaper *Vesti* publishes a list of the most influential one hundred people in the country at the end of every year, choosing Soros in 2019 as second to only President Volodymyr Zelensky. The prime minister took third place after Soros.

"Through the organizations financed by him, Soros can influence economic and political life in all of Ukraine," the Kyiv-based paper notes.[170]

They're hardly being hyperbolic.

Soros' influence in Ukraine kicked off in 1989, two years before the collapse of the USSR, when he was creating a series of NGOs.[171]

The most notable was in April 1990, when the International Renaissance Foundation (IRF), a part of the Open Society Foundations' international network, was established in Kyiv. Ukraine was still a struggling part of the Soviet Union at the time. Soros' influence would only grow in 1991 onwards when the country became fully independent. The IRF was disconnected from reality and worked only with the "NGO-cracy," whose leaders were busy networking with Western embassies rather than engaging with citizens. Detractors rebuked the narrow patronage network of NGOs where leadership used access to domestic policymakers and Western donors to influence public policies, yet were out of touch with the public at large.[172]

---

170   "George Soros Named Second-Most Influential Person in Ukraine," ReMix, December 20, 2019. https://rmx.news/article/article/soros-second-most-influential-person-in-ukraine

171   Caputo, Michael R., *The Ukraine Hoax: How Decades of Corruption in the Former Soviet Republic Led to Trump's Phony Impeachment*, Bombardier Books, 2020, page 41.

172   Lutsevych, Orysia, "How to Finish a Revolution: Civil Society and Democracy in Georgia, Moldova, and Ukraine," Chatham House, January 2013. https://www.chathamhouse.org/sites/default/files/public/Research/Russia%20and%20Eurasia/0113bp_lutsevych.pdf

The IRF became the biggest international donor to Ukraine by 1994 with an annual budget of $12 million, which it claims was for "projects that ranged from retraining tens of thousands of decommissioned soldiers to the creation of a contemporary arts center in Kyiv" named the Soros Center for Contemporary Arts. Today, its aid to Ukraine totals $7.8 million, with a reported spending breakdown of 42 percent going toward "Democratic practice and human rights," 24 percent to "health and rights" 15 percent to "justice system reforms," and the rest split between "economic governance and advancement," "education," and "equity and antidiscrimination."[173]

In the early 2000s, the IRF oriented itself around promoting European integration and later mobilized resources in the aftermath of Russia's invasion and annexation of Crimea in 2014. The OSF describes the IRF as a pro-democracy crusader, which has funded numerous organizations such as nonprofit civil-society group Statewatch.[174]

The Foundation claims to have supported over eighteen thousand projects during its lifetime. It ironically claims that "fighting corruption and strengthening transparency and accountability have always been a priority." The Foundation's mission is to "develop an open society" in Ukraine "where everybody has a sense of dignity, citizens are involved in the formation of the state, and the authorities are transparent and responsible."[175]

Soros has spent over $180 million in Ukraine since 1991.[176]

In addition to Soros' early endeavors in the country as the USSR collapsed, he financed Mikheil Saakashvili, the president of Georgia (2004–2013), who became governor of Ukraine's Odessa region (2015–2016), and Svitlana Zalishchuk, a former member of Ukrainian parliament. He's also given money to Mustafa Nayyem, an MP who was appointed VP of Ukroboronprom, a state association of the nation's major defense conglomerates.[177]

The epithet "sorosiata" was used to describe any subservient figure who sought to please Soros—portrayed as "the almighty leader of globalists." The derogatory term became popular in late February 2020 when a broadcast marathon called *Smells Like Soros* was televised. The expressive title translated to other variations such as *It Reeks of Soros* and *Stinks of Soros*.[178]

173   "The Open Society Foundations in Ukraine," *The Open Society Foundation,* January 28, 2020. https://www.open-societyfoundations.org/newsroom/the-open-society-foundations-in-ukraine
174   Ibid.
175   "About Us," International Renaissance Foundation. https://www.irf.ua/en/about/
176   Caputo, *The Ukraine Hoax,* page 38.
177   "George Soros Named Second-Most Influential Person in Ukraine."
178   Rybak, Vitalii, "Divide and Conquer: The 5 Most Popular Anti-Western Narratives in Ukraine So Far in 2020," *Ukraine World,* June 23, 2020. https://ukraineworld.org/articles/infowatch/5-most-popular-anti-western-narratives-ukraine-so-far-2020

Such messaging conveyed across political programming included phrases such as "Soros aims to control entire countries and he has succeeded the most in Ukraine," "He promotes degradation, destruction of traditional values and national identities," and "He supports class oppression."[179]

It's in Ukraine that Soros would be a rival to former Trump campaign chairman Paul Manafort. Manafort worked on behalf of then Ukrainian president (from 2010 to 2014) Viktor Yanukovych, while Soros backed former Ukrainian prime minister (in 2005 and again from 2007 to 2010) Yulia Tymoshenko, a populist firebrand of the Orange Revolution who was sentenced in 2011 to seven years in prison on charges of abuse of power and embezzlement over an alleged antieconomic deal to purchase natural gas from Russia.

The Orange Revolution was a series of protests that took place between November 2004 to January 2005 following the 2004 Ukrainian presidential election. Protesters alleged corruption and fraud after Yanukovych's victory, which was challenged following the mass protests. Viktor Yushchenko ended up winning by a nearly eight-point margin after a new vote was held.

In response to the 2005 sacking of the Tymoshenko government, Open Society Institute-New York regional director Leonard Benardo, now the executive vice president of programs for the Open Society Foundations, cowrote in an op-ed for *The Globe and Mail* that the Orange Revolution was "a victory for the democratic process" and "a beacon…around the world," especially for former Soviet Union countries. "To get [the Orange Revolution] back on track is crucial for Ukraine—and beyond," the editorial argued.[180]

Yanukovych would later receive 48.95 percent of the vote in the 2020 Ukrainian presidential election to Tymoshenko's 45.5 percent.[181]

If Soros wanted his revenge, he would get it from the Maidan protests of November 2013 to February 2014 that led to the ouster of Ukrainian President Yanukovych. The protests were sparked by Yanukovych's decision to not sign an association agreement with the European Union. Protesters then took to the streets to demand closer European Union relations and demonstrations in Maidan Nezalezhnosti—or Independence Square, the central square of Kyiv—formed to also denounce the post-Soviet politics of corruption and nepotism.

---

179   "Putin's Best Buddy in Ukraine Ramps Up Anti-Soros Smear Campaign." *EuroMaidan Press*, March 6, 2020. http://euromaidanpress.com/2020/03/06/putins-best-buddy-in-ukraine-ramps-up-anti-soros-smear-campaign/

180   Benardo, Leonard, and Laura Silber, "Ukraine's Dream Is Not Dead—Yet," *The Globe and Mail*, October 6, 2005. https://www.theglobeandmail.com/opinion/ukraines-dream-is-not-dead----yet/article739300/

181   Caputo, *The Ukraine Hoax*, pages 92–93.

Many of the main directors of the Maidan protests were tied to Soros-sponsored programs.[182] The IRF played a role in aiding the protests, with the OSF's website admitting they "ensured that legal aid was made available throughout the crisis to civic activists, protesters, and journalists; supplied victims of violence with medical care; enabled civil society solidarity and organization; supported channels like Hromadske TV in independent, live reporting about events on the Maidan; and documented cases of torture, beatings, and police and courts abuse."[183]

In one single climactic day for the history books, the political order of Ukraine was overturned when Ukrainian parliament voted to dismiss Yanukovych from office and to free Tymoshenko, the jailed opposition leader who went straight from prison after serving thirty months behind bars to addressing tens of thousands at Independence Square. Tymoshenko delivered an emotional, forceful speech on stage, honoring the eighty-two Ukrainians killed in street fighting.[184]

In an emergency session, the Ukrainian parliament voted 380 to zero to remove Yanukovych, maintaining he was guilty of gross human rights violations and dereliction of duty. Many of Yanukovych's allies were absent or abstained from voting. In a calculated statement, the Obama administration backed the swift political change, praised the "constructive work" of the Ukrainian parliament, and urged "the prompt formation of a broad, technocratic government of national unity." The White House also applauded Tymoshenko's release from prison.[185] With Yanukovych's ouster, President-Elect Petro Poroshenko would take office in June 2014.

In 2015, Poroshenko awarded Soros the Order of Liberty, one of Ukraine's highest awards. Poroshenko said of Soros upon giving him the award: "Your intense activities during recent years have extremely promoted the democratic change that we now have happening in Ukraine." He praised Soros' role in the country and the IRF's contributions to the establishment of a new Eurocentric Ukraine over the preceding twenty-five years.[186]

182   Ibid, page 38.
183   "Understanding Ukraine's Euromaidan Protests," The Open Society Foundation, May 2019. https://www.opensocietyfoundations.org/explainers/understanding-ukraines-euromaidan-protests
184   Booth, William, "Ukraine's Parliament Votes to Oust President; Former Prime Minister Is Freed from Prison," Washington Post, February 22, 2014. https://www.washingtonpost.com/world/europe/ukraines-yanukovych-missing-as-protesters-take-control-of-presidential-residence-in-kiev/2014/02/22/802f7c6c-9bd2-11e3-ad71-e03637a299c0_story.html
185   "Statement by the Press Secretary on Ukraine," The White House Archives, February 22, 2014. https://obamawhitehouse.archives.gov/the-press-office/2014/02/22/statement-press-secretary-ukraine
186   "Ukrainian President Gives High State Award to Soros," Radio Free Europe, November 13, 2015. https://www.rferl.org/a/ukrainian-president-gives-high-state-award-to-george-soros/27362587.html

The presidential decree commended Soros for working toward "the strengthening of the international authority of the Ukrainian state" and the "implementation of socio-economic reforms." This behavior could also roughly translate to "Thank you for making me president."

Soros had Poroshenko's ear; it made headlines that the two had met earlier in January of that year to discuss the European Union contributing to Ukraine's development and the prospect of increased economic assistance to the country.[187] "Ukraine is struggling to protect not only itself, but also Europe. Thus, Europe should help Ukraine implement reforms necessary for the country," Soros belabored, urging that the implementation of such reforms required financial assistance. By March, Soros announced his intent to invest $1 billion into Ukraine.[188] The following year, he joined Ukraine's National Investment Council.

At the same time, Soros emphasized that Ukraine must demonstrate commitment to the radical reform agenda. "You have to show that [the] new Ukraine is different from the old one," Soros said to Poroshenko while Euromaidan's supporters transitioned from being the opposition to nation building.

Soros was an ardent advocate of the "new Ukraine," led by "the cream of civil society," who claimed that the "old Ukraine" was entrenched in state bureaucracy and had conspired with the business oligarchy. He pontificated in the international press, flaunting a new Marshall Plan for Ukraine and urging European Union and United States leadership to "Save the New Ukraine" and "Keep the Spirit of the Maidan Alive." Soros romanticized Ukraine's transformation as a social experiment in participatory democracy that relied on checks and balances, "a noble adventure" of citizens turned toward modernity and democratizing the nation.[189]

Sensing the threat of Russian aggression from presidential strongman Vladimir Putin, he also urged Western powers to provide additional sums to strengthen Ukraine's military defense. "Russia looms, with its dominant military might...Putin believes in displays of force; he flexes his muscle, and expects people to fall in line. He will do what he can to thwart progress, to keep the country mired in its corrupt past," Soros wrote on the blog for Open Society Foundations.[190]

187   "Petro Poroshenko had a Meeting with George Soros," Consulate General of Ukraine in Chicago, January 13, 2015. https://chicago.mfa.gov.ua/en/news/31457-petro-poroshenko-proviv-zustrich-z-dzhordzhem-sorosom

188   "US Billionaire George Soros Ready to Invest $1 Billion in Ukrainian Economy," *Tass*, March 30, 2015. https://tass.com/economy/785780

189   Lévy, Bernard-Henri, and George Soros, "Save the New Ukraine," *New York Times*, January 25, 2015. https://www.nytimes.com/2015/01/27/opinion/bernard-henri-levi-george-soros-save-the-new-ukraine.html

190   Soros, George, "Keep the Spirit of the Maidan Alive," Open Society Foundations, April 7, 2014. https://www.opensocietyfoundations.org/voices/keep-spirit-maidan-alive

Soros classified the financial assistance from foreign entities, in which the IRF was placed in charge of seeing through the disbursements, as an immediate $15 billion need "to ensure Ukraine's survival and encourage private investment."[191]

Soros believed that the single most effective measure to counteract Putin was to offer free political risk insurance to those who invest in or do business with Ukraine. Despite political turmoil, the relationships would keep the economy running and signal to Ukrainians that the European Union and the United States are committed, Soros proposed in his instructional "How the EU Can Save Ukraine" op-ed.[192] "By acting promptly and convincingly, the EU could save Ukraine—and itself," Soros wrote, furthering his main gripe against Europe for not doing enough for the new Ukraine. "What I propose for Ukraine could also be implemented at home."

Soros warned Russia was emerging as a dangerous rival to the European Union, one with global geopolitical ambitions. "Europe needs to wake up and recognize that it is under attack from Russia," he rallied to reorient the European Union's policies to rescue Ukraine.

Soros felt that an injection of financial assistance to Ukraine would help to stabilize its economy and provide a much-needed stimulus to the European economy by encouraging exports and investment in Ukraine, which had experienced transitory shocks that led to its financial crisis. But once Ukraine recovers, Soros argued, it should be able to repay its creditors for the "defense expenditure." Soros declared that if the international authorities failed to match the radical Ukrainian reforms with an impressive assistance program, the new Ukraine will be destined to fail; "Europe will be left on its own to defend itself against Russian aggression," and "Europe will have abandoned the values and principles on which the European Union was founded."[193]

During Poroshenko's administration (2014–2019), Soros was able to get a number of desired changes to Ukrainian laws, which were achieved by bypassing Ukrainian parliament via the National Reforms Council (NRC) that was set up in 2014. Emboldening the post-Euromaidan reforms process, Soros provided an additional $3

---

191   Lévy, Bernard-Henri, and George Soros, "Save the New Ukraine."
192   Soros, George, "How the EU Can Save Ukraine," *The Guardian*, May 29, 2014. https://www.theguardian.com/business/2014/may/29/how-eu-can-save-ukraine-political-risk-insurance
193   Soros, George, "A New Policy to Rescue Ukraine," *The New York Review*, February 5, 2015. https://www.nybooks.com/articles/2015/02/05/new-policy-rescue-ukraine/

million in support of eight Strategic Advisory Groups (SAGs) within the NRC and its plethora of experts drafted eighty reform bills in education, health care, deregulation, energy security, decentralization, administrative reform, and e-governance.[194]

The NRC's chain of command includes the president and his cabinet, parliamentary committee chairs, a who's who of Soros-affiliated members of Ukraine's civil society, the European Bank of Reconstruction and Development, and representatives of EU and U.K. governments.[195] Soros spoke about what he expected from the new Ukrainian government in an interview with Ukrainian newspaper *Ukrayinska Pravda* arranged by the IRF. The elections gave "a clear mandate" to the elected representatives to form a coalition that would turn the new Ukraine into a reality, Soros said. A lot of the preparatory work had been done under the aegis of the NRCs with the help of the SAGs.[196]

Soros has a global vision, and his desire to fully integrate Ukraine into the European Union is part of his vision to once again turn Europe into a unified global power.[197] His influence in Ukraine has overlapped with his goals in America in recent years, particularly when it came to Donald Trump and his associates.

THE SOROS CIRCLE: ANTAC

In 2014, Soros' IRF and its grantees were active supporters in the creation of the Anti-Corruption Acter Centre (AntAC) of Ukraine, a powerful NGO.[198] Through the end of 2018, 17 percent of AntAC's funding was coming from Soros.[199]

AntAC is run by Daria Kaleniuk, an American-educated lawyer. Of note, White House logs say that Kaleniuk visited the White House on December 9, 2015, and reportedly met with Eric Ciaramella, a CIA employee that many suspect is the anonymous whistleblower that sparked Trump's first impeachment, the source of which was a phone call with Ukraine's president.

194   Smagliy, Kateryna, "Thank You, George!" *Atlantic Council*, December 14, 2015. https://www.atlanticcouncil.org/blogs/ukrainealert/thank-you-george/

195   Caputo, *The Ukraine Hoax*, page 44.

196   Musayeva-Borovyk, Sevhil, "George Soros: 'New Ukraine' It Is an Idea That Is Real," International Renaissance Foundation, November 14, 2014. https://www.irf.ua/en/jsoros_nova_ukraina_realnist/

197   Soros, George, "The Tragedy of the European Union," GeorgeSoros.com, March 11, 2014. https://www.georgesoros.com/2014/03/11/the-tragedy-of-the-european-union/

198   "Declaring Anti-Corruption Action Stories," AntAC, March 31, 2018. https://antac.org.ua/en/news/declaring-anti-corruption-action-stories/

199   Bongino, Dan, *Follow the Money: The Shocking Deep State Connections of the Anti-Trump Cabal*, Post Hill Press, 2020, pages 13–14.

AntAC was responsible for creating the National Anti-Corruption Bureau of Ukraine (NABU), a law enforcement group separate from the prosecutor general's office that was tasked with handling the biggest corruption cases. It has investigatory powers but cannot indict suspects unless it passes its findings to prosecutors. The agency was established in 2014 at the behest of the International Monetary Fund after its predecessor, the National Anti-Corruption Committee, was deemed a failure. Western governments funded NABU, and the FBI also supported it.[200] Like all the Orwellian-themed names of groups Soros had a part in, NABU acts independently in name only.

With the Obama DOJ's launch of the Kleptocracy Asset Recovery Initiative, which was aimed at battling large-scale public corruption in foreign states, the State Department, DOJ, and FBI began outsourcing some of their own work to AntAC.[201]

In February 2015, Viktor Shokin was appointed prosecutor general of Ukraine, and was soon scrutinized for helping the owner of the energy company Burisma. Shokin had helped owner Mykola Zlochevsky regain control of $23 million that was frozen by U.K. authorities. Burisma was made famous by Hunter Biden's involvement in the company, and Zlochevsky was the one who struck the deal to appoint Hunter to the company's board of directors in 2014 at a reported salary of up to $83,333 per month.[202]

AntAC's stance on Shokin was made clear; it tweeted on December 2015 that "One of the major goals of #AntAC for 2016 is to force #Shokin to resign."[203]

Shokin attempted to begin a probe into Burisma that "included interrogations and other crime-investigation procedures into all members of the executive board, including Hunter Biden." This never materialized because Joe Biden (then VP) threatened to withhold a $1 billion loan to Ukraine unless Skokin was removed as prosecutor general. Biden even bragged about it on video to the Council on Foreign Relations in 2018, stating that when he attended a meeting with Ukraine's president and prime minister, he said, "'I'm leaving in six hours. If the prosecutor is not fired, you're not getting the money.' Well, son of a bitch. He got fired. And they put in place someone who was solid at the time."[204]

200   Bongino, *Follow the Money*, page 14.
201   Solomon, John, "US Embassy Pressed Ukraine to Drop Probe of George Soros Group During 2016 Election," *The Hill*, March 26, 2019. https://thehill.com/opinion/campaign/435906-us-embassy-pressed-ukraine-to-drop-probe-of-george-soros-group-during-2016
202   Bongino, *Follow the Money*, page 138
203   AntAC Twitter account, December 25, 2015, https://twitter.com/ANTAC_ua/status/680314247923036160
204   Bongino, *Follow the Money*, page 14.

Biden had insisted that the U.S. wanted Shokin removed over corruption concerns, which were shared by the European Union. But tapes released by Ukrainian lawmaker Andrii Derkach allegedly containing calls between Biden and Poroshenko reveal that the Ukrainian president admitted to doing Biden's bidding, thus the extent to which the removal of Shokin was a quid pro quo is proven. "Despite the fact that (Shokin) didn't have any corruption charges, we don't have any information about him doing something wrong, I especially asked him…to resign," Poroshenko allegedly said in a recording dated February 18, 2016.[205]

In another recording from March 22, 2016, the two allegedly discussed who would be appointed prosecutor general of Ukraine, and then who would be their eventual replacement. Ukrainian former prosecutor Yuriy Lutsenko was mentioned. A White House press release confirms that the two talked on this date.[206]

At the end of the call, Biden said, "I'm a man of my word. And now that the new prosecutor general is in place, we're ready to move forward to signing that new $1 billion loan guarantee."[207]

Derkach would later be punished for allegedly exposing Biden's call with Poroshenko.

After the audio was made public, Poroshenko's successor Volodymyr Zelensky called for an investigation into the recordings, and our Treasury Department sanctioned Derkach, describing the audio as "unsupported information" part of a campaign to "discredit U.S. officials." They also accused Derkach, a member of Ukraine's parliament, of being a "Russian agent." [208]

The sanctions came less than a year after Derkach met with Rudy Giuliani in Kiev, which reports at the time said was to discuss possible misuse of U.S. tax dollars by Ukraine's government. "I can't think of anything [Derkach] gave me that you could consider meddling in the election. Indicting [Steve] Bannon is a lot more meddling in the election than this. My best recollection is it was all information we had already. I know I kind of got bored during the deposition because I had already heard it," Giuliani told Fox News. [209]

---

205 Ibid., page 15.
206 Ibid.
207 Ibid.
208 "Treasury Sanctions Russia-Linked Election Interference Actors," U.S. Department of the Treasury, September 10, 2020. https://home.treasury.gov/news/press-releases/sm1118
209 Fordham, Evie, "Ukrainian Lawmaker Who Leaked Biden Audio Sanctioned over Alleged Election Interference," Fox News, September 10, 2020. https://www.foxnews.com/politics/ukrainian-lawmaker-andrii-derkach-sanctioned-election-interference-biden

"I can't see how you can be accused of meddling in an election that is more than a year away," Giuliani continued. "The only new piece of information he gave…is the report that $5.3 billion in foreign aid [to Ukraine] is unaccounted for, $3 billion of which is American money and a big portion of that went to nongovernmental organizations controlled by George Soros," he continued.[210]

As the 2016 presidential race began to intensify, Ukraine's prosecutor general's office began an investigation into AntAC about the alleged misuse of $2.2 million of funds. An inquiry was sent to former U.S. ambassador Geoffrey Pyatt. George Kent, the second-in-command at the embassy, responded to Deputy Prosecutor General Yuriy Stolyarchuk with a two-page letter stating that the U.S. had "no concerns about the use of our assistance funds."[211]

Kent pressured Stolyarchuk about AntAC in the letter, writing "The investigation into the Anti-Corruption Action Center, based on the assistance they have received from us, is similarly misplaced." That was written on April 4, 2016—less than a week after Shokin was removed.

A few months later, Yuriy Lutsenko was named prosecutor general and met with U.S. Ambassador to Ukraine Marie Yovanovitch. Lutsenko recalls being stunned when the ambassador gave him a list of people who shouldn't be prosecuted. The list included a founder of AntAC, and two members of Ukrainian Parliament who supported AntAC's anticorruption agenda (while benefitting from corruption themselves).[212]

As John Solomon puts it, the implied message to Lutsenko was clear: "Don't target AntAC in the middle of an America presidential election in which Soros was backing Hillary Clinton to succeed another Soros favorite, Barack Obama."[213]

So what was motivating George Kent and Ambassador Yovanovitch to influence investigations in Ukraine of all places? The fact that Ukraine dealt with an organization created with the backing of the Obama administration, State Department, FBI, and George Soros. An investigation into AntAC could expose a whole chest of secrets—the least of which being that they're not all concerned with corruption like they claim.

---

210 Ibid.
211 Bongino, *Follow the Money*, page 16.
212 Ibid.
213 Solomon, "US Embassy Pressed Ukraine."

Memos uncovered by John Solomon from Soros' OSF before the 2016 election make that obvious. One advocates U.S. involvement in Ukraine and offers "behind the scenes advice and support to Ukrainian partner AntAC's efforts to generate corruption litigation in Europe and the U.S. respecting state assets stolen by senior Ukrainian leaders."[214]

Another memo describes AntAC's strategy of developing friendships in key government agencies to leverage within the countries Soros operates in. "We have broadly recognized the importance of developing supportive constituencies in order to make headway in tightening the global web of anti-corruption accountability. We first conceived of this in terms of fostering and helping to build a political environment favorable to high-level anti-corruption cases."[215]

One such contact was Karen Greenaway, the FBI supervisor who was one of the lead agents in investigating Paul Manafort in Ukraine. She's appeared at Soros-sponsored events and conferences before and joined AntAC's supervisory board after retiring from the FBI. The FBI also separately confirmed her contacts with AntAC before she joined them, saying they were part of her "investigative work."[216]

One memo reportedly had a chart of Ukrainians that should be investigated, including people with ties to Paul Manafort. While not mentioned by name, one of those mentioned is likely Dmytro Firtash, a Ukrainian billionaire with competing energy interests in Europe as Soros. Firtash previously beat civil charges alleging he had engaged in money laundering with Manafort.[217]

All of this pressure on Ukrainian prosecutors was happening in the spring of 2016 as Manafort joined the Trump campaign. At this time, Fusion GPS was just starting to conduct opposition research on Trump, and the DNC's Ukraine expert Alexandra Chalupa was searching for dirt on Manafort. Meanwhile, Soros-funded AntAC was looking to probe Manafort's Ukraine associates, and the U.S. embassy was trying to stop any and all inquiries that risk derailing AntAC's work. With AntAC having the potential to "uncover" more dirt on the prime contender to Hillary Clinton, the motivations become obvious.

---

214 Ibid.
215 Ibid.
216 Bongino, *Follow the Money*, page 21.
217 Solomon, "US Embassy Pressed Ukraine."

Prosecutor General Lutsenko himself suggested that the embassy applied pressure because it didn't want Americans to see who was being funded with our tax dollars. "At the time, Ms. Ambassador thought our interviews of the Ukrainian citizens, of the Ukrainian civil servants who were frequent visitors in the U.S. Embassy, could cast a shadow on that anti-corruption policy."[218]

Another Soros-funded group targeted Firtash in 2018. The Open Society-backed Campaign Legal Center filed a complaint with the FEC alleging that Ukrainian businessman Igor Fruman and Russian-born businessman Lev Parnas created a shell company called Global Energy Producers, LLC to anonymously donate $325k to a pro-Trump super PAC. The investigation that followed uncovered a $1 million payment to Parnas's wife from Firtash's lawyer. The hunt for any information that could possibly damage President Trump or anyone connected to him was on.[219]

THE LUTSENKO/KENT LEAKED EMAILS

Emails released to Citizens United as part of a Freedom of Information Act request for information in 2021 revealed that in the weeks leading up to the 2016 presidential election, Lutsenko told George Kent that he was pitched by a lobbying firm linked to Hunter Biden and Burisma access to the highest levels of the Clinton campaign. The lobbying firm was Blue Star Strategies, which is reportedly under federal investigation for potential illegal lobbying.[220] Blue Star had been hired by Burisma to help them fight corruption charges.

The email was sent by George Kent on September 4 to former assistant secretary for fossil energy Christopher Smith, former U.S. ambassador to Ukraine Marie Yovanovitch, and former Kiev embassy chief political officer Alan Purcell with the subject line "Lutsenko now likely not to go to DC with Blue Star, other Ukr issue comments." That's two impeachment witnesses on one email.

In the email, Kent writes that he met with Lutsenko "one on one after I'd SMSed him regarding stories that he was using a third-party lobbyist to pull together a planned trip to DC turned into a chat over Thai food at the DCR." Kent said they discussed a trip Lutsenko had

---

218   Bongino, *Follow the Money*, page 17.
219   Ibid., page 19.
220   Singman, Brooke, "Burisma-Linked Firm 'Pitched' Ukrainian Prosecutor 'Access' to 2016 Clinton Camp, Obama Officials' Emails Show," Fox News, June 4, 2021. https://www.foxnews.com/politics/blue-star-strategies-burisma-hunter-biden-ukraine-prosecutor-access-clinton-campaign-obama-official

been planning to the U.S. and that he "confirmed he has been pitched by Blue Star, not sought them out."

"He said he honestly didn't know how Blue Star was to get paid—he didn't have funds—and that some BPP MP that we probably didn't know 'and that's good' (Truhubenko??) had introduced them to him," Kent continued. It's unclear who Truhubenko is, but one potential person it could be is Serhii Truhubenko, a Ukraine parliamentarian that's part of the European Solidary Party (founded by Petro Poroshenko).

Kent then explained that Blue Star CEO Karen Tramontano pitched that she could get him access to "high levels" of the Clinton campaign, and said that it was appealing to him to "meet the possible next presidential chief of staff" (likely a reference to John Podesta). Kent explained the impracticality of such a meeting, though; "But I pointed out that wasn't too likely 6 weeks before the election, and that the embassies could arrange meetings at DOJ and State, and the Ukr[aine] embassy on the Hill," he continued. "As for the Hill, not many members would be around 6 weeks before an election when Congress would be in recess, and the attention of the chattering think tank class would be on UNGA. Not the best timing, apart from DOJ and State."

Kent went on to say that during their conversation, Lutsenko mentioned "the various money flows from Ukraine to lobbyists that had been prominently in the news this past month, whether Manafort/Klueyev via Brussels to Podesta Group and Weber/Mercury, Yanu's Justice Minister Lavrynovych to Skaden/arps-and Greg Caid—and Pinchuk to Clinton Foundation, and the media attention being paid at present to the Kyiv/ Washington lobbyist gravy train…And he got the drift. Not ideal timing, little receptive audience, and wrong facilitator."

Kent concluded: "He said he'd figure out a better time when there would be more traction/ better audience."

SOROS' SPHERE AND THE STEELE DOSSIER

Soros' sphere of influence in Ukraine extends beyond foundations he's helped found. In 2017, he donated $1 million to the Democracy Integrity Project (TDIP), a group founded by Daniel J. Jones to supposedly investigate election interference, which is ironic considering the level of election "interference" Soros does through his influence.[221]

Jones formally worked as an FBI analyst and a staffer for Senator Dianne Feinstein. His group paid just north of $3.2 million, nearly half its operating budget, in "research consulting" to Bean LLC, Fusion GPS's parent company.[222]

This transaction effectively amounted to Fusion GPS hiring themselves, as the TDIP was founded after Fusion GPS founder Glenn Simpson reached out to Jones. According to Simpson, who is referring to himself in third person for some unknown reason, "Simpson raised the idea of setting up a new group that could work with Fusion and other investigators around the world to expose Russian subversion operations in the United States and other western democracies. Jones said he thought it needed to be done—right away."[223]

This provides a Soros link to Fusion via Jones. Of note, Obama's Organizing for America PAC paid thousands of dollars to Perkins Coie in late April 2016 for "legal services" after the firm had hired Fusion GPS. Obama's group paid Perkins Coie $98,047 on April 25–26 and $700,000 on September 29, 2016. Fusion's contract with the firm ended in October 2016. By comparison, Obama's OFA paid Perkins Coie "only" $174,725 from January to August in 2017. The Clinton campaign had paid just under $5.1 million to Perkins Coie in 2016.[224]

Lefty journo Michael Isikoff in his book *Russian Roulette* confirmed that in the case of the Clinton campaign, just as the Obama campaign had done, the payments were "obscured on campaign disclosure reports filed with the Federal Election Commission." He wrote:

> The payments to Fusion GPS were reported as legal fees to the law firm. Over
>
> time, more than $1 million in Hillary for America and DNC funds would be paid to Fusion GPS in fees and expenses.

---

221 Bongino, *Follow the Money*, page 11.
222 Ibid.
223 Ibid.
224 Bongino, Denise McAllister, and Matt Palumbo, *Spygate: The Attempted Sabotage of Donald J. Trump*, Post Hill Press, 2018, page 72.

Yet many of the top officials at the Clinton campaign and the DNC were not aware of the arrangement and what Fusion GPS was up to. When, months later, Donna Brazile, then the interim DNC chair, picked up rumors about the firm's research in Russia, she confronted Elias and demanded an explanation. He brushed her off, according to Brazile, and said, "You don't want to know."[225]

Jones continued funneling money to Steele and Fusion GPS after the presidential election. $1.2 million was paid to Bean LLC in 2019 for "research consulting, and another $700k was paid for "research consulting" to Washington Partners, which is co-owned by dossier author Christopher Steele, the originator of the infamous "pee tape" myth, among many other discredited smears. The most recently available IRS forms show Jones sent Fusion $3.3 million in 2017 and $959k in 2018. Steele's company was sent $252k in 2017 and $198k in 2018.[226]

Jones also sent $218k in 2017, $167k in 2018, and $283k in 2019 to Edward Austin, a firm cofounded by Edward Baumgartner, a subcontractor for Fusion GPS.[227] Those who read *Spygate* may remember Baumgartner as the Fusion GPS subcontractor who worked on a legal case with Natalia Veselnitskaya, the woman at the center of the infamous Trump Tower meeting. It was the meeting at Trump Tower that fueled claims of "Russia hysteria" in the media, all while she was working for the firm funding the Steele dossier that pushed the same bogus narrative.[228]

The Zuckerman Spaeder law firm that represented Fusion GPS in dossier-related litigation received $148k from Jones.[229]

Texts from 2017 reveal that Jones was in contact with Russian oligarch Oleg Deripaska's D.C.-based lawyer Adam Waldman. Christopher Steele had previously worked with Deripaska in early 2016 to help recover money he claimed was stolen from him by Paul Manafort. This connects everyone involved through both their shared goals of taking down Manafort and Trump.[230]

225 Ibid., page 83.
226 Dunleavy, Jerry, "Feinstein's Former Staffer Helped Funnel Millions to Steele and Fusion GPS after 2016," *Washington Examiner*, May 11, 2021. https://www.washingtonexaminer.com/news/feinsteins-former-staffer-helped-funnel-millions-to-steele-and-fusion-gps-after-2016
227 Ibid.
228 Bongino, McAllister, and Palumbo, *Spygate*, pages 77–90.
229 Dunleavy, "Feinstein's Former Staffer."
230 Ross, Chuck, "EXCLUSIVE: Cabal of Wealthy Donors Financing $50 Million Trump-Russia Investigation." *Daily Caller*, April 27, 2018. https://dailycaller.com/2018/04/27/donors-50-million-steele-fusion-gps/

When the texts were made public, Waldman told the *Daily Caller* that Jones was working with Fusion GPS and that the research was funded by a "group of Silicon Valley billionaires and George Soros." He added that Fusion was a "shadow media organization helping the government."[231]

A Senate Intelligence Committee report further detailed Steele and Deripaska's relationship, revealing that Steele had worked on behalf of Deripaska from 2012 through part of 2017, and that Deripaska had "early knowledge of Steele's work" just a few months before he began compiling his dossier. It was that relationship that "provid[ed] a potential direct channel for Russian influence on the dossier," according to the report.[232]

"Steele declined to answer the Committee's direct questions on whether he worked for Deripaska, but he said no client would have known about the dossier or provided input, other than Fusion GPS," the report added.[233]

ANTAC TAKES DOWN PAUL MANAFORT

A headline over at Politico in the aftermath of the 2016 presidential election says it all: "Ukrainian Efforts to Sabotage Trump Backfire." For all the baseless Russia hysteria over Trump, there was no such coverage over Ukraine's attempted interference in the U.S. election for the benefit of Hillary Clinton.

As Politico's Kenneth Vogel wrote at the time:

> The Ukrainian antipathy for Trump's team—and alignment with Clinton's—can be traced back to late 2013. That's when the country's president, Viktor Yanukovych, whom Manafort had been advising, abruptly backed out of a European Union pact linked to anti-corruption reforms.[234]

Paul Manafort had a target on his back from the moment he joined the Trump campaign. The DNC's Ukrainian activist Alexandra Chalupa had him in her crosshairs since 2014 when he was working

231 Ross, "Back Channel to Christopher Steele Goes on the Record about Senate Testimony," *Daily Caller*, March 13, 2018. https://dailycaller.com/2018/03/13/back-channel-to-christopher-steele-talks-senate-testimony/
232 Dunleavy, "Senate Report Details Christopher Steele's Relationship with Putin-linked Russian Oligarch," *Washington Examiner*, August 27, 2020. https://www.washingtonexaminer.com/news/senate-report-details-christopher-steeles-relationship-with-putin-linked-russian-oligarch
233 Ibid.
234 Vogel, "Ukrainian Efforts to Sabotage Trump Backfire," *Politico*, January 11, 2017. https://www.politico.com/story/2017/01/ukraine-sabotage-trump-backfire-233446

for Ukrainian President Yanukovych. The moment Manafort joined the Trump team, Chalupa alerted the DNC that his hiring was "an early signal that Putin was trying to influence the U.S. election."[235] The Ukrainian embassy assisted Chalupa with her research, working directly with her.

Chalupa asked embassy staff to try to arrange an interview with the Soros-loving (then president) Poroshenko to discuss Manafort's ties to Yanukovych. The embassy denied the request, but Chalupa says there were other Ukrainian officials that were helpful with her research.

Chalupa's sister Andrea spread the word on a Ukrainian television show, calling Manafort's hiring a "huge deal" and describing him as the "puppet master of some of the most vile dictators around the world."[236] His hiring, she said, sent a "very, very, very, very, very serious warning bell going off."[237]

Such was the narrative, and it was soon "confirmed" through the invention of a bogus ledger supposedly belonging to Manafort. The origin of the ledger still remains a mystery.

Manafort lasted six months with the Trump campaign, stepping down days after a report in the *New York Times* about a mysterious black ledger that we know about only because of Soros' AntAC. "Handwritten ledgers show $12.7 million in undisclosed cash payments designated for Mr. Manafort from Mr. Yanukovych's pro-Russian political party from 2007 to 2012, according to Ukraine's newly formed National Anti-Corruption Bureau," AntAC reported. "In addition, criminal prosecutors are investigating a group of offshore shell companies that helped members of Mr. Yanukovych's inner circle finance their lavish lifestyles."[238]

Manafort's financial interests in Russia and Ukraine had already been reported in the press, but Manafort's job with the Trump campaign and the supposed hacking of the DNC emails by the Russians put them under the microscope. This examination revealed "new details of how he mixed politics and business out of public view and benefited from powerful interests now under scrutiny by the new government in Kiev."[239]

---

235 Ibid.
236 Ibid.
237 Hromadske International, "'Thanks To Russian DNC Hack, Now We Know How Dangerous Paul Manafort Really Is' – Andrea Chalupa," YouTube, December 6, 2017. https://www.youtube.com/watch?v=j4lOJQ8F19A
238 Kramer, Andrew, Mike McIntire, and Barry Meier, "Secret Ledger in Ukraine Lists Cash for Donald Trump's Campaign Chief," *The New York Times*, August 14, 2016. https://www.nytimes.com/2016/08/15/us/politics/paul-manafort-ukraine-donald-trump.html
239 Bongino, McAllister, and Palumbo, *Spygate*, pages 19–20.

The ledger appeared seemingly out of nowhere. Ukrainian Parliament member Sergii Leshchenko claimed that he received twenty-two pages of mysterious financial transactions in his mailbox in February of 2016. Three months later, the former deputy head of the Security Service of Ukraine said that the ledger had been left on his doorstep—eight hundred pages in total.[240]

Why such a ledger would even exist is an obvious question. Why leave a paper trail to document alleged wrongdoing?

A spokesperson for Poroshenko distanced his administration from AntAC, claiming that the Bureau is "fully independent." He also denied that there were any targeted efforts against Manafort. However, another Ukraine operative who formally worked as an adviser to Poroshenko was more candid, telling Politico: "It was something that Poroshenko was probably aware of and could have stopped if he wanted to."[241]

After taking a plea deal and becoming a cooperating witness, Manafort's business partner Rick Gates told the FBI and prosecutors from Robert Mueller's special counsel that the ledger was fake. He later summarized his interview with the special counsel to John Solomon: "The ledger was completely made up. The black ledger was a fabrication. It was never real, and this fact has since been proven true."[242]

Of the *New York Times* article revealing its existence, Gates said he told Mueller's team that it was "completely false." "As you now know, there were no cash payments. The payments were wired. The ledger was completely made up."

While we can't confirm this, Gates also claimed that ledger didn't fit with how Yanukovych's party kept records, and that even if it did, "All the real records were burned when the party headquarters was set on fire when Yanukovych fled the country."[243]

If the ledger was real, it would expose Manafort's failure to disclose income, exposing him to money laundering charges. It would also be proof that Manafort failed to register as a foreign agent working for Ukraine (and he was never prosecuted for that).

The bogus ledger served the purpose of targeting Trump's campaign—and would effectively force Gates and Manafort to co-

---

240   Bongino, *Follow the Money*, page 6.
241   Vogel, "Ukrainian Efforts to Sabotage Trump Backfire."
242   Ibid.
243   Ibid., page 7.

operate with prosecutors to tell investigators everything they knew. While Chalupa was confident that Manafort's hiring would be key to proving Russian collusion, for all the wrongdoing on the behalf of Manafort and Gates, no evidence of collusion ever surfaced.

UKRAINE AND IMPEACHMENT

The story of Donald Trump's first impeachment begins in Ukraine with a "perfect" phone call. It's in a call from July 25, 2019, that Trump is accused of a "quid pro quo." In the call, Trump requested at least eight times that Ukraine's president Volodymyr Zelensky investigate Hunter Biden. Trump is accused of dangling the prospect of him withholding military aid to Ukraine in front of Zelensky's face, hence the quid pro quo allegation. A whistleblower who we don't know the name of, and who didn't actually directly listen to the call itself, is responsible for elevating the call to such national importance that it justified a sham impeachment hearing.

While critics allege that President Trump threatened to withhold nearly $400 million in U.S. military aid if Ukraine didn't investigate potential corruption involving Joe Biden's son Hunter, the timeline on that thesis is murky. There's obvious irony here in that Biden himself was in a "quid pro Joe" situation with Ukraine when he threatened to withhold $1 billion in aid if Shokin wasn't fired. The whistleblower complaint itself makes note of this in a section with the header "Circumstances leading up to the 25 July Presidential phone call" without any indication of how damning it is to Biden or any acknowledgement of the hypocrisy.

The $400 million in aid was disbursed on September 11. The Trump administration initially planned on disbursing the aid in February, but did not. White House chief of staff Mick Mulvaney had told reporters in mid-July, a week before Trump's phone call with Zelensky, that aid to Ukraine was being withheld due to concerns over its necessity. Are we to believe that aid was withheld in February in anticipation of a phone call six months later? It seems unlikely.

The whistleblower cited "information from multiple U.S. government officials" for his claim that "the president of the United States is using the power of his office to solicit interference from a foreign country in the 2020 U.S. election." That's bogus, and there's yet a second bit of obvious irony in that the only Ukraine-related interference in an election we know about comes from the Left in

2016. The entire impeachment sham is yet another example of the Left leveraging Ukraine to themselves interfere in an election by impeaching a sitting president (who never was at risk of being removed from office) ahead of the 2020 election.

To bolster his case, the whistleblower's complaint makes multiple references to a report titled "Meet the Florida Duo Helping Giuliani Investigate for Trump in Ukraine," published by the Organized Crime and Corruption Reporting Project (OCCRP).[244] George Soros is one of OCCRP's top donors, and the project has published articles defending Soros against his critics before.[245]

Within the whistleblower complaint, the OCCRP report is cited relating to claims about Rudy Giuliani's alleged efforts to investigate Biden.[246] In the bizarre world of the whistleblower, we're to believe that investigating Biden for alleged crimes is a crime itself—but anything Biden may have allegedly done is not. That's why they're able to allege that Trump committed a quid quo pro while mentioning Biden's alleged quid pro quo while seemingly experiencing no cognitive dissonance.

The OCCRP article is referenced numerous times in the footnotes of the whistleblower complaint. As *The Epoch Times*'s Tom Ozimek chronicles:[247]

- Footnote #4 of the complaint reads: "In a report published by the Organized Crime and Corruption Reporting Project (OCCRP) on 22 July, two associates of Mr. Giuliani reportedly traveled to Kyiv in May 2019 and met with Mr. Bakanov and another close [President] Zelensky adviser, Mr. Serhiy Shefir."

- Footnote #9 reads: "In May, Attorney General Barr announced that he was initiating a probe into the 'origins' of the Russia investigation. According to the above-referenced OCCRP report (22 July), two associates of Mr. Giuliani claimed to be working with Ukrainian officials to uncover information that would become part of this inquiry."

244 Belford, Aubrey, "Meet the Florida Duo Helping Giuliani Investigate for Trump in Ukraine," OCCRP, July 22, 2019. https://www.occrp.org/en/investigations/meet-the-florida-duo-helping-giuliani-dig-dirt-for-trump-in-ukraine

245 Ozimek, Tom, "Whistleblower's Complaint against Trump Cites George Soros-Funded NGO," *The Epoch Times*, September 27, 2019. https://www.theepochtimes.com/whistleblowers-complaint-against-trump-cites-george-soros-funded-ngo_3098685.html

246 Belford, Aubrey, "Meet the Florida Duo Helping Giuliani Investigate for Trump in Ukraine."

247 Ozimek, Tom, "Whistleblower's Complaint against Trump Cites George Soros-Funded NGO."

- Footnote #10 reads: "See, for example, the above-referenced articles in Bloomberg (16 May) and OCCRP (22 July)." This footnote relates to the claim in the report that "Mr. Giuliani had met on at least two occasions with Mr. Lutsenko: once in New York in late January and again in Warsaw in mid-February. In addition, it was publicly reported that Mr. Giuliani had spoken in late 2018 to former Prosecutor General Shokin, in a Skype call arranged by two associates of Mr. Giuliani."

- Footnote #11 reads: "I do not know whether these associates of Mr. Giuliani were the same individuals named in the 22 July report by OCCRP, referenced above."

The OCCRP document is also anti-Zelensky, who has himself blasted Soros in the past.

The Left mobilized to respond to these facts—with slander.

The left-wing rag *Salon* headlined its article on former top National Security Council official Fiona Hill's testimony during the first impeachment hearing "Fiona Hill Lays Waste to George Soros Conspiracy Theory at the Heart of Trump's Ukraine Defense."[248]

This "laying waste" amounted to her calling theories about Soros an "absolute outrage," adding "This is the longest-running anti-Semitic trope that we have in history, and a trope against Mr. Soros was also created for political purposes, and this is the new Protocols of The Elders of Zion."

Of the criticisms of then Ukraine ambassador Marie Yovanovitch, Hill trotted out the same mindless argument. "When I saw this happening to Ambassador Yovanovitch again, I was furious, because this is, again, just this whipping up of what is frankly an anti-Semitic conspiracy theory about George Soros to basically target nonpartisan career officials, and also some political appointees as well, because I just want to say this: this is not indiscriminate in its attacks."[249] Apparently, noticing that Yovanovitch had a "do not prosecute" list is a fault of the people who noticed.

---

248   Derysh, Igor, "Fiona Hill Lays Waste to the George Soros Conspiracy Theory at the Heart of Trump's Ukraine Defense," *Salon*, November 22, 2019. https://www.salon.com/2019/11/22/fiona-hill-lays-waste-to-the-george-soros-conspiracy-theory-at-the-heart-of-trumps-ukraine-defense/
249   Ibid.

UKRAINE SURVEILLANCE (AMBASSADOR YOVANOVITCH)

It wasn't just members of Trump's sphere of influence being monitored during his 2016 campaign and after the election (Spygate); those who drew attention to Biden's Ukraine scandal were also surveilled.

We learned from Ambassador Yovanovitch's testimony during the first bogus Trump impeachment hearings that her embassy asked to monitor Americans after reading an article in *The Hill* exposing her "do not prosecute list."[250]

"So we, you know, we're interested in, you know, kind of keeping track of the story so that we would know what was going on." She said she received a "finished product" from the surveillance, which she justified on the basis that "Because, I mean, there's an interest, obviously, I had an interest since I was being directly attacked." The embassy asked State Department officials in Washington to assist with the monitoring, she testified, but "what we were told is that the folks in Washington were too busy to do this, etc., etc."

Previously redacted emails obtained by Just the News revealed that State Department officials were explicitly ordered in Spring 2019 to stop tracking thirteen Americans' social media accounts for info related to the Biden-Ukraine scandal using a tool called "CrowdTangle" because it violated federal law. "We are barred by law from actively monitoring the accounts of American citizens in aggregate—and particularly from identifying and monitoring individual, selected accounts" a State Department official wrote in one email.[251]

"We can use CrowdTangle to monitor terms as they pertain to Yovanovitch, but these search terms cannot be used to target a particular list if it includes American citizens," the email added. The individuals included Sean Hannity, Laura Ingraham, Lou Dobbs, Donald Trump Jr., Rudy Giuliani, John Solomon, and others.[252]

Other emails paint a picture of State Department officials under Trump that depicts them as worried before the 2020 election that the

250 Farrington, Dana, "Former Ukraine Ambassador Yovanitch's Testimony to Congress," NPR, November 4, 2019. https://www.npr.org/2019/11/04/776075849/read-former-ukraine-ambassador-yovanovitchs-testimony-to-congress

251 Solomon, "State Dept. Officials Told They Broke Law by Monitoring Americans During Ukraine Scandal," Just the News, October 6, 2020. https://justthenews.com/accountability/russia-and-ukraine-scandals/state-dept-officials-told-they-broke-law-monitoring

252 Ibid.

revelations about Biden in Ukraine may be "the mother load [sic] and main thread to play out, possibly thru Nov. 2020."[253]

According to John Solomon:

> Other unredacted emails also show that the search terms Yovanovitch's team sought to use included stories about herself as well as the liberal megadonor George Soros.
>
> They also expressed a desire to combat the narrative—later confirmed in testimony to be true—that State officials perceived Vice President Joe Biden had engaged in a conflict of interest in 2016 by continuing to preside over U.S. anti-corruption policy in Ukraine while his son Hunter served on the board of a Ukrainian gas company called Burisma Holdings that was under investigation for corruption.
>
> Deputy Assistant Secretary of State for European and Eurasian Affairs George Kent, then an official in the embassy, emailed the embassy team on March 27, 2019, imploring them to "get up to ramming speed" to counter four narratives in The Hill newspaper, including the Biden-Burisma controversy.
>
> "This story is being set up to both snowball and slow burn with now four separate storylines having been put into play the past week," wrote Kent, previously Yovanovitch's top deputy at U.S. Embassy Kiev.
>
> The emails don't explain why the embassy believed it had a policy reason to be concerned about the 2020 U.S. election or Biden.[254]

There's a strong possibility that it was the National Security Council's Lieutenant Colonel Alex Vindman, who was one of the driving forces behind the Ukraine impeachment hoax, who acted as the anonymous whistleblower's source. As Representative Lee Zel-

---

253 Ibid.
254 Solomon, "US Embassy Pressed Ukraine."

din puts it, "Vindman was the person on the call who went to the whistleblower after the call, to give the whistleblower the information he needed to file his complaint." One senior congressional aide commented that "for all intents and purposes," Vindman is the whistleblower in that light. [255]

Vindman was the only person at the NSC who listened into Trump's "perfect" call with Zelensky, and he testified that he spoke to only two people outside the NSC about it: someone whose name he didn't provide—and George Kent.[256]

So Kent pressured against investigating the Soros-funded Ukraine-based AntAC to avoid any explosive revelations from surfacing, and then reappeared as one of those the de facto whistleblowers contacted after Trump's call with Ukraine's president, sparking impeachment hearings.

What are the odds?

255 Hemingway, Mollie, "Vindman, Not Whistleblower, Was Driving Force behind Impeachment," *The Federalist*, September 8, 2020. https://thefederalist.com/2020/09/08/vindman-not-whistleblower-was-driving-force-behind-impeachment/
256 Ibid.

George Soros Infiltrates Higher Education

As if higher education's reputation for leftism wasn't bad enough, George Soros has entered the industry, and it's furthering his specific brand of progressivism.

Soros' Open Society Foundations budgeted $63.4 million, just over 5 percent of its budget, toward influencing higher education in 2020. Soros has been ramping up spending in this category at a pace of 45 percent per year since 2016.[257] Most of the spending ($50 million) is listed as "global" with no indication of where it's being spent. Of funds that are reported, Soros is spending the most in Eurasia.[258]

Through the OSF, Soros has funded over twenty thousand scholarships, invested hundreds of millions into American Far-Left colleges, and created a school of his own.

The OSF says "Our engagement in higher education issues has expanded considerably, to a broad effort to support the development of universities and colleges that are well governed, inclusive and responsive, and which promote academic freedom."[259]

Soros' first venture into higher education for the purpose of furthering his open society vision was with the founding of the Central European University (CEU) in Hungary in 1991. That serves as his ideological base of operations in the realm of higher education, one that he's since used for synergistic purposes with his venture into influencing American higher education.

It's also where his influence in Europe has been met with the fiercest resistance.

---

257 "What We Do: Higher Education," Open Society Foundations. https://www.opensocietyfoundations.org/what-we-do/themes/higher-education
258 Ibid.
259 Ibid.

CENTRAL EUROPEAN UNIVERSITY

The creation of CEU represents Soros' first journey into institution building.

Soros' idea for an "independent" university in Central Europe was spawned during a meeting at the Inter-University Centre in April 1989. Soros recalled of the meeting, "At that time I rejected [the idea of CEU] in no uncertain terms. 'I am interested not in starting institutions but in infusing existing institutions with content,' I declared. After the fall of the Berlin Wall, I changed my mind. A revolution needs new institutions to sustain the ideas that motivated it, I argued with myself. I overcame my aversion toward institutions and yielded to the clamor for a Central European University."[260] In other words, Soros seems to have changed his mind when he realized that he could use institutions as permanent fixtures to advance his agenda.

On the eve of the Soviet Union's dissolution, Soros published "Underwriting Democracy," in which he emphasized the importance of building institutions to advance his leftist agenda, and CEU would be his first project.

Soros and his advisers considered Bratislava, Prague, Warsaw, Budapest, Vienna, Trieste, Krakow, and Moscow to host the University. Soros said he was "anxious not to start the university in Hungary. Since I am myself Hungarian, the university would immediately become a Hungarian one," but that would quickly change.[261]

Soros initially wanted to create a university with "three legs" in Warsaw, Prague, and Budapest, but this plan would never materialize.[262]

In June 1990, Czechoslovakia's government agreed to provide buildings in Prague and Bratislava, pay for operating costs, and give them 50 million crowns in funding (about $6 million at today's exchange rate). Not coincidentally, Soros had a personal friendship with Czechoslovakian President Václav Havel. The government of Hungary promised to make a building available in Budapest for use as a third campus, which they never fulfilled, so Soros privately rented out a building in Budapest.[263]

---

260 "George Soros and the Founding of Central European University," Center for Strategic Philanthropy and Civil Society, April 9, 2007. https://cspcs.sanford.duke.edu/sites/default/files/SorosCEUOriginsfinal.pdf
261 Soros, George, *Soros on Soros: Ahead of the Curve*, page 134.
262 "Central European University (CEU)," *Influence Watch*. https://www.influencewatch.org/non-profit/central-european-university/
263 "George Soros and the Founding of Central European University."

After being offered a ten-story building by Petr Pithart, who was then the Czech prime minister, CEU's Prague campus opened in April 1991 with four departments: economics; environmental sciences; politics and sociology; and history. [264] CEU heavily focuses on the social sciences over hard sciences, and both campuses offered roughly the same number of programs. Eventually, the early curriculum would be expanded to include European studies, international relations, nationalism studies, and art history at Prague, and legal and gender studies at Budapest.[265]

At the school's opening ceremony, Soros committed to funding CEU $5 million per year for five years. A third foundation was established later in the year to serve as an umbrella for the two other campuses.[266] In 1992, Soros committed to including a permanent endowment.[267]

Soros outlines in CEU's statement of intent his vision:

> The Central European University has come into existence in response to the revolutionary changes that have occurred in Central and Eastern Europe recently. The primary impetus comes from Central European intellectuals who seek to understand their past and prepare for the future. But it has also received enthusiastic support from Western intellectuals who are concerned about the future of Europe. Everyone in Central Europe today wants a high-quality Western-style education. The CEU will provide for the region the academic equivalent of the best Western education, and thereby attract students of the highest caliber. It will also aim to provide a window of opportunity for some of the most able students whose studies should lead to a period of further study at a leading Western university.[268]

He listed four principal objectives for CEU: to develop a new curriculum, to help educating new central European leaders, to raise

---

264 Soros, George, *In Defense of Open Society*, page 96.
265 Ibid., 101.
266 Tereza Pospíšilová, "Transnational Philanthropy and Nationalism: The Early Years of Central European University." *Monde(s)* 2, no. 6., 2014, pages 139–140.
267 Ibid.
268 "George Soros and the Founding of Central European University."

the standards and methods of teaching and research in the region, and to "foster cooperation and understanding among the citizens and nations of the region."[269]

As Tereza Pospíšilová, a professor whose research areas include philanthropy, writes in a paper of CEU's early years, CEU is not just a network but perhaps an "international social movement."[270] CEU wasn't established solely as an educational institution, as it also investigated and held public discussions on their preferred political topics at conferences they held in the region. Many early conferences and workshops featured participants from Soros' inner circle.

The University has a number of notable faculty, including former minister of foreign of affairs of Hungary Péter Balázs, former president of the Supreme Court of Israel Aharon Barak, former minister of finance of Hungary Lajos Bokros, and former minister of culture of Hungary András Bozóki.

Soros further outlines CEU's forthcoming activities:

> The CEU will put far more into the educational system than it takes out. To ensure this, the CEU will also sponsor both teaching and research at existing institutions at the same times as it sets up and runs its own postgraduate centers. It will also sponsor and support research fellows of the highest caliber to work within their own institutions. The CEU intends to collaborate directly with a number of academic institutions: These will become "affiliated" with the University.[271]

The emphasis on research (to support Soros-backed and Soros-adjacent causes) could explain why the faculty-to-student ratio is so low. Today CEU is located in Vienna, Austria, and reports employing nearly as many staff as students. For the 2019–2020 year, CEU employed 367 faculty, ninety-three researchers, 395 permanent administrative staff, and 355 short term administrative staff,[272] all for a student body of 1,299.[273] In America, the national average faculty-to-student ratio is one to sixteen.[274] CEU officially boasts a facul-

269   Ibid.
270   Pospíšilová, "Transnational Philanthropy and Nationalism."
271   "George Soros and the Founding of Central European University."
272   "Faculty and Staff," Central European University. https://www.ceu.edu/about/facts-figures/staff
273   "Students," Central European University. https://www.ceu.edu/about/facts-figures/students
274   "What is a Good Student-to-Faculty Ratio for U.S. Colleges?" Best Value Schools, August 11, 2020. https://www.bestvalueschools.com/faq/what-is-a-good-student-to-faculty-ratio-for-u-s-colleges/#:~:text=The%20national%20average%20of%20students,Center%20for%20Educational%20Statistics%20report

ty-to-student ratio of one to three (only counting full-time faculty),[275] which only six schools in the entire U.S. can match.[276]

One hundred students enrolled in the first fall semester, and development continued with the construction of a library and five future academic programs. The school functions only as a graduate school.

Soros quickly ran into trouble due to a booming Prague real estate market when the trade union that owned CEU's Prague building decided they wanted to turn it into a hotel. Planning to evict the university, the building owners raised CEU's rent from nothing to $1 million per year. They also found a clause in the government's agreement with Soros that the university would need to get accredited within two years or be shut down.[277]

Despite a successful rush to accreditation, the opening of CEU's Budapest campus, and reaching an agreement with Poland's government to open a campus in Warsaw, Soros decided to move the Prague departments to Budapest. CEU Prague would cease to exist by January 1996 after Soros decided to end it the year prior. Soros' account of events is that he was kicked out of Prague by the new right-wing president, Václav Klaus, a man who considered Soros a socialist and would become a "lifetime enemy" of his. "In January 1993, the moment of the dissolution of Czechoslovakia, Klaus said that an optical illusion has finally disappeared from the map: the Czech Republic has nothing to do with Central Europe anymore. One of his first acts was to kick us out of the building."[278]

Despite a rocky start, CEU has since graduated nearly twenty thousand students from nearly 150 different countries, most of whom went on to work in business, research, education, and government.

Recent courses offered since 2020 show how the school looks to mold progressive activists. They include "Black Skin, White Masks: Decolonization through Fanon," "Confronting the Crisis: Refugees and Populism in Europe," "Gender and Sexuality in the Middle East," "Environmentalism of the Poor," "A History of Modern Police," "Capitalism and Slavery," and much more. Even in something as seemingly apolitical as an architecture degree are course offerings that include "Architectural Entanglements with Labor" and "The Politics of Infrastructure."

275   "Schools and Departments," Central European University. https://www.ceu.edu/academics/schools-depart-ments#:~:text=Students%20come%20from%2036%20countries,faculty%20ratio%20is%203%3A1
276   "Colleges with the Smallest Student-Faculty Ratios," Collegexpress. https://www.collegexpress.com/lists/list/colleges-with-the-smallest-student-faculty-ratios/2089/
277   "George Soros and the Founding of Central European University."
278   Soros, *In Defense of Open Society*, page 96.

The Soros family flag and their U.S. sphere of influence have firmly been planted in the university. George Soros' son Robert Soros was elected to the CEU board of trustees in 2012.[279] Other current and former members of the board include the OSF's London director, William Newton-Smith; the OSF's New York president, Christopher Stone; Bard College's president, Leon Botstein; Harvard Law School's Benjamin Heineman Jr.; and Harvard Professor Patricia Albjerg Graham.[280]

CEU is well intwined with Harvard. CEU's business school celebrated its twenty-fifth anniversary with the publication of a new book *Free Market in Its Twenties: Modern Business Decision Making in Central and Eastern Europe*, for which Soros wrote the intro. Soros also hosted a book launch event in Budapest, which featured Harvard Business School Dean Nitin Nohria.[281]

Notable CEU alumni include former president of Georgia Giorgi Margvelashvili, Members of European Parliament Lívia Járóka and Monica Macovei, former Georgian minister of defense Tina Khidasheli, Chairman of the Slovakian Party of the Hungarian Coalition József Berényi, and former Croatian minister of justice Orsat Miljenic.

Soros has only further developed the school over time.

In 2010, Soros pledged $5 million to create a new economics institute at the University of Oxford along with the left-wing Institute of New Economic Thinking—an organization that Soros himself launched with a $50 million donation. CEU hosted an institute event that brought together over two hundred academic, business, and government thought leaders in an attempt to replicate the famous 1944 Bretton Woods meeting that created the World Bank and IMF. Soros said there that he wants a "multilateral" economic system where America isn't dominant.

THE HUNGARIAN REVOLT

While Hungary served as the initial base for CEU, one of the seeds Soros planted would backfire decades later. In 1989 a young Viktor Orbán was on the receiving end of a Soros funded scholar-

---

279   "Robert Soros Elected to CEU Board of Trustees," Central European University, October 30, 2012, https://www.ceu.edu/article/2012-10-30/robert-soros-elected-ceu-board-trustees
280   "Central European University, Annual Report 2015," Central European University, 2016. https://www.ceu.edu/sites/default/files/attachment/basic_page/15437/ar2015final.pdf
281   "CEU Business School Marks 25th Anniversary with Book Launch with Soros, Harvard's Nohria," Central European University, June 23, 2014. https://www.ceu.edu/article/2014-06-23/ceu-business-school-marks-25th-anniversary-book-launch-soros-harvards-nohria

ship, and Soros also subsidized a student journal that Orbán edited. Soros was reportedly dazzled by Orbán's charisma enough to donate to the then year-old political party Fidesz that Orbán founded. At this time Orbán publicly called himself a liberal, and spoke out against attacks from nationalists against Soros' influence in the country.[282]

That would prove to backfire spectacularly for Soros as Orbán matured politically, and Fidesz gradually morphed into a right-wing nationalist party that now controls a majority of the seats in Hungarian parliament. Orbán has been president of Fidesz since 1993, and has been prime minister from 1998 to 2002, and again since 2010.

The migrant crisis spurred by the Syrian civil war, and Soros' support for mass refugee resettlement in Europe appears to be a turning point in 2015 that prompted Orbán to launch an all-out war on Soros and any vestige of influence he has, including CEU.[283] "The next year will be about squeezing out Soros and the power that he symbolizes," he declared in 2016.[284]

The government launched a €100 million anti-Soros ad campaign.[285] One billboard showed a black and white image of Soros with the caption "Let's not allow Soros to have the last laugh." One anti-Soros image was put on the floor of a train so that passengers would walk over it, which CEU's rector admits caused a "flicker of pain" across Soros' face when it was described to him.[286]

Public polling showed that Soros went from being a relatively unknown figure in Hungary to "diabolical figure" within a year and a half.[287]

No foreign leader has done more to combat the foreign influence of Soros in their country than Orbán. In part, he's criminalized advancing the Soros agenda, with one law dubbed the Stop Soros Law, criminalizing the advocacy of illegal migration in 2018.

The biggest impact Orbán would have would be in targeting CEU, which his government crushed in Hungary. In April 2017, the government passed a law affecting foreign branch campuses requiring them to have a campus in their home country, which CEU doesn't have (they're accredited in New York). An agreement was drafted

---

282 Foer, Franklin, "Viktor Orbán's War on Intellect," *The Atlantic*, June 2019. https://www.theatlantic.com/magazine/archive/2019/06/george-soros-viktor-orban-ceu/588070

283 Walker, Shaun, "'A Useful Punching Bag': Why Hungary's Viktor Orbán Has Turned on George Soros," *The Guardian*, June 22, 2017. https://www.theguardian.com/world/2017/jun/22/hungary-viktor-orban-george-soros

284 "Ruling Fidesz Party Wants Soros-Funded NGOs 'Swept Out' of Hungary," *Reuters*, January 11, 2017. https://www.reuters.com/article/us-hungary-fidesz-soros/ruling-fidesz-party-wants-soros-funded-ngos-swept-out-of-hungary-idUSKBN14V0P2

285 Patricolo, Claudia, "Hungary's Anti-Soros Campaign Cost 100 Million Euros," Emerging Europe, January 26, 2018. https://emerging-europe.com/news/hungarys-anti-soros-campaign-cost-100-million-euros/

286 Foer, "Viktor Orbán's War on Intellect."

287 Ibid.

between the Hungarian government and the State of New York, but the Hungarian government refused to sign it.[288]

Amid the crackdown, the Progressive Alliance of Socialists and Democrats (a political party in European Parliament that Soros has influence over) voiced its support for CEU [289]

CEU announced at the end of the year that it had been forced out of Budapest. "Because Hungary's Law of Higher Education forbids Central European University to accept new students after January 1, 2019, CEU is forced to announce today that it will launch all U.S.-accredited degree programs in Vienna in September 2019."[290]

With the move to Vienna, Soros announced the commitment of another $825 million to higher education, which would go toward CEU and New York's Bard College to "build a global network for colleges and universities to work together and support each other."

In total, the relocation to Vienna is expected to cost Soros a net €193 million over six years.[291]

Regardless, CEU president and rector Michael Ignatieff admitted defeat in what he called a "great battle." "We are definitely the only university in Europe, if not the world, that has been forced to move from one state to another—especially during a pandemic. I mean, honestly, it was really tough. Our people are very tired, very exhausted."[292]

At least Soros made one good investment in Orbán.

SOROS INFLUENCE ON AMERICAN CAMPUSES

From his first charitable grant in the late 1970s to the early 2010s, through his OSF Soros contributed over $400 million to colleges and universities, with 75 percent of it going to two schools; the aforementioned CEU, and Bard College. Over nineteen colleges had individually received at least $1 million from Soros.[293]

288 "CEU Forced Out of Budapest: To Launch U.S. Degree Programs in Vienna in September 2019," Central European University, December 3, 2018. https://www.ceu.edu/article/2018-12-03/ceu-forced-out-budapest-launch-us-degree-programs-vienna-september-2019

289 "The Group of the Progressive Alliance of Socialists and Democrats (the S&D Group) Supports CEU," *Central European University*, April 26, 2017, https://www.ceu.edu/article/2017-04-26/group-progressive-alliance-socialists-and-democrats-sd-group-supports-ceu

290 "CEU Forced Out of Budapest."

291 Foer, "Viktor Orbán's War on Intellect."

292 "'It was a Great Battle'—Michael Ignatieff, President and Rector of Central European University, on the Lost Fight Against Viktor Orban, His New Home in Austria, and the Miracle of the Viennese Tram," Central European University, April 13, 2021. https://www.ceu.edu/article/2021-04-13/it-was-great-battle-michael-ignatieff-president-and-rector-central-european

293 "Special Report: George Soros: Godfather of the Left," Media Research Center. https://web.archive.org/web/20210707043808/https://www.mrc.org/special-reports/special-report-george-soros-godfather-left

To give just a sampling of just a few programs that Soros has funded, Harvard received $60k in 2008 to develop an outreach program to promote the film *Secrecy*, a documentary on the war on terror. Georgetown received $1.8 million for the Justice at Stake Campaign, a group that believes it's a problem that there aren't enough "people of color, women, lesbian, gay, bisexual and transgender persons, and persons with disabilities" that are judges.[294] Ohio State University got over $100k for its Kirwan Institute for the study of race and ethnicity, which is now aiding in providing implicit bias training to Los Angeles City Workers.[295]

The funding is even greater than reported because some is indirect. The aforementioned Institute for New Economic Thinking (INET) was founded with a $50 million pledge from Soros, and within its first two years, INET disbursed fifty grants in over eleven countries. Among the beneficiaries was Duke University, which was given a $750k grant to its "Center for the History of Political Economy." We learned just how much an impact it would make in an announcement in *Duke Today*; the school's assistant director of media relations said: "The money will allow the Duke center to expand its programs, which include a fellowship and visiting scholars program, workshop and lunch series, a summer teaching institute, a speaker series, and annual conferences." The school will also be able to expand its summer institute.[296]

The rate of funding and number of institutions he bequeathed would only increase from there. From 2014 to 2018, Soros donated $184 million to 171 institutions of higher education in fifty-one countries, nearly a tenth of all Foundations-based giving.[297] The amount donated annually nearly doubled from 2014 ($32 million) to 2018 ($62 million). U.S. universities took in 72 percent of the money, reflecting a domestic shift in recent years.

Soros also backs institutes connected to universities, with his $4 million donating to the UConn Human Rights Institute in 2016 being the largest donation to the program. The funds are aimed toward students who want to major in human rights, and the school's graduates have landed a number of humanitarian jobs for various left-wing

---

294 Ibid.
295 "Soros-Funded Group to Provide 'Mandatory Implicit Bias Training' for City Workers in L.A." *Judicial Watch*, January 26, 2021. https://www.judicialwatch.org/corruption-chronicles/soros-funded-group-to-provide-mandatory-implicit-bias-training-for-city-workers-in-l-a/
296 Hartsoe, Steve, "Duke Joins Global Effort to Boost Economics Education," *Duke Today*, January 24, 2011. https://today.duke.edu/2011/01/soros.html
297 "History and Hungary: George Soros and His University Philanthropy," University Philanthropy, October 6, 2020. https://www.universityphilanthropy.com/our-blog/history-and-hungary-george-soros-and-his-university-philanthropy

social causes. According to the University of Connecticut, it boasts the largest number of students studying human rights in the U.S.[298]

Bard College had received nearly $80 million total from Soros when he announced in 2020 that he'd be awarding it an additional $100 million over the next decade.[299] In 2021 he offered another $500 million as soon as the college could find donors to match or exceed it, which Bard leaders believe they can pull off within five years. [300] This is one of the largest gifts in the history of American higher education.

Nowhere other than at the CEU and Bard does Soros have such a direct influence on the schools he backs, and the two schools are linked. CEU's chairman of the board, Leon Botstein, is also the president of Bard College. Botstein was later named chancellor of the Open Society University Network (CEU and Bard are the network's founding members).

Soros has family involved too. With $20 million from her former husband, Soros' ex-wife Susan Weber founded the Bard College Graduate Center for Studies in the Decorative Arts, Design, and Culture in 1993. Despite that, the media portrays her as self-made. One magazine described her as the "Renaissance woman at the helm of Bard's graduate center," quoting Weber as saying she "started this place because no one would hire me."[301] There was no mention of any assistance to the tune of $20 million from her then husband.

Bard's Institute for International Liberal Education offers joint degree programs in areas where Soros operates: South Africa, Kyrgyzstan, Hungary, Russia, and at the Palestinian Al-Quds University in Jerusalem, the only Arab school there. In Russia, Bard helped found the University of St. Petersburg, which Soros also pitched in nearly $6 million to fund. In Hungary, they partnered with CEU while still active there.

Soros funds student activists through the "Trustee Leader-Scholar" program at Bard, which the college says has had its students leave an impact "from Red Hook to the West Bank." (Bard College is located in Red Hook). Projects include the "Black Body Experience," "Bard Palestinian Youth Initiative," "Migrant Labor Project," "Pal-

298 Merritt, Grace, "Largest Human Rights Gift to UConn to Provide Scholarships, Build Endowment," UConn Foundation, January 2016. https://www.foundation.uconn.edu/largest-human-rights-gift-to-uconn/
299 "Open Society Foundations Invest $100 Million in Bard College: Strengthening the Global Network," Bard College, July 1, 2020. https://www.bard.edu/news/osf-100-million-bard-college-strengthening-global-network
300 Adams, Susan, "George Soros Is Giving $500 Million to Bard College," Forbes, April 1, 2021. https://www.forbes.com/sites/susanadams/2021/04/01/george-soros-is-giving-500-million-to-bard-college/?sh=2d2d4d512ba7
301 Milgrom, Melissa, "The Renaissance Woman at the Helm of Bard's Graduate Center," Metropolis, January 7, 2014. https://www.metropolismag.com/design/arts-culture/susan-weber-renaissance-woman-bard-graduate-center/

estine Awareness Project," and the "Trans Action Initiative," among numerous left-wing causes.[302]

The school's 2020–2021 course catalogue thanked Soros for a recent effort near the end of an introductory section titled "History of Bard":

> The Open Society University Network (OSUN), created with support from George Soros's Open Society Foundations, launched in January 2020 with the goal of integrating teaching and research across higher education institutions worldwide. Leon Botstein will serve as the first chancellor of the network, which is anchored by Bard and Central European University (CEU) and includes educational and research partners in Europe, Russia, Asia, Africa, the Middle East, South America, and the United States. Within the framework of OSUN, Bard's Human Rights Project, the Fisher Center, and CEU are developing a graduate program in human rights and the arts."[303]

We also get some insight into the school's priorities, which heavily favor so-called "social justice." Course initiatives include the "Hate Studies Initiative," "Migration Initiative," and "Racial Justice Initiative."[304]

One new course that will debut in the fall 2021 semester as part of the "Hate Studies Initiative" promotes the Far Left's national defund-the-police hysteria. The course is titled "Abolishing Prisons and the Police" and will teach students "how to sell abolition to the masses and design a multimedia ad campaign to make prison abolition go viral."[305]

The course description elaborates that "Through the figure of abolition (a phenomenon we will explore via movements to end slavery, the death penalty, abortion, gay conversion therapy and more) we will explore how and why groups of Americans have sought to bring an absolute end to sources of human suffering. In turn, we will explore a history of the punitive impulse in American social policy and seek to discern means of intervening against it."[306]

302 "Trustee Leader Scholar," Bard CCE. https://cce.bard.edu/community/tls/
303 "Catalogue," Bard CCE. https://www.bard.edu/catalogue/
304 Ibid.
305 Kaminsky, Gabe, "George Soros-Backed Bard College Offers Class Called 'Abolishing Prisons and The Police,'" *The Federalist*, July 1, 2021. https://thefederalist.com/2021/07/01/george-soros-backed-bard-college-offers-class-called-abolishing-prisons-and-the-police/
306 Ibid.

The course will be taught by Kwame Holmes, who has a history of calling for the abolition of law enforcement, and penned an op-ed called "Why Abolish the Police?"[307]

Within the U.S. and Europe, the universities Soros funds share his left-wing social justice agenda and are known for creating the kinds of future leaders to spread them.

Many universities under the Soros umbrella are closely linked, like CEU and Bard, or CEU and the London School of Economics, which are both part of CIVICA, an alliance of eight European schools in the social sciences.[308]

Bard has established a network of six partner institutions that includes other Soros beneficiaries such as the American University of Central Asia and European Humanities University.[309]

Schools are also networked into the OSF. Board members of the OSF's "Open Society Justice Initiatives" include individuals who teach at or are affiliated with American University in Washington, the University of Nairobi, Fordham University, and Middlesex University (all of which receive funding from the Foundation to Promote Open Society).[310]

OTHER INTERNATIONAL FUNDING (EUROPE, ASIA, AFRICA)

By continent, European universities receive the most from Soros after the U.S. in recently years, and the U.K. is the largest beneficiary by country there. Soros disbursed nearly $12 million to twenty-five U.K. universities, including Oxford and the London School of Economics (all numbers in this section are from 2014 to 2018).[311]

Asian universities are the third-biggest beneficiary of Soros backing. Excluding CEU, the biggest non-U.S. beneficiary of Soros' higher education splurge is the American University of Central Asia (in Kyrgyzstan).[312]

Latin American universities received $7.6 million, with Columbian and Venezuelan universities taking in the most funding. African and Australasian universities were on the bottom of the funding list,

307   Ibid.
308   Soros, George, "Opinion: George Soros Explains How Democracy Can Overcome Authoritarian Nationalism." MarketWatch, January 24, 2020. https://www.marketwatch.com/story/george-soros-explains-how-democracy-can-overcome-authoritarian-nationalism-2020-01-24
309   "Bard International Network," Bard CCE. https://cce.bard.edu/international/
310   "History and Hungary."
311   "Funding by George Soros and the Foundation to Promote Open Society," University Philanthropy. https://www.universityphilanthropy.com/funding-by-george-soros-and-open-society
312   "History and Hungary."

with Soros still making donations to the University of Cape Town, the beneficiaries of his first donations in the realm of higher education.[313]

Funding of foreign universities is rising at the fastest pace, more than doubling from thirty-one non-U.S. universities funded in 2014 to sixty-four by 2018.[314]

THE OPEN SOCIETY UNIVERSITY NETWORK

Like all his influence campaigns, Soros' influence over universities is global. In the words of the Open Society Foundations, Soros is launching a "global network" to "transform" higher education.

As per one of OSF's press releases in January 2020:

> Soros announced today that he is creating a new university network to better prepare students for current and future global challenges. He is endowing the network with one billion dollars ($1 billion) and asking other philanthropists to contribute.
>
> The network, which will operate throughout the world, is named the Open Society University Network (OSUN). It will integrate teaching and research across higher education institutions worldwide.
>
> .....
>
> Mr. Soros said: "I believe our best hope lies in access to an education that reinforces the autonomy of the individual by cultivating critical thinking and emphasizing academic freedom. I consider the Open Society University Network to be the most important and enduring project of my life and I should like to see it implemented while I am still around."[315]

---

313   Ibid.
314   Ibid.
315   "George Soros Launches Global Network to Transform Higher Education," Open Society Foundations, January 23, 2020. https://www.opensocietyfoundations.org/newsroom/george-soros-launches-global-network-to-transform-higher-education#:~:text=DAVOS%2C%20SWITZERLAND%E2%80%94George%20Soros%20announced,asking%20other%20philanthropists%20to%20contribute

CEU and Bard College were named as the "core" of the new network and will partner with Arizona State University (a leader in distance learning) and other global institutions such as American University of Central Asia in Kyrgyzstan and BRAC University in Bangladesh.

President of Bard College Leon Botstein was named as chancellor of OSUN, who described it as one of the "most transformative initiatives in higher education I have witnessed in my career" before expressing his gratitude toward Soros.

Just days before the announcement, Soros spoke to the World Economic Forum where he railed against the rise of nationalism in the U.S., U.K., Hungary. Nationalism is, in his words, the "great enemy of the open society." He blasts Trump in the speech as the "ultimate narcissist"—which is rich coming from Soros, who wrote in his 1987 book *The Alchemy of Finance* "I have always harbored an exaggerated view of my self-importance…to put it bluntly, I fancied myself as some kind of God."[316]

We already know his solution: "I believe that as a long-term strategy our best hope lies in access to quality education, specifically an education that reinforces the autonomy of the individual by cultivating critical thinking and emphasizing academic freedom" he told the audience. "30 years ago I set up an educational institution that does exactly that (cultivating critical thinking and emphasizing academic freedom). It is called the Central European University (CEU) and its mission is to advance the values of the open society."[317]

The OSUN is yet another organization Soros set up when he reasonably can expect to have only years to live, indicating that it's a network he's organizing to keep his grip on higher education from beyond the grave. The odds of losing influence over any one university are reduced when they're bound together.

Excluding Bard and CEU, CEU's global network includes twenty-four colleges and universities and fifteen research and educational institutions. As one organization that tracks university philanthropy observes, "The objective appears to be leveraging the resources of universities around the world to provide a common curricula for teaching and facilitating partnerships to explore and research global issues."[318]

316   Soros, George, *The Alchemy of Finance*, page 372.
317   Christian, "The Open Society University Network (OSUN)," AALEP, January 25, 2020. http://www.aalep.eu/open-society-university-network-osun
318   "History and Hungary."

George Soros and the Media

Hundreds of millions of people worldwide are exposed to one form of media or another influenced by George Soros whether they're aware of it or not. Soros and those he backs would rather you don't notice—but have a baseless charge of anti-Semitism handy if you point out a Soros connection.

Soros has his tentacles in most forms of media: radio, print, television, investigative outlets, supposedly independent media, blogs, and more.

Besides funding activist groups to do his bidding, Soros uses the media as another primary tool of influence. His activists take a stance—and his media arms make their narrative a "reality" by repeating it. Highlights include the racial hysteria that underpins the Black Lives Matter movement (and the activists themselves), the campaigns to take down Fox News, the push for open borders, campaigns for mass refugee resettlement, anti-law-and-order narratives, and more.

It's through Soros' narrative-pushing that he can convert the unsuspecting to his worldview without them knowing it. After all, the best propaganda is propaganda that the audience doesn't recognize as such.

SOROS LIFELONG FASCINATION WITH MEDIA

Soros' history with journalism dates back to his upbringing in Hungary. He served as the editor-in-chief, publisher, and vendor of his own publication "The Lupa News" (named after Lupa Island, where his family would spend summer holidays). At the time was only in fourth grade.[319]

It was from money earned from that paper that Soros made his first political donation. In 1939, the Budapest newspaper *8 Orai ujsag* (*8 O'clock News*) ran a story about the then nine-year-old Soros arriving to their office and handing them two-pengő notes over the counter. When asked what they were supposed to do with the money, Soros replied "I brought this money for the Finnish people. There is a war in Finland at the moment. Daddy told me." Soros would later tell one of his biographers that he doesn't remember the event, but that his father probably put him up to it.[320]

The Soros media empire has grown from a small paper to hundreds of media organizations that receive his funding. According to one estimate reporters, writers, and bloggers backed by Soros at just the top thirteen operations he funds (out of 180 at the time) reach an estimate three hundred thirty million people around the world every month (a size roughly equal to the population of the U.S.).[321] Presumably, that reach has only grown with time. That estimate (which is the only one available of its kind) is from 2011—and Soros hasn't slowed down since then.

THE SOROS MEDIA STOCK PORTFOLIO

Soros' funds are required to file a Form 13F, which is a quarterly report all investment managers with at least $100 million under management are required to file. Through one, we can glean insight into exactly what Soros Fund Management is invested in at the end of any quarter.[322]

At the end of the first quarter of 2021 Soros' biggest stock holding was Liberty Broadband, which had a market value of $621 million and accounted for 12 percent of his entire portfolio, and a roughly 2.2 percent stake in the company.[323] Liberty Broadband's largest asset is Charter Communications and its subsidiaries, which together are the second-largest cable operator in the U.S.[324]

319 Kaufman, *Soros: The Life and Times of a Messianic Billionaire*, pages 25–26.
320 Ibid.
321 Gainor, Dan, "Soros-Funded Lefty Media Reach More Than 300 Million Every Month," mrcNewsBusters, May 25, 2011, https://www.newsbusters.org/blogs/business/dan-gainor/2011/05/25/soros-funded-lefty-media-reach-more-300-million-every-month
322 Vincent, John, "George Soros's Portfolio—Q1 2021 Update," *SeekingAlpha*, May 24, 2021. https://seekingalpha.com/article/4430793-george-soros-portfolio-q1-2021-update
323 "Liberty Broadband Corporation (LBRDA) Valuation Measures & Financial Statistics," Yahoo Finance, July 20, 2021. https://finance.yahoo.com/quote/LBRDA/key-statistics/
324 "Investor FAQS," Liberty Broadband Corporation, https://ir.libertybroadband.com/investor-faqs

Another large media holding is ViacomCBS, of which Soros owned just over $194 million, representing 3.64 percent of his portfolio, and a 0.7 percent stake in the company. ViacomCBS and its subsidiaries include Viacom and CBS (duh), Paramount Pictures, and Simon & Schuster, among others.

Soros Fund Management took part in a $250 million debt funding round for VICE Media, a left-wing digital media company known for its "Mad Libs" headlines.[325] Soros Fund Management also owns a 10 percent stake in the company.

THE SOROS MEDIA INFLUENCE EMPIRE

As is standard for Soros, his influence began in Europe before America. By 1994 Soros had thirty supposedly independent radio, TV stations, and publications under his influence just in Eastern Europe, and that's a drop in the bucket compared to his modern American influence.[326]

From 2004 to 2011 Soros spent nearly $50 million funding about 180 media organizations, and "news infrastructure" such as journalism schools and industry organizations. The funding figures are derived from tax forms and news stories and understate the true extent of his funding, because they don't include indirect funding (Soros funding an organization that then donates to media).[327]

Today, the OSF budgets $25.8 million a year (in 2020) toward journalism, and its website claims that 0 percent of it goes toward U.S. outlets. As was the case when the OSF provided numbers on its funding of higher education, a large share of the spending (in this case nearly-half) was unclassified as "global."[328]

Internationally, the OSF says it has regional foundations in "Africa, Asia, Latin America, and the Middle East that support innovative and courageous independent media, from the Afghan newspaper *Etilaatroz* to *El Faro* in El Salvador."[329]

Contributions are made through the OSF's "Program on Independent Journalism," which claims it "supports journalism that verifies, exposes, and explains reality while inspiring the kind of self-reflection and critical thinking that open society requires."[330]

325   Spangler, Todd, "Vice Media Gets $250 Million in Debt Funding from George Soros, Other Investors," Yahoo Finance, May 4, 2019. https://finance.yahoo.com/news/vice-media-gets-250-million-060719192.html

326   Gainor, Dan, "George Soros: Media Mogul," Media Research Center, August 15, 2011. https://web.archive.org/web/20210708020915/https://www.mrc.org/special-reports/george-soros-media-mogul

327   Ibid.

328   "Journalism," Open Society Foundations. https://www.opensocietyfoundations.org/what-we-do/themes/journalism

329   Ibid.

330   "Open Society Program on Independent Journalism," Open Society Foundations. https://www.opensocietyfoundations.org/who-we-are/programs/program-on-independent-journalism

As the Media Research Center's Dan Gainor notes of Soros' massive investments in media infrastructure:

> [He's] bought him[self] connections to the under-pinnings of the news business. The Columbia Journalism Review, which bills itself as "a watchdog and a friend of the press in all its forms," lists several investigative reporting projects funded by one of Soros foundations.
>
> The "News Frontier Database" includes seven different investigative reporting projects funded by Soros's Open Society Institute. Along with Pro-Publica, there are the Center for Public Integrity, the Center for Investigative Reporting and New Orleans' The Lens. The Columbia School of Journalism, which operates CJR, has received at least $600,000 from Soros, as well.[331]

Columbia University President Lee Bollinger also sits on the Pulitzer Price Board and the board of directors of the *Washington Post*.

Industry associates funded by Soros include the National Federation of Community Broadcasters, the national Association of Hispanic Journalists, and the Committee to Protect Journalists.[332]

Even the Organization of News Ombudsmen, which exists to "encourage transparency" and "assist media organizations to provide mechanisms to ensure they remain accountable to consumers of their news" is partially funded by Soros. The organization has members from twenty-two countries, with U.S. members including employees of the Associated Press, NPR, Columbia University, PBS, Voice of America, UC Berkeley School of Journalism, Fourth Estate, and more.[333] It formally included members from the *LA Times*, USA Today, ESPN, and the *Washington Post*.

Soros funded the Investigative News Network (INN), a collaborative effort that includes the Investigative Reporting Workshop at American University, liberal publication MinnPost, National Institute for Computer-Assisted Reporters, National Public Radio, and the Wisconsin Center for Investigative Journalism.[334]

---

331 Gainor, "Why Is Soros Spending over $48 Million Funding Media Organizations?" *Fox News*, May 18, 2011. https://www.foxnews.com/opinion/why-is-soros-spending-over-48-million-funding-media-organizations.

332 Ibid.

333 "ONO Members Around the World," Organization of News Ombudsmen. https://www.newsombudsmen.org/regular-members/

334 Gainor, "George Soros."

The Media Research Center has found links between Soros at over thirty mainstream news outlets.[335]

ABC's Christiane Amanpour and former *Washington Post* executive editor Leonard Downie Jr. both serve on boards of companies that take Soros money.

In 2010 and 2011, Soros contributed $250k to ProPublica, an investigative outlet whose advisory board includes former *New York Times* executive editor Jill Abramson, president of Univision Isaac Lee, former *Wall Street Journal* publisher L. Gordon Crovitz, Harvard professor of public service David Gergen, Berkeley Graduate School of Journalism director Tom Goldstein, the executive editor at publisher Simon & Schuster, the senior vice president for editorial quality at ABC News, *Fortune Magazine*'s senior editor at large, among others.[336]

ProPublica has addressed its Soros funding by adopting the default argument that any concerns over funding involving Soros can be considered a "vaguely anti-Semitic epithet meant to connote left-wing bias."[337]

The Center for Public Integrity (CPI) is another left-wing media organization funded by Soros. It received nearly $1 million from Soros between 2003 and 2008, and over $650k in 2009 alone. Speaking of integrity, CPI was found to have knowingly violated the law in pursuit of a story despite multiple warnings from its legal counsel in 2012.[338]

Their CPI board includes NBC/CBS/PBS veteran Richard Lobo, CBS's Wesley Lowery, former *Washington Post* correspondent Amit Paley, among others. Past directors included ABC's Christiane Amanpour, *HuffPost*'s founder Arianna Huffington, former NBC executive Paula Madison, and former NPR editorial product manager Matt Thompson.

Other publications and news companies represented by journalists that serve on Soros-funded boards include the following:

- Advisory Council: Vista, *Sacramento Bee*, ABC News, NPR.

335 "Over 30 Major News Organizations Linked to George Soros," Media Research Center. https://web.archive.org/web/20210513132805/https://www.mrc.org/commentary/over-30-major-news-organizations-linked-george-soros
336 "Leadership," ProPublica. https://www.propublica.org/leadership
337 Engelberg, Stephen, "A Free Press Works for All of Us," ProPublica, August 16, 2018. https://www.propublica.org/article/a-free-press-works-for-all-of-us
338 Howley, Patrick, "IHack News," *Washington Free Beacon*, April 18, 2012. https://freebeacon.com/national-security/ihack-news/

- Journalism Advisory Board: *New York Times*, *Seattle Times*, *LA Times*, *Baltimore Sun*, *Wall Street Journal*, CNN, *Atlanta Journal-Constitution*, Sunlight Foundation, *Fortune Magazine*, ABC.

- Business Advisory Council: ALM Media, National Federation of Community Broadcasters.[339]

The full list of publications that have staffers on the boards of Soros-funded media outlets is as follows:

- Print: *Atlanta Journal-Constitution*, *Arizona Daily Star*

- Associated Press, *El Nuevo Herald*, *Fortune*, Gazette Communications, Hearst Newspapers, *Houston Chronicle*, *New York Times*, *The New Yorker*, *Sacramento Bee*, *Seattle Times*, Simon & Schuster, *Toronto Star*, USA Today, Vista, *Washington Post*

- Ratio: KQED, NPR, Radio-Canada

- Online: AOL/*HuffPost*, *St. Louis Beacon*, Voice of San Diego, YouTube

- TV: ABC, CBS, CNN, Danish Broadcasting Corporation, PBS, WTVF-TV

- Education: American University School of Communication Investigative Reporting Workshop, Columbia University Graduate School of Journalism's *Columbia Journalism Review*, Duke University Sanford School of Public Policy, Toni Stabile Center for Investigative Journalism at Columbia University's Graduate School of Journalism, University of Illinois, University of Michigan, University of Pennsylvania Annenberg School for Communication, and the University of Southern California's Annenberg School for Communication School of Journalism

---

339   Gainor, and Iris Somberg, "Top Journalists That Serve on Soros-Funded Boards of Directors or Advisers," Media Research Center, August 15, 2011. https://web.archive.org/web/20210614020257/https://www.mrc.org/special-reports/top-journalists-serve-soros-funded-boards-directors-or-advisers

- Other: ALM Media, James L. Knight Foundation, Madison Media Management, Maynard Institute, National Federal of Community Broadcasters, Nieman Foundation, Poynter Institute, Sunlight Foundation, and the Tides Foundation.[340]

The Washington Post has appeared numerous times here, and not coincidentally, they're quick to run to Soros' defense. *Post* writer Emily Tamkin penned an article in 2017 on the "Five Myths about George Soros," attempting to convince us that he's not "plotting a revolution or paying people to protest." In it, she provides cover for Soros aiding the Nazis in Hungary, denies that he pays people to protest by naming protests that he didn't fund and ignoring the ones that he does, claims the fact that Soros broke the Bank of England is a myth, and says that Soros isn't "plotting a destructive resolution in America" because he's "simply a large political donor."[341] The piece reads as if Soros himself handed the author a list of the most common criticisms of him and asked them to play defense.[342]

Other outlets funded by Soros include $7.3 million to the Center for American Progress, Media Matters ($1 million in 2010), Sundance Institute ($9.6 million from 1996 to 2009),[343] NPR ($3.4 million from 1997 to 2020),[344] and much more. He's also funded Democracy Now, a progressive show that airs on 1,444 stations.

The Columbia Journalism Review called the contribution to NPR problematic due to the political nature of Soros. "Perception is NPR's currency they put it. While they're right to criticize NPR on that front—the CJR article makes no mention that they too are Soros funded.[345]

Soros' donation to Media Matters after years of them denying any sort of connection to him coincides with former Fox News host Glenn Beck doing a series of reports exposing him. Soros fired back at an International Crisis Center dinner that the likes of Fox, Beck, and the Tea Party may lead "this open society to be on the verge of

---

340 Ibid.
341 Tamkin, Emily, "Five Myths About George Soros," *The Washington Post*, August 25, 2020. https://www.washingtonpost.com/outlook/five-myths/five-myths-about-george-soros/2020/08/06/ad195582-d1e9-11ea-8d32-1eb-f4e9d8e0d_story.html
342 Ibid.
343 "Open Society Institute Awards $5 Million to Support Sundance Institute and Documentary Films," Open Society Foundations, July 14, 2009. https://www.opensocietyfoundations.org/newsroom/open-society-institute-awards-5-million-support-sundance-institute-and-documentary
344 Shepard, Alicia C., "Worthy Cause, Controversial Funding Source," NPR, May 24, 2011. https://www.npr.org/sections/ombudsman/2011/05/24/136216017/worthy-cause-controversial-funding-source
345 Meares, Joel, "A Soros Problem at NPR," *Columbia Journalism Review*, May 25, 2011. https://archives.cjr.org/campaign_desk/a_soros_problem_at_npr.php

some dictatorial democracy" before making a cliched reference to *1984*. In attendance at the dinner were CNN's Fareed Zakaria, Bill Clinton, the chancellor of Oxford University Lord Christopher Patten, and multibillionaire Paul Tudor Jones.[346]

Soros called his donation to Media Matters "symbolic"—but he'd immediately fight a proxy war through them against Fox News, launching what Media Matters founder David Brock called a campaign of "guerrilla warfare and sabotage" against the network in 2011. The strategy was outlined in an article in Politico:

> Media Matters, Brock said, is assembling opposition research files not only on Fox's top executives but on a series of midlevel officials. It has hired an activist who has led a successful campaign to press advertisers to avoid Glenn Beck's show. The group is assembling a legal team to help people who have clashed with Fox to file lawsuits for defamation, invasion of privacy or other causes. And it has hired two experienced reporters, Joe Strupp and Alexander Zaitchik, to dig into Fox's operation to help assemble a book on the network, due out in 2012.[347]

Media Matters declared victory in the war in 2013—though Fox's ratings indicate zero casualties.[348]

The war against Fox News included thirty Soros-funded belligerents, including *Mother Jones*, *ThinkProgress*, and AlterNet, among others. While the war escalated in the early 2010s, this is no new effort from Soros. The Soros-funded BraveNewFilms produced the anti-Fox News documentary called *Outfoxed* back in 2004, which the Soros-funded MoveOn.org distributed.[349]

When the conservative Sun News Network was set to enter the Canadian market, Soros took part in a "Stop Fox News North" campaign. While the network has no formal connection to Fox, it modeled its network after it. After a Sun Media newspaper column connected Soros' opposition to Sun TV News to his experience as a Jew

346   Lenzner, Robert, "Soros Warns U.S. Could Be on Verge of Dictatorial Democracy, Slams Fox, Glenn Beck," *Forbes*, December 8, 2010. https://www.forbes.com/sites/robertlenzner/2010/12/07/soros-warns-us-could-be-on-verge-dictatorial-democracy-slams-fox-glen-beck/?sh=2e726564a7dc

347   Smith, Ben, "Media Matters' War Against Fox," Politico, March 26, 2011. https://www.politico.com/story/2011/03/media-matters-war-against-fox-051949

348   Chumley, Cheryl K., "George Soros-Affiliated Media Matters Calls Off Fox News Attack: 'We Won,'" *The Washington Times*, December 16, 2013. https://www.washingtontimes.com/news/2013/dec/16/george-soros-group-calls-fox-news-attack-we-won/

349   Gainor, "George Soros."

during WWII (making mention of the salacious details outlined in the introductory chapter of this book), Soros threatened to sue.[350] He never followed through with the threat, probably because he knew he would lose.

Soros funds the Investigative News Network, which bills itself as a collaboration of over three hundred "independent news organizations," with the vision of ensuring "all people in every community have access to trusted news."[351] The organizations under this umbrella include the pro-open borders *Borderless*, the Center for Public Integrity, the Center for Sustainable Journalism, the *Dallas Free Press*, Delaware Public Media, Detroit Public Television, *Forward*, the Indigenous Media Freedom Alliance, *Maryland Reporter*, and countless niche publications and news companies.[352] *HuffPost* formally took grants from them too.

Soros' media influence ranges from local to national and has greatly impacted the national narrative when it comes to the latter.

The "independent, nonpartisan, and nonprofit" Wisconsin Center for Investigative Journalism took $185k from Soros between 2009 and 2011, and $900k from 2012 to 2016, accounting for over 40 percent of its funding, the vast majority of which comes out of the state of Wisconsin.[353] Another $320k was given in 2016. The publication launched a project titled Scott Walker's Wisconsin in which it published over two dozen stories critical of Walker, including a grand total of zero statements critical of Democrats.

On a national level, Soros played an outsized role in the 2014 Ferguson protests and the narrative shaped around them that followed the entirely justified police shooting of Michael Brown, who robbed a convenience store before assaulting Officer Darren Wilson and trying to steal his weapon. One witness during Officer Wilson's trial, who is described as a "biracial female," said she would've shot Michael Brown sooner, while a seventy-four-year-old black male witness said Officer Wilson did what he had to do, adding that he would've "shot that f***ing boy too."[354]

350 Vlessing, Etan, "George Soros May Sue Fox News North Player," *The Hollywood Reporter*, September 17, 2010. https://www.hollywoodreporter.com/business/business-news/george-soros-may-sue-fox-27984/
351 "Who We Are," Institute for Nonprofit News. https://inn.org/about/who-we-are/
352 "Member Directory," Institute for Nonprofit News. https://members.inn.org/directory
353 Benson, Dan, "Hidden Agenda?" Badger Institute, October 22, 2018. https://www.badgerinstitute.org/Diggings/Fall-20181/Hidden-agenda.htm
354 "Department of Justice Report Regarding the Criminal Investigation into the Shooting Death of Michael Brown by Ferguson, Missouri Police Officer Darren Wilson," Department of Justice, 2015. https://www.justice.gov/sites/default/files/opa/press-releases/attachments/2015/03/04/doj_report_on_shooting_of_michael_brown_1.pdf

But if you heard anything about the case on the media, you likely heard the discredited "hands up don't shoot" narrative—a narrative still heard at protests today. Soros funds both activists and the narratives the underpin them.

Soros gave at least $44 million to so-called "racial justice" groups to add fuel to the fire started following Brown's death in 2014. All the organizations Soros funded had a synergistic relationship with one another, using each other's talking points, referencing articles published by the others, and helping create an echo chamber by coordinating certain hashtags on social media.[355]

Soros is practically an angel investor in the Black Lives Matter movement, donating $100k to the Black Alliance in 2011.[356] The Black Alliance is run by Opal Tometi (who also goes by Ayo Tometi), one of the women responsible for creating the "#Blacklivesmatter" hashtag following the also justified shooting of Trayvon Martin, which morphed into a violent national antipolice movement.

Soros also cut a $200k check in 2011 to Colorlines, a website that heavily pushes the Black Lives Matter narrative and published constantly in support of the Ferguson riots. Soros gave $5.4 million to "grassroots" efforts in Ferguson and Staten Island to fund police reform, with half of the funds earmarked for Ferguson.[357]

The Hands Up Coalition, named after the aforementioned false narrative about Mike Brown having his hands in the air while being shot, was established by two groups funded by Soros, and a third funded by the Soros-backed Tides Foundation. The group bills itself as "grassroots" and recruits young people to start events to spread the Ferguson protests nationally. Seldom is it the case that even a group's name is a lie.[358]

One group that became a key source of video and stories from Ferguson (with a pro-Black Lives Matter agenda) was a group called Millennial Activists United, which received training on civil disobedience from a Soros-backed group called the Advancement Project. The Advancement Project helped organize a meeting between Ferguson community organizers and then president Barack Obama.[359]

355   Riddell, Kelly, "Video: George Soros Funds Ferguson Protests, Hopes to Spur Civil Action," Make the Road New York, January 14, 2015. https://maketheroadny.org/video-george-soros-funds-ferguson-protests-hopes-to-spur-civil-action/
356   Ibid.
357   Ibid.
358   Ibid.
359   Ibid.

Soros would later pour a massive $220 million into "racial equity" groups following the death of George Floyd in 2020.[360]

The influence of Black Lives Matter today is impossible to ignore, with seemingly every U.S. corporation on the face of the Earth emailing its customers following the death of Floyd to clarify that they're not racists in a bizarre national repentance ritual. Many made promises to fund Black Lives Matter-adjacent organizations and make vague commitments to representation. Regardless of one's opinion on the Floyd case, there's never been a case where an individual death caused such a seemingly coordinated response from corporate America.

As you'll see in coming pages, Soros was here to help kick it all off.

With friends everywhere in the media, Soros has been able to create and fuel countless high-profile narratives. The rest of this chapter documents some notable examples.

THE "ANTI-SEMITISM" NARRATIVE

One obvious benefit of Soros' direct media influence is that it enables him to use them as his own personal reputation management firm. Whenever there is any backlash against Soros, his media companies and publications all coordinate to push a unified narrative in his defense. In an era where baseless accusations of racism are the norm, the media has opted for an "any criticism of George Soros is anti-Semitism" strategy.

One particularly hilarious example comes from *Moment Magazine*, which accuses Jewish former prime minister Benjamin Netanyahu of the Jewish state of Israel of pushing "common anti-Semitic canards" in his criticism for Soros.[361] Another absurd take in a similar vein comes from Buzzfeed in an article with a truly incredible subheading: "How two *Jewish* American political consultants helped create the world's largest *anti-Semitic* conspiracy theory [emphasis added]."[362]

And they're just echoing what Soros-connected outlets are saying.

During the Kavanaugh hearings, the Soros-funded *ThinkProgress* called reports that Soros was paying people to protest against

---

360 Herndon, Astead W., "George Soros's Foundation Pours $220 Million into Racial Equality Push," *The New York Times*, July 13, 2020. https://www.nytimes.com/2020/07/13/us/politics/george-soros-racial-justice-organizations. html

361 Epstein, Nadine, "The Vilification of George Soros in Israel," *Moment Magazine*, 2019. https://momentmag.com/the-vilification-of-george-soros-in-israel/

362 Grassegger, Hannes, "The Plot Against George Soros," BuzzFeed News, January 20, 2019. https://www.buzzfeednews.com/article/hnsgrassegger/george-soros-conspiracy-finkelstein-birnbaum-orban-netanyahu

then president Donald Trump an "anti-Semitic conspiracy theory," and accused Trump himself of "getting in on the anti-Semitic action."[363] Meanwhile, Soros was spending $5 million on the effort to thwart Brett Kavanaugh's Supreme Court nomination, and his accuser Christine Blasey Ford's lawyer Debra Katz was vice chair of the Project on Government Oversight, which has been directly funded by Soros' OSF.[364]

The Soros-funded NPR described a fifteen-minute television segment criticizing Soros on a federally funded Spanish-language broadcaster Radio and Television Martí anti-Semitic for describing Soros as a "multimillionaire Jew" who uses his wealth to "finance anti-system political movements that fill his pockets," and approvingly reported on the U.S. Agency for Global Media launching an investigation into them as a result[365]

The *Washington Post* misinformed its readers that "Conspiracy theories about Soros aren't just false. They're anti-Semitic," because the rhetoric "draws on old, and deep-rooted, anti-Semitic ideas that have been deployed by the right for decades."

The Associated Press dismissed attacks against Soros during the Ukraine impeachment saga, opting to decry them as anti-Semitic.[366]

An article published in the *New York Times* opinion section finds the criticism for Soros both "deeply disturbing" and "anti-Semitic."[367]

No such concern has been expressed by these outlets for the criticism of Jewish Republican megadonors such as the late Sheldon Adelson.

While serving as president of the Open Society Foundations, Patrick Gaspard himself made the argument that was being laundered through the media during an appearance on PBS where he discussed Soros and anti-Semitic tropes.[368]

Even those who don't invoke the default anti-Semitism argument shield Soros with story selection.

363 Dale, Frank, "Trump Promotes Anti-Semitic Conspiracy Theory on Twitter," *Think Progress*, October 5, 2018. https://archive.thinkprogress.org/donald-trump-george-soros-anti-semitic-conspiracy-theory-7962b3d02a86/

364 Chumley, "Brett Kavanaugh, Christine Blasey Ford and the Links to George Soros," *The Washington Times*, September 18, 2018. https://www.washingtontimes.com/news/2018/sep/18/brett-kavanaugh-christine-blasey-ford-and-links-ge/

365 Dwyer, Colin, "U.S. Agency Investigates 'Taxpayer-Funded Anti-Semitism' Against George Soros," NPR, October 30, 2018. https://www.npr.org/2018/10/30/662052937/u-s-agency-investigates-taxpayer-funded-anti-semitism-against-george-soros

366 Schor, Lana, "Soros Attacks in Impeachment Saga Spark Anti-Semitism Debate," *Associated Press*, December 11, 2019. https://apnews.com/article/george-soros-donald-trump-anti-semitism-race-and-ethnicity-impeachments-5610d6a5be82e5bcc7ff2a58fbffbb54

367 Gajowski, Cheryl, "Vilifying George Soros," *The New York Times*, November 6, 2018, https://www.nytimes.com/2018/11/06/opinion/letters/george-soros.html

368 "Patrick Gaspard on George Soros and Anti-Semitic Tropes," *WETA*, PBS, https://weta.org/watch/shows/amanpour-and-company/patrick-gaspard-george-soros-and-anti-semitic-tropes-c7a18d

The Soros-linked *Seattle Times* runs stories on Soros only to provide cover for him or portray him as a victim. A sampling of headlines includes "George Soros Conspiracy Theories Surge as Protests Sweep US," "Soros, the Far Right's Boogeyman, Is Again a Target," "Bomb Found at Philanthropist George Soros's Suburban Home," "Hungarian Official Retracts Comparing George Soros to Hitler," and "US Agency Vows to Investigate Broadcast Report That Called George Soros a 'Multimillionaire Jew.'"

IRAN NUCLEAR DEAL ECHO CHAMBER

During an interview with the *New York Times Magazine*, Deputy National Security Adviser Ben Rhodes openly bragged about creating a media echo chamber of journalists and NGOs to push the lie that Iran's leaders are moderate.[369] Contradicting the narrative were the endless chants of "Death to America" from Iran's leadership.

One of the key NGOs involved in this effort is the Ploughshares Fund, whose stated mission is to "reduce and ultimately eliminate the world's nuclear stockpiles" (apparently except Iran's). White House officials described Ploughshares as the chief architect of the media campaign, which ushered in a barrage of "experts" touting the deal in the press. Ploughshares also gave a $70,000 grant to Princeton University to underwrite the activities of Iran's nuclear spokesman Seyed Hossein Mousavian, effectively subsidizing Iran's own talking points.

Ploughshares requested and got $700,000 from Soros with the funding proposal "Defending Iran Nuclear Diplomacy" to promote Obama's Iran nuclear deal. Other Soros-linked NGOs that aided the echo chamber included J Street and the National Iranian American Council.

In total, Ploughshares president Joe Crincione says his group has a network of eighty-five organizations and two hundred individuals that was "decisive in the battle for public opinion." Or as Rhodes put it, "they were saying things that validated what we had given them to say."[370]

According to a Ploughshares funding request to Soros, Ploughshares's efforts were to use the funds to "broaden and better coor-

---

369   Phillips, James, "How the Liberal Echo Chamber Sold the Lie of 'Moderate' Iranian Leaders," The Heritage Foundation, May 27, 2016. https://www.heritage.org/global-politics/commentary/how-the-liberal-echo-chamber-sold-the-lie-moderate-iranian-leaders

370   Post Editorial Board, "How Big Money Funded the 'Echo Chamber' That Pushed Obama's Iran Deal," *New York Post*, May 23, 2016. https://nypost.com/2016/05/23/how-big-money-funded-the-echo-chamber-that-pushed-obamas-iran-deal/

dinate circle of experts and validators who support diplomacy, including prominent US, European and Israeli military and diplomatic personalities, as well as Iranian human rights and civil society leaders." The request further states that the funds will be used to aid "mainstream and social media outreach by validators along with other public and private efforts to shape the debate in support of an agreement and continued diplomacy," and "increase outreach by coalition members and validators to policymakers with focus on long-term impact of the deal on regional and global security issues where potential cooperation with Iran could be beneficial."[371]

Those advancing the Ploughshares agenda didn't identify themselves as such. One *Washington Post* op-ed by a contributor employed by an organization that takes money from Ploughshares argued in favor of a $400 million cash payment to Iran, and made no mention of the author's conflict of interests. NPR also took money from Ploughshares and conducted interviews with proponents of the deal, but cancelled interviews with top congressional opponents of it.[372]

Meanwhile, Obama was busy complaining that "well-funded lobbyists" would defeat his deal, and encouraged Congress to vote based on the national interest, not based on lobbyists.

THE SOROS IMPEACHMENT ECHO CHAMBER

Soros backed the Washington-based Democracy Integrity Project with $1 million, which played a large role in spreading Russiagate hysteria and making the case for impeachment. The group's origins can be traced back to 2016, but it didn't incorporate until eleven days after Trump took office.[373]

Among the group's activities was placing news stories alleging back-channel communications and meetings between Trump's inner circle and Russian spies while influencing related investigations and reports that Congress was producing. The group created daily briefings that were then sent out to Washington journalists and congressional staffers to bolster their bogus narrative. Among those who

---

371 Kredo, Adam, "White House Partner Asked Soros for $750k to Fund Pro-Iran Deal 'Echo Chamber,'" *Washington Free Beacon*, August 18, 2016. https://freebeacon.com/national-security/wh-partner-asked-soros-to-fund-echo-chamber/

372 Ibid.

373 Sperry, Paul, "Soros-Funded Media Echo Chamber Pushes Impeachment," *The Federalist*, March 25, 2019. https://thefederalist.com/2019/03/21/soros-funded-pr-shop-constructing-media-echo-chamber-push-impeachment/

received their reports included *New York Times* and *Washington Post* staffers, alleged investigative reporters at Buzzfeed, ProPublica, and McClatchy, and news producers at CNN and MSNBC.

Information was also fed to the FBI and congressional investigators—which the project would then tip off to journalists who would in turn report that authorities are investigating those leads. One inside source told *The Federalist*: "Dan Jones does more than just send out these briefs. He's working with the FBI and [the] Senate Intelligence [Committee]." In other words, he created fake news, then attempted to use government and media to legitimize the narrative and bring consequences.

The Project is headed by Dan Jones, a former FBI investigator, Clinton administration volunteer, and top staffer to Senator Dianne Feinstein. Jones joined the Democrat staff of the Senate Intelligence Committee in 2007, and when he back-channel stepped down from the committee in December 2015, Feinstein praised him on the Senate floor.

The group employs key figures linked to the Russia hoax, such as Fusion GPS founder Glenn Simpson and bogus dossier author Christopher Steele to continue digging up fictitious dirt on Trump. While he was chairman of the Senate Judiciary Committee, Senator Chuck Grassley took note, writing of an interview with jones that "Mr. Jones stated he planned to push the information he obtained from Fusion and Steele to policymakers on Capitol Hill, the press and the FBI."

Senate Judiciary Committee investigators suspect that Jones may have also been involved in the efforts to create and disseminate Steele's dossier. After Glenn Simpson testified before the Senate Judiciary Committee in 2018, Feinstein went behind Grassley's back and released a three-hundred-page transcript of the closed-door testimony—with the names of all Fusion GPS employees redacted, or any mention of the connection between her former top staffer Jones and Simpson.

The Project partnered with cybersecurity firm New Knowledge, which actively worked to create the illusion of Russian interference in congressional elections for the 2018 midterms. One strategy the Project previously deployed in 2017 was Project Birmingham—

which swarmed the Twitter account of Alabama Senate special election candidate Roy Moore with fake Russian Twitter accounts—and then drew attention to the supposed Russian support for Moore. Jones personally promoted New Knowledge on his social media accounts.

Jones would collaborate with New Knowledge's director of research Renée DiResta for a report on Russian disinformation that was released by the Senate intelligence committee claiming that Trump was aided by a Russian social-media plot. Jones and DiResta also claimed that this plot went as far as attempting to influence Senate voting on the confirmation of Brett Kavanaugh, and alleged "Russian influence networks" have conspired with "domestic right-wing disinformation networks" and publications such as Fox News, Breitbart, *The Hill*, and *the Daily Caller*. Phrased differently, Jones and company are accusing the aforementioned outlets of pushing disinformation—just as they're actively doing.

George Soros Goes Local

All politics is local, and it's local politics where George Soros has had the most success.

Unlike presidential races where even tens of millions of dollars in spending will only amount to a few percent of overall spending, Soros has been able to drown local races in cash, making it virtually impossible for anyone to compete with his desired candidate.

Soros first began dabbling in local politics in 2006 with the Secretary of State Project.[374]

Founded to advance so-called "election protection measures," the organization's sole effort was to get Democrats elected as secretaries of state in swing or battleground states, particularly those who had a margin of victory below one hundred twenty thousand votes in the 2004 presidential election.

Many Democrats placed the blame for Al Gore's loss on the former Ohio Secretary of State Kenneth Blackwell, whom they branded a political operative for his ruling that provisional ballots in the state wouldn't be counted if they were submitted in the wrong precinct (which the U.S. Court of Appeals upheld).

In other words, the goal of this organization is to get Democrats elected so those Democrats can do what they accused Republicans of doing in the 2000 election.

The project grew out of the Democracy Alliance, of which Soros is a founding member and donor. The DA was founded with the long-term objective of raising $200 million to fund progressive groups. The project ended up shutting down in 2010.

---

374   "Secretary of State Project," Ballotpedia. https://ballotpedia.org/Secretary_of_State_Project

In an age when the Left views everything as racist, Soros began in the mid-2010s backing state prosecutors who embrace that vision and look to change the criminal justice system accordingly.

Underpinning the ideology of Soros and those he backs in these sorts of races is one that paints the American legal system as not only systemically racist, but founded upon racist principles, requiring the complete abolition and "reimagination" of the justice system.

Soros gave at least $33 million in one year to help support various groups that spurred the protests and riots in Ferguson following the justified police shooting of Michael Brown. Among those aided included "buses of activists from the Samuel Dewitt Proctor Conference in Chicago; from the Drug Policy Alliance, Make the Road New York and Equal Justice USA from New York; from Sojourners, the Advancement Project and Center for Community Change in Washington; and networks from the Gamaliel Foundation—all funded in part by Mr. Soros—descended on Ferguson starting in August and later organized protests and gatherings in the city."[375]

The purpose of propaganda isn't to be logical, it's to convince, and even at a time where America is objectively the least racist it's ever been, the narrative of "systemic white supremacy" has practically become conventional wisdom among the ruling class.

With the death of George Floyd and the subsequent moral panic that followed, Soros began upping his donations to so-called "racial justice" causes into the hundreds of millions. Soros committed $220 million to "emerging organizations and leaders building power in Black communities across the U.S." The biggest share of the funds, $150 million, is to be distributed over a five-year period to black-led organizations while the remaining $70 million was spent as a lump sum on "more immediate efforts to advance racial justice."

According to an Open Society Foundations press release about the $70 million in immediate funding, that money will go toward "Investments in a set of cities as they reimagine public safety, moving beyond the culture of criminalization and incarceration, and aiming to create safe, healthy, and racially just communities," "A further set of investments will go toward nurturing the civic engagement of young people, many of whom have engaged in activism for the first

---

375   Feldt, Brian, "Billionaire Funded Groups That Spurred Ferguson Protests: Report," *St. Louis Business Journal*, January 15, 2015. https://www.bizjournals.com/stlouis/blog/2015/01/billionaire-funded-groups-that-spurred-ferguson.html

time," and "Support for ongoing efforts to fight voter suppression and disinformation, and ensure safe and secure elections."[376]

In the years between the surges in Black Lives Matter activism after the deaths of Brown and Floyd, Soros began backing candidates positioned to exploit unrest and implement an anti-law-and-order agenda through his Justice & Public Safety PAC. In 2016, he spent money in fifteen races, and his candidates won twelve. He spent $2 million toward defeating Joe Arpaio that year. Since then, he's continued funding candidates who've had massive success in implementing fact-free progressive policies.

The rise of social justice-oriented lawyers getting elected to public office is part of a "progressive prosecutors movement," and Soros has been funding it all.

Soros' first strategy to influence law and justice in America was to stack the courts by advocating for replacing elections for judges with selection by committee, in which a committee made up of lawyers appoints judges to the bench as opposed to voters in elections, which is how most nonfederal judges nationwide are selected. Soros' Open Society Institute fund has spent at least $5 million from 2005 to 2015 toward this goal, though the figure could be as high as $45 million according to one report. It's disputed because some of the funds went to legal issues that had no position on merit selection.[377]

Most of Soros' money has gone toward funding candidates directly, and the damage they're doing to law and order nationwide is undeniable.

ARIZONA

As previously mentioned, Soros contributed $2 million to Maricopa Strong with the aim of getting Sheriff Joe Arpaio out of office. It was the single largest donation he made in a local race in 2016, and it was successful, leading to Arpaio being replaced by Sheriff Paul Penzone, ending Arpaio's twenty-four-year reign.

Penzone ran on a platform of undoing Arpaio's legacy of being extremely tough on crime and illegal immigration. Just a month after

---

376 "Open Society Pledges $220 Million for Building Black Power in the U.S," Open Society Foundations, July 13, 2020. https://www.opensocietyfoundations.org/newsroom/open-society-foundations-announce-220-million-for-building-power-in-black-communities

377 Lott, Maxim, "Billionaire George Soros Trying to Stack the Courts, Critics Say," *Fox News*, June 27, 2011. https://www.foxnews.com/politics/billionaire-george-soros-trying-to-stack-the-courts-critics-say

he took office, illegal aliens were being released by Penzone at a rate of four hundred criminal illegals every ten days.[378]

One of the first major policies Penzone enacted after taking office in was to end the practice of keeping immigrants in jail longer to give immigration authorities time to determine if they were in the country illegally.[379] He also ended the jail known as Tent City, which was the result of Arpaio's first act as Sheriff back in 1993.

Fast-forward four years and Penzone was interfering with the Maricopa County 2020 election audit, refusing to comply with a subpoena to hand over data, claiming it would compromise "the security of sensitive, protected and critical data."[380]

PENNSYLVANIA

Soros pumped nearly $1.5 million into backing Larry Krasner in the Democrat primary for the Philadelphia district attorney election, which Krasner won.[381] He campaigned on "social reform" and reducing the prison population. Chants of "f*** the police" could be heard at his victory party.[382]

As a lawyer in Philadelphia, Krasner sued the police department seventy-five times (representing groups including Occupy Philadelphia and Black Lives Matter) and called law enforcement "systemically racist."[383]

Philadelphia has an accelerated rehabilitative disposition (ARD) program, which is a pretrial program for some first-time offenders that allows them to get off with a lighter probationary sentence. In the year before Krasner's election, only twelve cases qualified for diversion. During his first year in office, seventy-eight were referred to ARD.[384]

378 "Arizona Sheriff Releasing 400 'Criminal Illegal Immigrants' Every 10 Days," Judicial Watch, February 22, 2017. https://www.judicialwatch.org/corruption-chronicles/arizona-sheriff-releasing-400-criminal-illegal-immigrants-every-10-days/

379 Duara, Nigel, "Elected as the Anti-Arpaio, New Phoenix Sheriff Finds Himself at Center of Nation's Immigration Debate," *Los Angeles Times*, March 10, 2017. https://www.latimes.com/nation/la-na-phoenix-sheriff-20170310-story.html

380 Piper, Greg, "Soros Kicked in $2M to Elect Maricopa County Sheriff Now Stonewalling Election Audit," Just The News, May 19, 2021. https://justthenews.com/politics-policy/elections/soros-kicked-2m-elect-maricopa-county-sheriff-now-stonewalling-election

381 Brennan, Chris, "$1.45 Million Soros Investment in Philly DA's Race Draws Heat for Krasner," *The Philadelphia Inquirer*, May 6, 2017. https://www.inquirer.com/philly/news/politics/Soros-145-million-investment-in-DAs-race-draws-heat-for-Krasner.html

382 Pomper, Steve, "The George Soros War Against Tough-on-Crime, Law and Order Prosecutors," National Police Association, November 5, 2019. https://nationalpolice.org/the-george-soros-war-against-tough-on-crime-law-and-order-prosecutors/

383 Schultz, James D., "The Disastrous Consequences of DA Larry Krasner's "Reforms,"" *Philadelphia Magazine*, June 27, 2019. https://www.phillymag.com/news/2019/06/27/larry-krasner-reforms-philadelphia/

384 Ibid.

One such case involved a man charged with carrying a concealed gun in what was his first arrest in June. He qualified for ARD and was given two years of probation. In the following March of 2019, he was arrested again on gun-possession charges, released from jail after the judge granted a defense motion for unsecured bail, and then by June, a full year after his first arrest, he was charged with murder.[385]

Oddly, these sort of "weak on crime" leftists will support every gun control measure in the book against law-abiding gun owners, but think exceptions are worth making when it comes to enforcing the law for criminals.

Krasner ordered assistant district attorneys to request cash bail less often, and to provide a "cost analysis" of incarceration when making sentencing recommendations. He fired veteran prosecutors and replaced them with inexperienced lawyers who share his ideology. U.S. Attorney William McSwain observed that Krasner "is not even pretending to be a prosecutor. He calls himself a public defender with power. It's almost like letting a fox into the hen house. Once he's in, he's trying to cause as much havoc as possible."[386]

The numbers tell the same story; Krasner has dropped charges on over 60 percent of shooting cases and 37 percent of illegal firearms cases in the two years after taking office.[387] Not coincidentally, shootings and homicides have spiked since then. In 2020, Philadelphia prosecuted the lowest number of felony cases in thirty years, while the city saw 499 homicides, more than New York City has with five times the population. For reference, there were 351 homicides the year he took office.[388]

Jack Stollsteimer became the first Democrat ever elected as the DA for Pennsylvania's Delaware county, taking office in January 2020. Soros spent $165k backing him.[389] Unlike nearly everyone else on this list, Stollsteimer hasn't proposed anything radical as of writing, though he did create a Criminal Justice Reform Task Force following the death of George Floyd, which could produce radical proposals.[390]

---

385 Shaw, Julie, "Under DA Krasner, More Gun-Possession Cases Get Court Diversionary Program," *The Philadelphia Inquirer*, June 23, 2019. https://www.inquirer.com/news/philadelphia-district-attorney-larry-krasner-gun-possession-cases-diverted-ard-probationary-program-20190623.html

386 Nolan, Pat, "Beware of George Soros's Trojan Horse Prosecutors," *The American Conservative*, September 11, 2020. https://www.theamericanconservative.com/articles/beware-of-george-soros-trojan-horse-prosecutors/

387 Ibid.

388 Hogan, Thomas, "Larry Krasner, Philadelphia D.A., Presides over Homicide Spike," *City Journal*, May 13, 2021. https://www.city-journal.org/larry-krasner-district-attorney-presides-over-philadelphia-homicide-spike

389 Mooney, Kevin, "Soros-Funded Prosecutors Said to Put 'Social Justice' over Law and Order," *The Daily Signal*, October 18, 2020. https://www.dailysignal.com/2020/10/18/soros-funded-prosecutors-put-social-justice-above-law-and-order-analysts-say/

390 Lee, Jaclyn, "Delaware County DA Announces Criminal Justice Reform Task Force," WPVI-TV, June 16, 2020. https://6abc.com/criminal-justice-reform-policing-delaware-county-da-jack-stollsteimer/6250625/

CALIFORNIA

Soros spent over $2.5 million backing George Gascón, who assumed office as Los Angeles DA in December 2020.[391] During Gascón's prior tenure at San Francisco's DA, a position he held until January 2019, property crime increased by 49 percent and misdemeanor charges were filed in only 40 percent of cases presented by the police. [392] He was once chief of the Mesa Police Department and frequently clashed with Sheriff Joe Arpaio.

Gascón announced that he would no longer prosecute crimes that he says are "associated with poverty." Most crimes are committed disproportionately by the poor, so this kind of reasoning opens up Pandora's box in legalizing most crimes. Gascón said that crimes such a trespassing, disturbing the peace, driving without a license, driving on a suspended license, drug and paraphernalia possession, drinking in public, public intoxication, loitering to commit prostitution, and resisting arrest will all "be declined or dismissed before arraignment and without conditions."[393]

Gascón disdain for consequences doesn't stop with nonviolent crime either, as he eliminated sentencing enhancements for convicted criminals, issuing a directive statement that said "sentence enhancements or other sentencing allegations, including under the Three Strikes law, shall not be filed in any cases, and shall be withdrawn in pending matters."[394]

Another Soros-backed candidate in California is Chesa Boudin, the son of two left-wing radicals convicted for their role in a 1981 armored-car robbery that resulted in the murders of two police officers and a Brinks guard. His mother Kathy was sentenced to twenty years to life (and was paroled in 2003); his father remained in prison until being granted clemency by a disgraced Andrew Cuomo in his final days as governor. Boudin was adopted and raised by Weather Underground radicals Bill Ayers and Bernardine Dohrn. Ayers and Dohrn were friends with Boudin's parents through Students for a Democratic Society and later the Weather Underground.[395]

391   Grimes, Katy, "Soros Dumps Another $2.5 Million into George Gascón's Race for Los Angeles DA," *California Globe*, September 28, 2020. https://californiaglobe.com/section-2/soros-dumps-another-2-5-million-into-gascons-race-for-los-angeles-da/

392   Whalen, Bill, "Crime and Punishment? Not so Much in California," *Hoover* Institution, January 14, 2021. https://www.hoover.org/research/crime-and-punishment-not-so-much-california.

393   Smith, Perry, "Gascon Announces Sweeping Changes to County Criminal Justice," *The Santa Clarita Valley Signal*, December 9, 2020. https://signalscv.com/2020/12/gascon-announces-sweeping-changes-to-county-criminal-justice/

394   Girdusky, Ryan, "The Real Radicals Aren't in Washington | Opinion," *Newsweek*, May 17, 2021. https://www.newsweek.com/real-radicals-arent-washington-opinion-1591769.

395   Hendrickson, Matthew. "Chesa Boudin, Raised by Radicals Bernardine Dohrn, Bill Ayers, about to Become San Francisco's Top Prosecutor," *Chicago Sun-Times*, January 3, 2020. https://chicago.suntimes.com/politics/2020/1/3/21033388/chesa-boudin-bernardine-dohrn-bill-ayers-san-francisco-sds-weather-underground-brinks-robbery.

After graduating high school, Boudin traveled to South America, where he'd return numerous times over the decade that followed. During graduate school, he traveled to Venezuela to learn about the nation's "revolutionary upheaval."[396]

The man whom the San Francisco Police Officer's Association called the "#1 choice of criminals and gang members" would squeak out a slim victory by fewer than three thousand votes to become DA. Like Krasner, chants of "f*** the police" were to be heard at his victory party.[397] He pulled off his victory with $620k from Soros and other backers including Chloe Cockburn, a Democracy Alliance partner, and the Tides Foundation.[398]

As Boudin himself admitted, he was the only DA candidate who had never tried a case before. Upon taking office, he fired the most seasoned prosecutors and replaced them with inexperienced public defenders who had never tried murder cases. His office pled out twenty of eighty-five pending murder cases for less than murder.

From the time he took office in January 2020 until March 2021, Boudin tried twenty-three cases resulting in sixteen convictions. In 2019, during the same time frame, his predecessor (interim DA Suzy Loftus) tried 294 cases and got 203 convictions.[399] In 2020, the San Francisco Police Department presented 6,333 felonies to Boudin's office, and 40 percent of cases were dropped. In neighboring Alameda, only 11.4 percent of cases were dropped.

A number of individuals who had their charges dropped or reduced by Boudin later went on to be charged for homicides just months later.[400]

Boudin got rid of "gang enhancements" (additional punishment to an initial felony if it's committed for a gang), and refuses to try any juveniles as adults, regardless of how serious the crime. Cash bail was scrapped, as was the city's "life unit," which involved two senior attorneys who handled life sentences.

Boudin promised to "keep San Francisco safer by emptying the jail"—and made good on the second half of that promise, emptying half of the city's prison population.[401]

396   Ibid.
397   Ho, Vivian, "Son of Jailed Radicals, Reviled by the Police Union. Now, Chesa Boudin Is San Francisco's Top Cop," *The Guardian*, November 17, 2019. https://www.theguardian.com/us-news/2019/nov/16/son-of-jailed-radicals-reviled-by-the-police-union-now-chesa-boudin-is-san-franciscos-top-cop.
398   Fuller, Clayton, "These Radical Democrat Prosecutors Are Breaking Their Oaths to Prosecute Criminals." Association of Mature American Citizens, June 10, 2021. https://amac.us/these-radical-democrat-prosecutors-are-breaking-their-oaths-to-prosecute-criminals/
399   Reynolds, Susan D., "Chesa Boudin by the Numbers," *Marina Times*, April 2021. https://www.marinatimes.com/chesa-boudin-by-the-numbers.
400   Ibid.
401   Meyer, Maxwell, "Checking in on Chesa Boudin," *The Stanford Review*, February 8, 2021. https://stanfordreview.org/chesa-boudin-san-francisco-crime/

By summer, homicides were already up 25 percent, burglary up 42 percent, motor vehicle theft up 31 percent, and arson up 45 percent compared with the same time period the year before he took office.[402]

The lack of enforcement against theft had the pharmacy chain Walgreens reporting thefts at its San Francisco stores at eight times the national average. That led it to close its seventeen stores in the city[403] (and if a corporation worth over $100 billion as of writing is being affected by Boudin, you can imagine how small businesses are faring). Shortly after, every Target store in San Francisco reduced hours in an attempt to curb theft.[404]

A recall campaign quickly sprung up in response to Boudin, and despite laughable claims that it's a Republican campaign (in San Francisco of all places), 60 percent of signatories are Democrats, and 88 percent are non-Republicans.[405]

Soros spent $275k backing Contra Costa County DA Diana Becton.[406]

Becton was selected by a board of supervisors to serve the rest of her predecessor Mark Peterson's term through the end of 2018 after he was forced to resign after being convicted of felony perjury stemming from illegal personal use of campaign funds. Part of the selection process to fill the vacancy included an extensive questionnaire in which Becton repeatedly plagiarized responses.[407] Among the plagiarized responses included Martin Luther King Jr. quotes she somehow thought wouldn't get recognized. Three of five members of the board selected her anyway, and she later won a DA race in 2018.

Becton had never served as a prosecutor before, and read from a binder of statements during her public appearances during the selection process. Even during a telephone interview with the *East Bay Times* (prior to her appointment) she said she wanted to pull out her notes before responding, and the rustling of paper could be heard during the conversation. When asked about her plagiarism, she said she "owns the mistake" before blaming a colleague who told her "it was OK."[408]

---

402   Nolan, "Beware of George Soros's Trojan Horse Prosecutors."

403   Polumbo, Brad, "Here's Why San Francisco Is Experiencing a Shoplifting Surge That's Putting Some Stores Out of Business," Foundation for Economic Education, May 25, 2021. https://fee.org/articles/why-san-francisco-is-experiencing-a-shoplifting-surge-that-s-putting-some-stores-out-of-business/

404   "All 5 San Francisco Target Locations Reducing Operating Hours Due to Recent Spike in Crime," ABC7, July 2, 2021. https://abc7news.com/target-hours-san-francisco-crime-shoplifting-sf/10851794/

405   Reynolds, "Chesa Boudin by the Numbers."

406   DeSoto, Randy, "Billionaire Soros Backs Plagiarist in Contra Costa DA's Race: Candidate of 'Integrity,'" *Contra Costa Herald*, May 24, 2018. https://contracostaherald.com/05271801cch/

407   Borenstein, Daniel, "Borenstein: Contra Costa Replaces Perjurer with Plagiarist as DA," *East Bay Times*, September 15, 2017. https://www.eastbaytimes.com/2017/09/15/borenstein-contra-costa-replaces-perjurer-with-plagiarist-as-da/

408   Ibid.

THE MAN BEHIND THE CURTAIN

She's a friend of St. Louis's Kim Gardner and Chicago's Kim Foxx, and shares their weak-on-crime philosophy. In a Politico op-ed she penned with Gardner, Foxx, Durham County DA Satana Deberry, and Suffolk DA Rachael Rollins, our criminal justice system is described as one "constructed to control Black people and people of color." They continue "Its injustices are not new but are deeply rooted in our country's shameful history of slavery and legacy of racial violence. The system is acting."[409]

In a line that encapsulates their weak-on-crime philosophy, they admit that "We ran for public office on progressive platforms to *shrink the system* and create a more equitable and just society." Then they lay out eleven commitments that include not prosecuting what they consider to be peaceful protesters, not accepting funding from police unions, banning no-knock warrants, advancing discussions of divestment from the criminal legal system, and other vague progressive nonsense.

In August 2020, *Red State* obtained an internal "Looting Guidelines" document from Becton's office that listed factors to consider before charging someone. Among them was "Was the theft committed for financial gain or personal need?"—which would legalize looting for the poor, or anyone claiming to be motivated by necessity.[410]

The next month, that had become policy, with Becton announcing that she wouldn't be filing charges for low-level drug possession, shoplifting, and other misdemeanors.[411]

Another policy of hers makes law enforcement navigate a bureaucratic labyrinth to hold criminals who assault cops accountable. According to the directive that applies to "related charges that allege use of force, threats or violence against law enforcement":

> When reviewing allegations of force, threats or violence against a law enforcement officer or when reviewing allegations of resisting, delaying, or obstructing a law enforcement officer, the reviewing Deputy District Attorney must review all available and material body worn camera footage and any

---

409   Becton, Diana et al., "Opinion | 'Prosecutors Are Not Exempt from Criticism,'" Politico, August 25, 2020. https://www.politico.com/news/magazine/2020/08/25/black-prosecutors-11-ideas-393577.

410   Van Laar, Jennifer, "Soros DA Diana Becton Requires Officers Consider Whether a Looter "Needed" Stolen Goods Before Charging," Redstate, August 27, 2020. https://redstate.com/jenvanlaar/2020/08/27/soros-da-diana-becton-requires-officers-consider-whether-a-looter-needed-stolen-goods-before-charging-n252621

411   "Contra Costa DA Will Not File Charges for Low-Level Drug Possession, Shoplifting, Other Misdemeanors," CBS San Francisco, September 24, 2020. https://sanfrancisco.cbslocal.com/2020/09/24/contra-costa-da-misde-meanors-no-charges-drug-possession-shoplifting/

other material videos, as well as all relevant evidence before a charging decision is made. Prior to making a final charging decision, a supervisor must approve the charge(s) after reviewing the body worn camera footage, along with any other material videos, and any other relevant evidence."[412]

While graffiti is a misdemeanor (and thus a crime Becton doesn't prosecute), she will prosecute it as a hate crime if you have the wrong political opinions. After a couple allegedly painted over a Black Lives Matter mural, she filed three misdemeanor charges against them including violation of civil rights (a hate crime charge), vandalism, and possession of tools to commit vandalism.[413]

The charges were entirely politically motivated. A day after the initial vandalism, one of Becton's favored deputies, Nichelle Holmes, posted on Facebook for help identifying the "two racists who defiled the BLM mural." She posted a link to an article describing the two as "white trash Trumpers." She added that "we want more than a citation for vandalism," seeming to allude to her boss.[414]

Soros dumped $659k into the Loudoun County race backing Buta Biberaj for commonwealth's attorney,[415] which she won and was sworn into the position in January 2020.

On the campaign trail, Biberaj said she favored new pretrial diversion programs for perpetrators of lower-level charges to earn a "dismissal" of their case, backed restoring voting rights of felons, and argued that prosecutors shouldn't be involved in immigration enforcement on the nonsensical basis that it would make it look like the officer was "much more forceful in trying to bully or take advantage of somebody's status by threatening them with that."[416]

She also called for the attorney's office to start collecting racial and demographic data for charging and sentencing decisions. In her words, this is to make sure police are not "over policing on one side" while "not doing the same investigation into others."[417]

412   Van Laar, "Exclusive: Soros DA Diana Becton's New Policy Protects Criminals Who Assault Law Enforcement Officers," Redstate, September 2, 2020. https://redstate.com/jenvanlaar/2020/09/02/soros-da-diana-bectons-new-policy-protects-criminals-who-assault-law-enforcement-officers-n253257

413   "Pair Charged with Hate Crime for Vandalizing Martinez Black Lives Matter Mural," CBS Sacramento, July 8, 2020. https://sacramento.cbslocal.com/2020/07/08/martinez-black-lives-matter-mural-hate-crime-charges/

414   Van Laar, "Facebook Posts from Deputy DA Whose Office Charged Couple with 'Hate Crime' for Painting over BLM Mural Confirm Political Motivation," Redstate, August 19, 2020. https://redstate.com/jenvanlaar/2020/08/19/facebook-posts-from-deputy-da-whose-office-charged-couple-with-hate-crime-for-painting-over-blm-mural-n251672

415   Greene, Renss, "Super PAC Pumps $659K into Loudoun's Commonwealth's Attorney's Race; Whitbeck Approaches $1M," *Loudoun Now*, November 1, 2019. https://loudounnow.com/2019/11/01/super-pac-pumps-659k-into-loudouns-commonwealths-attorneys-race-whitbeck-approaches-1m/

416   Nichanian, Daniel, ""How Are You Keeping My Community Safe If You're Stealing My Resources?"" *The Appeal*, October 24, 2019. https://theappeal.org/politicalreport/virginia-loudoun-county-buta-biberaj-interview/

417   Ibid.

While in office, she was one of twelve Virginia prosecutors who signed onto a letter calling for "automated, automatic, and free expungement of criminal records for formerly system-involved community members," the end of mandatory minimum sentences, the end of cash bail, the abolition of the death penalty, and the end of "three strikes" felony enhancements for petty larceny offenses.[418]

The Loudoun County Board of Supervisors decided to give her office a smaller budget increase than requested in 2021 due to high turnover and her handling of domestic-violence cases. Of 735 cases brought to her office, she dismissed 491, bringing only 8 percent to trial.[419]

Biberaj defended herself by saying that prosecution is more than just taking cases to trial, "it's the whole process of examining cases and working with all parties involved to find the right outcome." Apparently, the right outcome is no outcome.

In June 2021, Los Angeles Mayor Eric Garcetti said that the Open Society Foundations expressed interest in funding a local reparations program. The comment was made to the *Los Angeles Times* on the same day he announced the creation of the LA Reparations Advisory Commission to create a "pilot reparations program targeted at a cohort of Black Angelenos." Garcetti told the *Times* that Soros had interest in funding the endeavor, and that he hoped banks and corporations would join in it to "reckon with a complicity that we saw in American capitalism, slavery, and post-slavery racism."[420]

FLORIDA

George Soros backed Aramis Ayala to become Orlando's state attorney for the Ninth Judicial Circuit Court of Florida, donating $1.4 million toward that goal. Her husband David Ayala had been convicted of drug conspiracy and counterfeiting checks and spent seven years in jail for it before being released in 2006 (before the two met).[421]

418 "Virginia Progressive Prosecutors Call for Ending Cash Bail, Abolishing Death Penalty, Ending Mandatory Minimums, Etc.," *Blue Virginia*, January 4, 2021. https://bluevirginia.us/2021/01/virginia-progressive-prosecutors-call-for-ending-cash-bail-abolishing-death-penalty-ending-mandatory-minimums-etc

419 Burk, Eric, "Loudoun Board of Supervisors Criticizes Commonwealth's Attorney for Handling of Domestic Violence Cases," *The Virginia Star*, March 30, 2021. https://thevirginiastar.com/2021/03/30/loudoun-board-of-supervisors-criticizes-commonwealths-attorney-for-handling-of-domestic-violence-cases/

420 Cawood, Jeffrey, "Report: L.A. Mayor Says George Soros's Foundation Expressed Interest in Funding Reparations Program," *The Daily Wire*, June 19, 2021. https://www.dailywire.com/news/report-l-a-mayor-says-george-soros-foundation-expressed-interest-in-funding-reparations-program

421 Willingham, A. J., and Madison Park, "Traffic Stop Is Just the Latest Controversy for State Attorney Aramis Ayala," CNN, July 13, 2017. https://edition.cnn.com/2017/07/13/us/aramis-ayala-traffic-stop-who-is-profile-trnd/index.html

Ayala's office moved to reduce the number of people prosecuted for resisting arrest without violence on the sole basis that "Black people are disproportionally arrested on such charges." There are virtually no crimes that every racial demographic commits in exact proportion to their share of the general population, and thus such illogic could be used to justify abolishing the penalties for virtually any crime (and they will try).[422]

The new policy came to the rescue of many arrested during the George Floyd riots. Ayala framed the arrests of the rioters as attempts to "silence" and "crush" their First Amendment rights. Orange County Sheriff John Mina says he was never informed of the policy change, and had to learn from the media.

In lieu of actual consequences, Ayala seeks to punish criminals like kindergarteners by giving them an adult time-out and having their charges dropped in exchange for watching an educational video about resisting crime and the dangers associated with breaking the law. Ironically, that very exercise teaches them that there aren't many dangers associated with breaking the law.

Defendants are allowed to take part in the program once every six months, proving that its purpose is ideological, and not simply to give first-time offenders a warning.

Or as Ayala puts it, "we do lead with common sense."

Another one of her "common-sense" ideas was to create a list of police officers that have credibility issues. The supposed purpose of the list was to identify unreliable witnesses to bar them from testifying in criminal cases.

The policy was completely ambiguous and few details were given about how it would be administered. The committee tasked with creating the list were given only the viewpoint of witnesses but not police themselves. Ayala offered no description of how investigations would be conducted,[423] nor was any insight offered into what the exact criteria to end up on the list is.

Despite what Ayala billed the program as, it has the obvious potential of becoming nothing more than a blacklist of cops that the defund-the-police crowd doesn't like. She eventually released her bad cops list in July 2020.[424]

422   Cordeiro, Monivette, "Aramis Ayala to Drop More Resisting Arrest Cases," *Orlando Sentinel*, October 6, 2020. https://www.orlandosentinel.com/news/crime/os-ne-state-attorney-resisting-officer-without-violence-20201006-zbdqxmweyvhjddc7hs3ltdgnnm-story.html
423   Sheets, Tess, "Orlando Police Union Bristles at State Attorney's Plan to Make List of Unreliable Witnesses, Including Cops," *Chicago Tribune*, August 2019. https://www.chicagotribune.com/os-ne-aramis-ayala-brady-policy-20190802-d2nqqsokbjhrzgdltrtt6vvh6a-story.html
424   Sheets, and Jeff Weiner, "State Attorney Aramis Ayala Releases List of Central Florida Cops with Questionable Credibility as Witnesses," *Orlando Sentinel*, July 14, 2020. https://www.orlandosentinel.com/news/breaking-news/os-ne-orange-osceola-brady-list-aramis-ayala-20200714-rtoj6cmyfnd5rpiqsuvttt3g4u-story.html

When she took office, she said she wouldn't seek the death penalty in any cases. Former Florida Governor Rick Scott reassigned twenty-nine death penalties to his state attorney as a result, and slashed Ayala's budget by $1.3 million. Ayala lost the subsequent legal battle she waged in response.[425]

As she prepared to depart office, she dropped the death penalty in three murder cases, including a man accused of killing his wife and three children, and a man accused of killing an Orlando police officer.[426]

Soros is one of four backers who spent nearly $2.2 million supporting Monique Worrell, the candidate who successfully ran to replace Ayala and took office in 2021.[427] Less than two weeks before election day, Ayala hired Worrell, adding her to her office's Conviction Integrity Unit with a $50k salary.[428]

Worrell wants to reform the criminal justice system because it "disproportionately affects people of color and poor people," which, again, seems to just be an excuse to legalize various crimes that her favored minority groups disproportionately commit.[429] No one is calling for DUI laws to be abolished because a disproportionate share of that offense is committed by whites, but such a ridiculous argument could be justified by her logic.

She's kept Ayala's bad cops list in effect and created a new unit to investigate allegations of police brutality and misconduct.[430]

She's used the coronavirus to justify changes to bail, calling for prosecutors to "recommend defendants accused of non-violent offenses be released without having to post bail if they are over age 60, have a body mass index over 30, have a high risk of complications if infected with COVID-19, are a primary caretaker or are an essential worker."[431]

425 Cutway, Adrienne, "Gov. Rick Scott Wins Legal Battle Against State Attorney Aramis Ayala," ClickOrlando, August 31, 2017. https://www.clickorlando.com/news/2017/09/01/gov-rick-scott-wins-legal-battle-against-state-attorney-aramis-ayala/
426 "Florida's Aramis Ayala Drops Death Penalty in 3 Murder Cases as She Departs Office," Tampa Bay Times, January 5, 2021. https://www.tampabay.com/news/crime/2021/01/05/floridas-aramis-ayala-drops-death-penalty-in-3-murder-cases-as-she-departs-office/
427 Powers, Scott, "Desmond Meade's New PAC Pours $1.5 Million into Orlando's State Attorney Race," Florida Politics, August 18, 2020. https://floridapolitics.com/archives/358913-desmond-meades-new-pac-pours-1-5-million-into-orlandos-state-attorney-race/
428 Weiner, "Monique Worrell Hired by Aramis Ayala Before Election," Orlando Sentinel, October 30, 2020. https://www.orlandosentinel.com/news/breaking-news/os-ne-monique-worrell-hired-by-aramis-ayala-20201030-ul2d-3wxwqnf25pg6co6lxxoc3i-story.html
429 Cordeiro, "Monique Worrell to Push Progressive Policies as State Attorney," Orlando Sentinel, November 13, 2020. https://www.orlandosentinel.com/politics/2020-election/os-ne-2020-monique-worrell-state-attorney-20201113-qfocscit5vczzmgo42i7mujf6a-story.html
430 Jones, Daralene, and Sarah Wilson, "New Orange-Osceola County State Attorney Creating New Unit to Investigate Allegations of Police Brutality, Misconduct," WFTV, January 9, 2021. https://www.wftv.com/news/local/orange-county/new-orange-osceola-county-state-attorney-creating-new-unit-investigate-allegations-police-brutality-misconduct/6B77KFPH7FCPJCICYVSTQVWO2Q/
431 Cordeiro, "Worrell Aims to Rethink Bail, Pleas After COVID Outbreak at Orange Jail," Orlando Sentinel, February 19, 2021. https://www.orlandosentinel.com/news/crime/os-ne-monique-worrell-orange-osceola-jails-20210219-jhptx7dyv5grzgpiupvnbemqly-story.html

The biggest recipient of PAC money in the Broward state attorney race was Joe Kimok, who made no effort to hide the $750k he received from Soros' Justice & Safety PAC in just a three-week period. "We, like many candidates, have run a campaign unapologetically seeking to dismantle the system of mass incarceration. We want to encourage a new understanding of law enforcement and prosecution," he said after identifying Soros as his main donor. He said of Soros, "We welcome the help. He's supporting what we've been fighting for, not asking us to change to accommodate his beliefs."[432]

GEORGIA

Shalena Cook Jones received at least $80k in support from Soros, leading to her becoming district attorney for Chatham County in Georgia.[433] She took office in January 2021.

Of violent protests, Jones has stated "I think that marching, and rioting, and burning—they all have their place." She further claimed "I recognize that rioting, marching, and burning may work some." [434]

In her words, rioting is merely a "widely accepted form of civil disobedience," which she justifies on the basis that a "heart that elevates property over the value of human life is debased and morally corrupt."[435]

She opposed President Trump's decision to send federal law enforcement to major cities to squash rioting, which enabled more chaos.

On social media, she's voiced opposition to prohibitions against sanctuary cities, increased penalties for gangs, and a peace officers bill of rights. She supports ending cash bail and has said on video that "virtually no one should be in jail." She opposed HB 994, an anti-gang bill, and represented an alleged member of the Bloods in the past. She also supports removing qualified immunity for cops.[436]

---

432   Olmeda, Rafael, "Secret Money, Soros Money Shake up State Attorney's Primary," *South Florida Sun-Sentinel*, August 15, 2020. https://www.sun-sentinel.com/news/politics/fl-ne-broward-sao-pac-money-20200814-phgj6qy-tuzevhmths3w2drsul4-story.html

433   Nussbaum, Katie, "Rep. Jesse Petrea Says Chatham County DA Candidate Shalena Cook Jones' Campaign Connected to Soros PA,." *Savannah Morning News*, October 15, 2020. https://www.savannahnow.com/story/news/politics/elections/2020/10/15/rep-jesse-petrea-says-chatham-county-da-candidate-shalena-cook-jonesrsquo-campaign-connected-to-soro/43056709/

434   "Shalena Cook Jones," Landmark Communications Inc, October 2020. https://landmarkcommunications.net/wp-content/uploads/2020/10/The-Real-Shalena-Cook-Jones.pdf

435   Ibid.

436   Ibid.

MISSOURI

Kimberly Gardner is best known among conservatives for her injudicious decision to charge Mark and Patricia McCloskey after they stood outside of their home with firearms to defend it against a mob of Black Lives Matter rioters who forcibly entered their neighborhood. She was removed from the case after she sent out an email fundraising off of it.[437]

That all came not long after Gardner dropped all charges against thirty-six people arrested when St. Louis saw mass violence, rioting, arson, and looting following the death of George Floyd.

Soros spent $190k backing her in 2016 to become circuit attorney of St. Louis, and $116k backing her reelection.[438] Conviction rates fell from about 80 to 85 percent from when Gardner was elected to 54 percent by 2019. The only other place in the entire country that has a comparably low conviction rate is in Orlando under Amaris Ayala's watch.[439] Kristi Flint, a St. Louis defense attorney who worked as a prosecutor for ten years in the Circuit Attorney Office said the reason for the drop in convictions is simple: nobody wants to work there anymore. "They came in acting as if the police are the enemies, very combative. Then everything breaks down, and the people who are suffering the most are the victims of these crimes."

Upon taking office, Gardner fired veteran prosecutors and replaced them with inexperienced lawyers, with her office losing an estimated combined 470 years of experience in the process. The conviction rate for the Circuit Attorney's Office fell from a historical average of 72 percent to as low as 51 percent under Gardner.[440]

While not solely due to Gardner specifically, St. Louis now boasts the highest murder rate in the U.S. (as of 2020), and it is due largely to the ideological vision Gardner favors. Mayor Tishaura Jones seconds her vision, and vowed to cut $4 million from police (costing nearly one hundred jobs) and close a city jail in light of a

---

437 Byers, Christine, "Judge Dismisses St. Louis Circuit Attorney Kim Gardner from Mark McCloskey Case," KSDK, December 10, 2020. https://www.ksdk.com/article/news/local/kim-gardner-mccloskey-case-judge-dismiss/63-779eab2f-32d7-4f8e-b171-5d77307b89b7

438 Varney, James, "George Soros-Funded DAs Oversee Big Cities with Skyrocketing Crime," *The Washington Times*, August 20, 2020, accessed July 24, 2021. https://www.washingtontimes.com/news/2020/aug/20/george-soros-funded-das-oversee-big-cities-skyrock/

439 Trager, Lauren, "Records Show Trial Conviction Rate for Circuit Attorney's Office Has Fallen Nearly 20% in 2 Years," KMOV4, February 26, 2020. https://www.kmov.com/news/records-show-trial-conviction-rate-for-circuit-attorneys-office-has-fallen-nearly-20-in-2/article_a1c0f8d2-5842-11ea-b7f6-d7598e1fc94e.html

440 Ibid.

homicide rate of eighty-seven victims per hundred thousand people. For reference, Baltimore, which ranks second, has a murder rate of fifty-seven per hundred thousand (and the national average is roughly eight per hundred thousand).[441]

In one case that the mother of the homicide victim describes as "incompetent" and "criminal," the man charged with her son's murder was set free after Gardner's office failed to show up at hearings.[442]

Gardner's legal career could soon come to a close, as she's now at risk of losing her law license for alleged misconduct in a case involving former Missouri governor Eric Greitens. According to court documents, the Missouri Chief Disciplinary Counsel has concluded there is probable cause that Gardner is "guilty of professional misconduct" in the case in May of 2021. Gardner will have to defend her actions in front of a disciplinary hearing panel that is likely to take her law license if she's found guilty. Gardner is alleged to have concealed investigation details from her team, failed to disclose facts to Greitens's legal team, and misrepresented evidence to a court.[443]

The prior July, a St. Louis judge named Christopher McGraugh ordered Gardner to turn over all emails and text messages between Gardner and people of influence including George Soros.[444] This came after John Solomon won a default judgement against Gardner in an open-records lawsuit he filed concerning her 2018 investigation into Greitens. She failed to respond, leading to the judge blasting her in a court order. "This didn't just happen once. This is a consistent behavior," he wrote, "I think it's the office that's attempting to obfuscate this process."[445]

What do you think she was trying to hide?

441   Ruiz, Michael, "St. Louis' Murder Rate, Already Highest in US, Soared Last Year; Mayor Vows to Defund the Police," Fox News, May 23, 2021. https://www.foxnews.com/us/st-louis-murder-rate-defund-police-mayor-tishaura-jones

442   "Mother Calls for Kim Gardner's Resignation over Handling of Son's Murder Case," CBS St. Louis, July 23, 2021. https://patch.com/missouri/stlouis/mother-calls-kim-gardners-resignation-over-handling-sons-murder-case

443   Dima, Jake, "St. Louis Prosecutor Who Charged McCloskeys Faces Professional Misconduct Allegations," *Washington Examiner*, May 5, 2021. https://www.washingtonexaminer.com/news/kim-gardner-mccloskey-prosecutor-professional-misconduct-investigation-law-license

444   Hayes, Chris, "Judge Orders Release of Circuit Attorney's Communications During Investigation of Former Governor," FOX 2 Now, July 30, 2020. https://fox2now.com/news/fox-files/judge-orders-release-of-circuit-attorneys-communications-during-investigation-of-former-governor/

445   Hayes, "Judge Calls Out Gardner's Office for 'Consistent Behavior' to 'Obfuscate the Process,'" FOX 2 Now, October 8, 2020. https://fox2now.com/news/fox-files/judge-calls-out-gardners-office-for-consistent-behavior-to-obfuscate-the-process/

ILLINOIS

Kim Foxx assumed office in December 2016, now heading the second largest prosecutor's office in the United States. To her aid was $300k from George Soros,[446] who donated an additional $2 million in 2020 toward her reelection campaign.[447] She is the first DA to be backed by Soros.[448]

Foxx became a household name shortly after actor and Subway sandwich enthusiast Jussie Smollett claimed to have been the victim of a hate crime after picking up a sandwich in Chicago at 2:00 a.m. in −11-degree weather when he was then confronted by two Trump-hat-wearing white men who recognized him from the show *Empire* and then proceeded to beat him (leaving almost no injuries in the process), and pour bleach on him before putting a noose around his neck that he kept wearing until police arrived at his apartment.

The narrative was premised on two impossibilities: that there are Trump supporters in Chicago; and that white people know what the show *Empire* is. Regardless, the media mindlessly ate up the story, but police didn't, and they turned toward investigating Smollett, eventually leading to him being indicted on sixteen felony counts by a grand jury. Foxx dropped all of them.

Likely due to the outrage in response to the dropped charges, Smollett was later indicted by a Cook County grand jury on six counts of making false police reports, and a judge struck down Smollett's claim that this violated his right against double jeopardy.

While this looks a lot like special treatment for a celebrity, Foxx is just as generous to other alleged criminals too. Foxx dropped 30 percent of all charges in felony cases her first three years as Cook County state's attorney, compared with 19.4 percent for per predecessor's last three years. In total, 25,183 defendants saw their felonies cases dropped under Foxx, compared with 18,694 for her predecessor. Foxx's conviction rate was only 66 percent compared with her predecessor's 75 percent.[449]

446   Stecklow, Sam, "A Look at the 'Dark Money' behind Kim Foxx's States Attorney Campaign," The Chicagoist, March 10, 2016. https://chicagoist.com/2016/03/10/kim_foxx_funding.php

447   Hinton, Rachel, "George Soros Gives $2 Million to PAC Backing Kim Foxx," *Chicago Sun-Times*, February 21, 2020. https://chicago.suntimes.com/politics/2020/2/20/21146269/george-soros-kim-foxx-bill-conway-states-attorney

448   Smith, Zack, and Charles Stimson, "Meet Kim Foxx, the Rogue Prosecutor Whose Policies are Wreaking Havoc in Chicago," Heritage Foundation, November 3, 2020. https://www.heritage.org/crime-and-justice/commentary/meet-kim-foxx-the-rogue-prosecutor-whose-policies-are-wreaking-havoc

449   Eustachewich, Lia, "Kim Foxx, Former Jussie Smollett Prosecutor, Drops Felony Cases at Alarming Rate: Report," *New York Post*, August 10, 2020. https://nypost.com/2020/08/10/kim-foxx-ex-jussie-smollett-prosecutor-drops-cases-at-high-rate-report/

Only a month after taking office, Foxx announced that shoplifting would no longer be a felony if the stolen items were worth less than $1,000 (three times higher than current state law). That resulted in an immediate drop of around three hundred felony shoplifting cases being charged each month to about seventy. Shoplifting dropped from being the second most frequent offense to the eighth due to the new rules (even as the frequency of the crime increased).[450] Simply refusing to define certain crimes as crimes is just the latest trick of progressive prosecutors in reducing crime—but only on paper.

When mass looting broke out during the George Floyd rioters, Foxx dropped charges against 817 defendants.[451]

In 2021, Foxx declared support for House Bill 163, proposed legislation that would eliminate qualified immunity and end cash bail. Critics refer to it as a "defund the police" bill.[452]

In October 2021, Foxx refused to press charges following a public gang shootout, claiming that the incident was "mutual combat."[453]

LOUISIANA

Soros donated a total of $406k to a PAC backing James Stewart in the Caddo Parish DA race[454] He was first elected in November 2015 and he won reelection in November 2020. Most of his efforts that align with the Soros agenda have been in trying to abolish use of the death penalty,[455] though Louisiana hasn't put anyone to death since 2010.

MASSACHUSETTS

In Suffolk County, Soros backed DA Rachael Rollins, a woman reportedly "exhausted" because police officers "shoot us in the street as if we were animals." She assumed office in January 2019.

She doesn't have a high view of police, but criminals can do little wrong in her eyes.

450   Daniels, Matt, "The Kim Foxx Effect: How Prosecutions Have Changed in Cook County," The Marshall Project, October 24, 2019. https://www.themarshallproject.org/2019/10/24/the-kim-foxx-effect-how-prosecutions-have-changed-in-cook-county

451   Flannery, Mike, "Foxx Confirms FOX 32 Report That Charges Will Be Dropped against Hundreds of Protesters," FOX 32 Chicago, July 1, 2020. https://www.fox32chicago.com/news/foxx-confirms-fox-32-report-that-charges-will-be-dropped-against-hundreds-of-protesters

452   Gaskins, Nikki, "Orland Park Mayor: 'I Strongly Oppose the Defund Police Bill,'" Patch, January 11, 2021. https://patch.com/illinois/orlandpark/orland-park-mayor-i-strongly-oppose-defund-police-bill

453   Rios, Blanca. "What Is Impact of Mayor Lightfoot, Kim Foxx Feud Over 'Mutual Combat' Argument in Austin Shooting?" ABC7 Chicago, October 10, 2021. https://abc7chicago.com/kim-foxx-lightfoot-mutual-combat-ants-combat/11100664/

454   Litten, Kevin, "George Soros Puts Another $150,000 into Caddo DA Race," Nola, October 21, 2015. https://www.nola.com/news/politics/article_2e8bce41-547c-5781-80c7-d6fbcdfab885.html

455   Young, Yolanda, "America's Death Penalty Capital: Can a Black DA Really Change the System?" The Guardian, March 13, 2016. https://www.theguardian.com/us-news/2016/mar/13/caddo-parish-louisiana-death-penalty-capital-district-attorney

In an op-ed titled "The Public Safety Myth," Rollins argues that "We have been told that our communities are safer with each criminal that our local law enforcement locks up—often for low-level offenses like drug possession, shoplifting, or loitering. The problem with this narrative is that it's largely false, predicated on a pervasive and pernicious myth known as 'broken windows' theory."[456]

Within a month after Rollins was elected, the National Police Association filed a formal complaint with the Office of the Bar Counsel in Massachusetts against her, alleging that she had "reckless disregard for the laws enacted by the Massachusetts General Assembly mandate." They were specifically referring to a campaign promise of hers not to prosecute entire classes of crimes that would "adversely and will foreseeably impact the safety and well-being of those that she is soon charged to represent." [457]

Rollins disregarded those concerns and published a policy memo she claimed was "data driven" and "grounded in science." In it, fifteen categories of crimes are outlined that she says should either be "outright dismissed prior to arraignment," or, where appropriate, "diverted and treated as a civil infraction."

Those fifteen crimes are trespassing, shoplifting, larceny under $250, disorderly conduct, disturbing the peace, receiving stolen property, driving with a suspended or revoked license, breaking and entering into a vacant property or property for the purpose of "sleeping or seeking refuge from the cold," wanton or malicious destruction of property, threats, minors in possession of alcohol, drug possession, drug possession with intent to distribute, resisting arrest (when the only charge is resisting arrest), and resisting arrest (if the other charges include only charges that fall under the list of charges for which prosecution is declined).[458]

This policy prevents criminals who would later commit more serious crimes from having those prior offenses on their record, so a sentence enhancement can't be sought.

As the Heritage Foundation's Charles Stimson puts it "In other words, in Boston, a violent career felon can break into your home, be in possession of cocaine, plan to distribute that cocaine to others,

---

456   Feldman, Cassi, "The Public Safety Myth," *The Appeal*, August 29, 2019. https://theappeal.org/the-public-safety-myth/

457   Stimson, Charles, and Zack Smith, "Meet Rachael Rollins, the Rogue Prosecutor Whose Policies Are Wreaking Havoc in Boston," Heritage Foundation, November 12, 2020. https://www.heritage.org/crime-and-justice/commentary/meet-rachael-rollins-the-rogue-prosecutor-whose-policies-are-wreaking

458   Ibid.

and resist arrest after you call the police, and all the charges will be 'outright dismissed,' so long as the reason he broke into your house—and terrified your family—was because he wanted 'to sleep' or was 'seeking refuge' from the cold."[459]

Rollins' memo also established a new policy on cash bail and pretrial release of "presumptive recommendation of release on personal recognizance without conditions. This presumption will be rebutted only if there is clear evidence of a flight risk." She ordered that her office apply her cash bail and pretrial release policy retroactively to anyone held on cash bail of $25k of less.[460]

In response to criticism of her insane policies, Rollins assures us that she doesn't "have much time for more white men telling me what of communities of color need, because they don't know." She also cited her body's possession of "actual melanin" in her defense.[461]

As of August 2020, the number of shootings in Boston was up 29 percent from the year prior, and deadly shootings were up 34 percent. Boston Police Commissioner William Gross blamed Rollins's policy of releasing prisoners due to coronavirus hysteria.[462]

MISSISSIPPI

With $326k in backing from Soros, Scott Colom was elected district attorney for Circuit Court District Sixteen in 2015.[463] He scored a historic win over a twenty-six-year incumbent, who raised only $49k for his race.

Speaking to Politico, Colom explained that he wanted to reduce reliance on jails. "I'm sure there are plenty of people out there who think prison is too nice and we need to spend more on it." Colom continued, "But it seems like a large majority of people out there get it and realize there have to be priorities. Just because a fella commits a crime doesn't mean the best outcome is sending them to jail...As much as possible, I want to take people from being tax burdens to taxpayers."[464]

459 Ibid.
460 Stimson and Smith, "'Progressive' Prosecutors Sabotage the Rule of Law, Raise Crime Rates, and Ignore Victims," Heritage Foundation, October 29, 2020. https://www.heritage.org/crime-and-justice/report/progressive-prosecutors-sabotage-the-rule-law-raise-crime-rates-and-ignore.
461 Stimson and Smith. "Meet Rachael Rollins."
462 Corrado, Kerri, "Commissioner Fumes About Release of Violent Criminals after Roxbury Triple Shooting," WHDH, May 4, 2020. https://whdh.com/news/commissioner-fumes-about-release-of-violent-criminals-after-roxbury-triple-shooting/
463 Gates, Jimmie E., "Billionaire Money Used in Dem Races," The Clarion-Ledger, October 16, 2015. https://www.clarionledger.com/story/news/2015/10/15/billionaire-money-used-da-races/73994362/
464 Bland, Scott, "George Soros's Quiet Overhaul of the U.S. Justice System," Politico, August 30, 2016. https://www.politico.com/story/2016/08/george-soros-criminal-justice-reform-227519

The reelection campaign of Robert Shuler Smith, a Hinds County district attorney, got $56k from Soros, which he won in 2015.[465]

By 2016, he would be arrested by the Mississippi Attorney General's Office on charges of providing improper advice to two people facing criminal charges (which he was later acquitted of).[466] In 2017, a grand jury indicted him on four charges: two domestic-violence misdemeanor charges and two felony charges, one for aggravated stalking and another for robbery, but he ultimately wasn't convicted.[467] Regardless, he'd later step down in 2019, mired in controversy.

NEW MEXICO

Soros spent $107k backing Raul Torrez to become Bernalillo County's DA, and he was sworn in January 2017. His Republican opponent dropped out of the race due to Soros' backing, commenting "New Mexicans cannot afford to challenge anyone who has unlimited resources and support from a multibillionaire from another country."[468]

On his campaign website, Torrez pitched a platform of "reform, rebuild, renew," calling for adopting "modern, community-based prosecution strategies that target the particular public safety priorities of every neighborhood in Bernalillo County."

Unlike Soros' other backed candidates, Torrez hasn't implemented any notable radical policy changes (so far), though his office has had some incredible acts of incompetence. In one case, a female imposter scammed them by falsely claiming to be a victim in a case, demanding the charges be dropped against the violent defendant and that he be released from jail. The defendant, Freddie Trujillo, pled guilty in a 2017 aggravated assault case, and was put on probation but jailed in 2018 for violating it. The charges were dropped when the imposter walked into the courthouse and demanding the charges to be dropped—and Trujillo was released. Nobody bothered to check if the imposter was the actual victim.[469]

---

465   Gates, "Billionaire Money Used in Dem Races."

466   Vicory, Justin, "Why Robert Shuler Smith Was Acquitted," *The Clarion-Ledger*, August 13, 2017. https://www.clarionledger.com/story/news/politics/2017/08/12/behind-robert-schuler-smith-not-guilty-verdict/552488001/

467   Vicory, "Hinds DA's Third Criminal Trial: No Conviction," *The Clarion-Ledger*, September 12, 2018. https://www.clarionledger.com/story/news/local/2018/09/12/hinds-da-robert-shuler-smith-contradicts-two-witnesses-stand/1273563002/

468   Boetel, Ryan, "Republican Candidate Drops Out of Race for DA," *Albuquerque Journal*. https://www.abqjournal.com/796843/republican-candidate-drops-out-of-da-race.html.

469   Pete Dinelli, "Two Very Bad News Stories and Acts of Pettiness by DA Raul Torrez," PeteDinelli.com, February 22, 2019. https://www.petedinelli.com/2019/02/22/two-very-bad-news-stories-and-acts-of-pettiness-by-da-raul-torrez/

OREGON

Portland DA Mike Schmidt was backed with $230k from Soros.[470] Schmidt was appointed to be director of the Criminal Justice Commission by Oregon Governor Kate Brown in 2015. He advocated ending cash bail and investing in "alternative programs" to incarceration and has campaigned on the elimination of mandatory minimum sentencing. His job as DA began in August 2020.

Ten days after taking office, he announced that he'd refuse to prosecute the city's rioters, defending them as people who "represent the instinctive reactions of people who have been gassed repeatedly, who have been struck with kinetic projective weapons." Even though rioting is a felony, he doesn't prosecute those cases.[471]

He refuses to prosecute individuals for "interfering with a peace officer, disorderly conduct in the second degree, criminal trespass in the first or second degree, escape in the third degree, and harassment and riot when it isn't accompanied by a separate charge."[472]

Before being sworn in as DA, he sat down for an interview with the online antifa personality "Awkword," whom we learned he was "old buddies" with for over twenty years during the interview. The two had met at Vassar College. Awkword currently leads the Ten Demands for Justice movement, which lists defunding and demilitarizing the police among its demands to set the stage for the full abolition of prisons.[473]

In the interview, Awkword asks what Schmidt considers fair punishment, prefacing his question by stating that "the majority of perpetrators have been victims themselves," and thus these "victims" deserve "reparative justice" in the form of social services instead of imprisonment. Schmidt responded by claiming that the U.S. prison system is built on "white supremacist culture."

Awkword told Schmidt that as a prison abolitionist he "definitely see[s] you as an ally in that effort." Schmidt expressed that he ran on a campaign of "needing to shrink the criminal justice system."

Awkword then asked Schmidt about his forthcoming policy of not prosecuting rioters, whom he described as individuals simply exercising their first amendment rights (apparently the first time one of these crazies cares about the constitution). Schmidt replied that the rioters are "nothing like the Armageddon that the Trump Adminis-

470 Nolan, "Beware of George Soros's Trojan Horse Prosecutors."
471 Ibid.
472 Ibid.
473 Cathell, Mia, "New DA in Portland Admits He Is 'Old Buddies' with an Antifa Militant," *The Post Millennial*, August 15, 2020. https://thepostmillennial.com/new-portland-da-admits-he-is-old-buddies-with-an-antifa-militant

tration is trying to portray our city," and called protesters blocking off a bridge as part of a "die in" protest a "beautiful demonstration."

TEXAS

Kim Ogg won her race in 2016 after campaigning on bail reform and promising to create a "system that doesn't oppress the poor." She defeated the incumbent by eight points, becoming the first Democrat DA in forty years for Harris County (whose county seat is Houston). Soros initially backed Morris Overstreet, who lost in the Democratic primary, then funded Ogg to the tune of $500k.[474]

Ogg has declared herself part of the "national reform movement," and dropped nearly eight hundred criminal charges made against 654 protesters during the George Floyd riots. Most of the offenses were characterized as involving trespassing and obstructing highways. Even that wasn't enough for some leftists, who complained that Ogg didn't also offer an apology to the protesters for being charged in the first place.[475]

While she'll give them a pass, Ogg pursued charges against Dr. Hasan Gokal for giving away free doses of a coronavirus vaccine that was going to expire. The price tag of the vaccines was $135 for the doses, far less than the cost of property damage associated with your typical Black Lives Matter protester. The charges were later dropped amid outrage, but it shines insight into Ogg's priorities.[476] As does Ogg dismissing charges against a Houston doctor accused of molesting a child patient in 2014.[477]

The percentage of misdemeanor defendants released on general order or personal bond increased from 11.2 percent in 2016 to 72.4 percent by 2020. The number of violent offenders released on personal recognizance bonds increased from 239 in 2018 to 1,097 in 2020. Harris County reported a 28 percent year-over-year increase in murders from 2019 to 2020, while Houston reported a 42 percent increase.[478]

474 "Billionaire Soros Makes $500K Ad Buy for Democratic DA Candidate Ogg," *Houston Chronicle*, October 14, 2016. https://www.chron.com/politics/article/Billionaire-Soros-makes-500-000-ad-buy-for-9970130.php

475 Edwards, Schaefer, "Harris County District Attorney's Office Drops Nearly 800 Charges against Non-Violent Protesters," *Houston Press*, June 10, 2020. https://www.houstonpress.com/news/harris-county-district-attorney-kim-ogg-dismisses-charges-against-non-violent-protesters-11476173

476 Homer, Michelle, "Update: Charge Dropped Against Harris Co. Doctor Who Had Been Accused of Stealing Vial of COVID Vaccine," KHOU, January 21, 2021. https://www.khou.com/article/news/health/coronavirus/vaccine/harris-county-doctor-charged-theft-covid-19-vaccine/285-48ba88ad-c6e7-4ba9-a97b-7f5c14f42b58

477 Rogers, Brian, "Charges Dropped against Doctor Accused of Child Molestation," San Antonio Local News, April 28, 2017. https://www.mysanantonio.com/news/houston-texas/article/Charges-dropped-against-doctor-accused-of-child-11107402.php

478 Arrajj, Shawn. "Harris County Officials Take Aim at Rise in Violent Crime," *Community Impact*, April 20, 2021. https://communityimpact.com/houston/spring-klein/public-safety/2021/04/20/harris-county-officials-take-aim-at-

In her only bout of sanity, Ogg at least violated her campaign promise to bring so-called bail reform to the county.

Soros spent $652k on José Garza, who won his race to become DA of Travis County.[479] Garza is a member of the Democratic Socialists of America.[480]

Garza's definition of public safety is "stability, good jobs, access to health care, access to mental health care, access to good education." Noticeably missing is law enforcement, members of which he says lock up "as many working-class people and people of color as they can." [481]

Garza took office in January 2021 and immediately progressed with plans to abolish cash bail and "diversion plans" to make it easier for people charged with some nonviolent crimes to go into intervention programs instead of jail.[482]

Three weeks into the job, Garza indicted Officer Gregory Gentry (and another cop involved in the same incident) on use of force charges, even though his 2019 case was investigated by the previous DA and he wasn't indicted. The political stunt failed and Garza ended up having to drop charges after another review of the incident. Garza claimed that "new evidence" was behind his decision to drop the charges he brought—but the supposed "old evidence" had already led to the same conclusion years prior.[483]

Another case where Garza played loose with the facts is that of Sergeant Daniel Perry, who was doing a ride for Uber when his car was surrounded by rioters during the George Floyd protests. Police did not block off streets so people could protest. Already surrounded by a mob, Perry was approached by Garrett Foster, who was open carrying an assault weapon and minutes earlier was videotaped saying people who have a problem with him and his comrades are "pussies and won't do anything about it." Shortly after, Foster confronted Perry and was fatally shot after allegedly pointing his gun at him.

A lead investigator on the case told pundit Matt Christiansen that the best detective in the department determined that probable cause

rise-in-violent-crime/

479   Clifton, Jo, "Is Money Going to Decide Travis County Races?" *Austin Monitor*, July 10, 2020. https://www.austinmonitor.com/stories/2020/07/is-money-going-to-decide-travis-county-races/

480   Day, Meagan, "Austin's Likely Next District Attorney Vows to End the Drug War," *Jacobin*, July 25, 2020. https://jacobinmag.com/2020/07/jose-garza-travis-county-district-attorney-texas/

481   Barajas, Michael, "José Garza Redefines 'Progressive Prosecutor,'" *The Texas Observer*, November 2, 2020. https://www.texasobserver.org/jose-garza-redefines-progressive-prosecutor/

482   Hall, Katie, "New Travis County DA Plans to Move More Defendants Out of Jail, into Diversion Programs," *Austin American-Statesman*, January 29, 2021. https://www.statesman.com/story/news/2021/01/29/jose-garza-plans-move-people-out-jail-into-diversion-programs/4295580001/

483   Preston, Bryan, "SHOCK: Radical Travis County DA Garza Drops Indictment against Cop, Claims 'New Evidence,'" PJ Media, July 19, 2021. https://pjmedia.com/news-and-politics/bryan-preston/2021/07/19/shock-radical-travis-county-da-garza-drops-indictment-against-cop-claims-new-evidence-n1463048

didn't exist to charge Perry with a crime after an investigation that involved reviewing video, fifty witness statements, and forensic and ballistic evidence from the scene.[484] A grand jury ended up indicting Perry on murder charges after a twisted presentation of the evidence by Garza.[485] Garza described Foster as someone "shot while participating in a protest," and made no mention of the mob surrounding Perry, or Foster allegedly pointing a rifle at him. No video showing Foster allegedly pointing his gun at Perry or witness statements saying at much were shown to the jury. Perry's defense team says they weren't allowed to make a written presentation to the grand jury, which is unusual in Texas.

The indictment of Perry came shortly after Garza let off two of three suspects in a shooting near a playground, with the third charged with murder, and providing neither evidence that the other two are cooperating nor an explanation for why they were set free.[486]

VIRGINIA

Soros scored two wins in Virginia in November of 2019 after pouring nearly $1 million into the campaigns of two prosecutors who successfully ousted incumbent Democrats. He funded this through his ironically named Justice and Public Safety PAC.

The candidates he backed were Parisa Dehghani-Tafti, who received $583k, and Steve Descano, who received $392k. The two incumbents raised a combined $404k. Former Virginia governor Terry McAuliffe also supported the Soros-backed candidates because the incumbents were sane enough to push back against his effort to restore felons' voting rights.[487]

Descano is Fairfax County's commonwealth's attorney, while Dehghani-Tafti is the commonwealth's attorney for Arlington County and the City of Falls Church.

In this case, money did buy an election—unless there's a better explanation for how two candidates who never prosecuted a case in state court defeated incumbents with sixty years of combined experience. A consultant for one of the incumbents said after the race "We were outspent 3 to 1. Our candi-

---

484   Christiansen, Matt, "Army Sergeant Indicted for Murder in Austin AK Self-Defense Case | DA Gets Choosy with the Evidence," YouTube video, July 7, 2021. https://www.youtube.com/watch?v=VEeJT_tYy9U&ab_channel=MattChristiansen

485   Coronado, Acacia, "Texas Soldier Who Shot Protester Indicted on Murder Charge," Military, July 2, 2021. https://www.military.com/daily-news/2021/07/02/texas-soldier-who-shot-protester-indicted-murder-charge.html

486   Preston, "SHOCK: Radical Travis County."

487   Shaw, Adam, "Left-Wing Billionaire George Soros Scores Wins in Virginia Elections, as Opponents Say Race Was 'Bought,'" Fox News, June 14, 2019. https://www.foxnews.com/politics/george-soros-scores-wins-in-virginia

date was in the hospital for nearly a week. This is an election that was bought, not won." A former state delegate commented "I think it is foreboding for local elections because we're going to have people clamoring to get money from George Soros—that's what I fear greatly." And it was a rational fear.[488]

Descano formally eliminated cash bail in December 2020, claiming "It creates a two-tiered system of justice—one for the rich and one for everybody else. It exacerbates existing racial inequities."[489]

The demand for bail in the first place was reduced by Descano's other policies legalizing various crimes. Her "do not prosecute" list gives Rachael Rollins a run for her money, allowing criminals to avoid prosecution for shoplifting goods valued at up to $1k, assault and battery, insurance fraud through arson if the property burned is worth less than $1k, setting off smoke bombs, prostitution or solicitation of prostitution, participating in a riot, obstructing the legal process, obstructing emergency medical services personnel, accepting bribes, obstructing justice by threats or force, knowingly and willfully making materially false statements to a law enforcement officer, resisting arrest, knowingly making a false police report, using a police radio during a crime, some forms of jury tampering, some forms of extortion as a governmental officer, aiding the escape of a prisoner, indecent exposure, reckless driving, possession of schedule III, IV, V, or VI drugs, and possession of drugs with intent to distribute.[490]

By April 2021 a recall campaign aimed at ousting Descano was launched.

Dehghani-Tafti campaigned on eliminating cash bail, implementing diversion programs to prioritize treatment over jail, "protecting immigrants" (which seems to be a synonym for supporting sanctuary policies), never seeking the death penalty, raising the threshold for felony larceny, and other promises.[491]

Fortunately, her agenda was met with resistance shortly after she took office. On March 4, 2020, the Arlington County Circuit Court enacted an order requiring her to justify all charging decisions regarding whether to dismiss, charge, or settle cases.[492] The Circuit

488   Ibid.
489   Jouvenal, Justin, "Virginia Prosecutor Formally Ends Cash Bail, Joining Growing Movement," *Guam Daily Post*, December 23, 2020. https://www.postguam.com/the_globe/nation/virginia-prosecutor-formally-ends-cash-bail-joining-growing-movement/article_42fb9188-43fe-11eb-9180-3718dc750728.html
490   Smith and Stimson, "Meet Steve Descano, the Rogue Prosecutor Whose Policies Are Wreaking Havoc in Fairfax County, Virginia," Heritage Foundation, December 14, 2020. https://www.heritage.org/crime-and-justice/commentary/meet-steve-descano-the-rogue-prosecutor-whose-policies-are-wreaking
491   "On the Issues," Parisa For Justice. https://parisaforjustice.com/on-the-issues/
492   Greenwald, David, "Virginia Prosecutor Threatened with Power Stripped for Advocating Reform," *Davis Vanguard*, August 15, 2020. https://www.davisvanguard.org/2020/08/now-virginia-prosecutor-threatened-with-power-stripped-for-advocating-reform/

Court and Dehghani-Tafti have also clashed on relatively minor issues, such as rejecting a plea bargain that would place a Maryland man on two years of probation for allegedly bringing fifty pounds of marijuana and four hundred cartridges of hashish oil into the country. This indicates that the Circuit Court has very little patience for Dehghani-Tafti's agenda.[493]

Soros donated a small $5k to James Hingeley's campaign for commonwealth attorney in Albemarle County.[494]

In July 2020, Hingeley formed a group with ten other commonwealth's attorneys to back criminal justice reform. The group's agenda includes an "end to mandatory driver's license suspensions on drug convictions; give defendants the ability to have past convictions expunged; eliminate mandatory sentences; and clarify "the discretionary powers of prosecutors." Other proposals include an end to no-knock warrants, which they justified by citing the death of Breonna Taylor, who wasn't killed in a no-knock warrant raid.[495]

In April 2021, he signed a letter along with other DAs on this list including Chesa Boudin, Shalena Cook Jones, Kimberly Gardner, Kim Foxx, Steve Descano, Parisa Dehghani-Tafti, Rachael Rollins, and others, calling for the automatic expungement or sealing of criminal records after one completes a sentence.[496]

"Research has shown that people with criminal records are no more likely than the general population to commit a new crime if they have avoided contact with the criminal justice system for four to seven years," they wrote, without considering that perhaps their proposal should apply only to people who've been out of the system for four to seven years without reoffending.

They do make an exception for felonies, which they say should be expunged after a "reasonable" amount of time—but the word "reasonable" doesn't mean the same to these kind of ideologically driven kooks as it does to you and me.

493   DeVoe, Jo, "Rejected Plea Deal Part of Tug-of-War Between Arlington Courts, Prosecutor," ARLnow, November 5, 2020. https://www.arlnow.com/2020/11/05/rejected-plea-deal-part-of-tug-of-war-between-arlington-courts-prosecutor/

494   Schoffstall, "Soros-Backed Prosecutor Candidates Sweep Virginia Races," *Washington Free Beacon*, November 6, 2019. https://freebeacon.com/politics/soros-backed-prosecutor-candidates-sweep-virginia-races/

495   Oliver, Ned, "11 Commonwealth's Attorneys Form Group to Back Criminal Justice Reform," *Virginia Mercury*, July 21, 2020. https://www.virginiamercury.com/2020/07/20/11-commonwealths-attorneys-form-group-to-back-criminal-justice-reform/

496   "Joint Statement on Supporting Clean Slate Initiatives April 2021: Fair & Just Prosecution," *Yellow Scene Magazine*, April 26, 2021. https://yellowscene.com/2021/04/26/joint-statement-on-supporting-clean-slate-initiatives-april-2021-fair-just-prosecution-boulder-das-office-press-release/

SOROS' 2021 RACES

Soros' involvement at the local level continued into 2021, with him quietly investing nearly $200k into far-left prosecutor Ramin Fatehi to make him Norfolk, Virginia's commonwealth attorney. He donated $157k through his Justice & Safety PAC, and $41.5k from his Democracy PAC. Fatehi won a three-way Democrat primary in June and will head to the November general election as the only candidate on the ballot. Buta Biberaj endorsed him after his victory.

Fatehi opposes strict law enforcement and subscribes to the false view that crime is a "symptom of structural racism." Fatehi's campaign website advocates abolishing cash bail, abolishing the jury trial penalty, and making the criminal justice system "honor the principle that Black Lives Matter."[497]

Fatehi explained his twisted philosophy in a recent interview with *The Appeal*. "The old-fashioned view about public safety was not taking into account externalities. It was focused on the idea of crime as an evil unto itself. Where I part ways is in recognizing that crime is a symptom. It's a symptom of structural racism, of systematic community disinvestment, of redlining, unequal school policy, the lack of jobs, lack of transportation, a lack of opportunities, intergenerational barriers to wealth building, the disinvestment in the treatment of the mentally ill."[498]

Like all progressives, Fatehi bends over backward to create enough excuses for criminal behavior so criminals themselves receive no share of the blame. Instead, the "system" is blamed, rarely with coherent elaboration. A commonality between all of Soros' prosecutors is that they all treat criminals as if they're the real victims.

The causes for crime Fatehi blames are deliberately vague enough so that he always has something to blame. How do we do define "intergenerational barriers to wealth building" and quantify when they've disappeared? There's never any threshold or criteria given to determine when a problem attributed to racism has been solved.

Further proving that any excuse is useable, Fatehi blames a lack of jobs for crime during an unprecedented labor shortage. Even if we were to solve the problems Fatehi lays out, progressives would still blame them for any disparity they see fit.

497   "Legislative and Office Priorities," Ramin Fatehi for Norfolk Commonwealth's Attorney. https://fatehinorfolk.com/priorities/
498   Nichanian, "Norfolk Elects Prosecutor Who Says Crime Is a 'Symptom of Structural Racism,'" *The Appeal*, June 10, 2021. https://theappeal.org/politicalreport/norfolk-elects-prosecutor-who-says-crime-is-a-symptom-of-structural-racism/

Fatehi also complains that we put criminals in prison: "It's incredibly expensive, imprisoning people, jailing them, supervising them. We are disinvesting from our own community. We're pulling human capital and dollars away from things like mental health treatment, drug treatment, education, housing contracts, and so on."[499]

Soros has also invested in New York City's mayoral race, backing far-left Maya Wiley, who serves as The New School's Senior Vice President of Social Justice and is a professor at the university's graduate school of policy, management, and environment.

Wiley boasts an endorsement from socialist Alexandria Ocasio-Cortez, who said in support of her "If we don't come together as a movement, we will get a New York City built by and for billionaires, and we need a city for and by working people." Wiley shared the quote on her Twitter account and fundraised from it.[500]

Despite the rhetoric, Wiley is fine taking billionaire money. Soros put $500k into an independent expenditure group backing Wiley's campaign.[501]

NYC Mayor Bill de Blasio gutted nearly $1 billion from the NYPD's $6 billion budget in 2020, a year that saw more homicides than the prior two combined. And in the wake of that policy failure, Wiley called for cutting another billion in funding at a time when shootings in 2021 were already 74 percent higher than they were at the same time in 2020.[502]

Wiley's campaign website called for "reimagining policing," which really means "imagine no policing." She also wants to freeze the number of incoming cadet classes for the NYPD and NY Department of Corrections and remove police from traffic enforcement and school safety.

Meanwhile, Wiley's Brooklyn home is protected by a private security patrol that she pays for (as do about half of her neighborhood's two hundred households). Crime in her Precinct (the 70th) has actually declined year-over-year, while the adjacent precinct (and rest of the city) has seen a surge.[503]

---

499   Ibid.

500   Wiley, Maya, Twitter account, June 7, 2021. https://twitter.com/mayawiley/status/1401702651524431873

501   Marsh, Julia, Campanile, and Nolan Hicks, "Maya Wiley Rails against Billionaires—Despite Big-Bucks Backing by George Soros," *New York Post*, June 14, 2021. https://nypost.com/2021/06/13/maya-wiley-rails-against-billionaires-despite-george-soros-backing/

502   Ruiz, "NYC 'Defund the Police' Mayor Candidate Helped Suppress Reform Recommendation as Head of Review Board: Report," Fox News, June 12, 2021. https://www.foxnews.com/politics/nyc-maya-wiley-defund-the-police-suppress-reform-ccrb

503   Marsh, Craig McCarthy, and Bruce Golding, "Maya Wiley Wants to Defund the NYPD—While Her Home Is Protected by Private Security Patrol," *New York Post*, June 7, 2021. https://nypost.com/2021/06/07/wiley-wants-to-defund-nypd-while-her-home-protected-by-security/

Fortunately, she lost in the Democrat primary to former NYPD officer Eric Adams.

THE GREAT POLICE SHORTAGE

Soros' Foundation to Promote Open Society earmarked $1.5 million in 2019 for the Community Resource Hub for Safety and Responsibility (CHR). The group backs the defund the police movement, and goes even further, engaging in research to review "alternatives to policing in the context of police abolitionist frameworks." It provides a tool kit to help activists defund their local sheriffs, which it says is an "essential step towards building a more safe and just communities across this country."[504]

A spokesperson for Open Society confirmed that the Foundations back those specific goals, telling the *Washington Free Beacon* "OSF supports the exploration and development of alternatives to current policing practices, and the Hub serves as a clearinghouse of ideas and resources to help advocates determine how best to improve police practices in their communities. We defer to communities regarding what alternatives make sense for them, including substantially shifting funding for the current approach to policing/law enforcement into services that address societal challenges while doing less harm."[505]

Soros funded CHR through his New Venture Fund, acting as its fiscal sponsor. CHR doesn't provide any individual tax forms to the IRS, so the rest of its financial information is unknown.[506]

Soros donated $1 million to the Color of Change PAC during the 2020 election cycle, and his Soros Super PAC kicked in an additional $2.5 million. Color of Change is behind a petition calling for all elected officials to cut ties with the Fraternal Order of Police, which they brand the "deadliest frat in the world." "The time has come for these officials to make a choice: you are either with the people, or you are in support of systemic police violence and mass incarceration," the PAC wrote.[507]

This is a separate group from the aforementioned Color of Change nonprofit, which Soros has continued giving to, backing with

504   Schoffstall, "Soros Gets Behind Abolishing the Police," *Washington Free Beacon*, January 6, 2021. https://free-beacon.com/national-security/soros-gets-behind-abolishing-the-police/
505   Ibid.
506   Ibid.
507   Vazquez, Joseph, "Financing Hate: George Soros Dumps $1 Million into Anti-Police Group Color of Change PAC," mrcNewsBusters, June 21, 2021. https://newsbusters.org/blogs/business/joseph-vazquez/2021/06/21/financing-hate-george-soros-dumps-1-million-anti-police

at least $1.4 million in 2018 and 2019 alone. He donated another million in 2021 amid a continuing rising crime wave.[508]

Then AG William Barr had warned of this in December of 2019. "There's this recent development [where] George Soros has been coming in, in largely Democratic primaries where there has not been much voter turnout and putting in a lot of money to elect people who are not very supportive of law enforcement and don't view the office as bringing to trial and prosecuting criminals but pursuing other social agendas."[509]

Barr predicted that violent crime will increase as a result, but added (incorrectly) that he doesn't believe police will withdraw from communities.

Seattle saw sixty-six departures in the first months of 2021, bringing the total number of police who left since racial justice protests began over the summer of 2020 to over two hundred, leaving the city with a record low 1,080 deployable officers. The police department in Louisville, Kentucky saw a 20 percent decrease in the size of their police force, while New York lost 15 percent. Portland lost 115 cops and has 140 vacancies with a force of under eleven hundred officers.[510]

Leftists will often point to America's relatively high prison population as proof of over policing, but an international comparison renders that argument moot. Relative to the world average, the U.S. employs 35 percent fewer police officers per capita. While the U.S. does have an outsized prison population (302 percent of the world average), this is in part linked to under policing. As economist Alex Tabarrok notes:

> Increasing the number of police on the street, for example, would increase capture rates and deter crime and by doing so it would also reduce the prison population. Indeed, in a survey of crime and policing that Jon Klick and I wrote in 2010 we found that a cost-benefit analysis would justify

---

508 Miller, Andrew Mark. "Soros Hands $1 Million to Group Attempting to Defund Police as Violent Crime Skyrockets Nationwide," Fox News, July 25, 2021. https://www.foxnews.com/politics/soros-hands-1-million-to-group-attempting-to-defund-police-as-violent-crime-skyrockets-nationwide

509 Creitz, Charles, "AG Barr: Soros-Funded Dem Prosecutor Candidates Will Lead to Increased Crime, Fewer Police Officers," Fox News, December 21, 2019. https://www.foxnews.com/media/ag-barr-soros-funded-democratic-prosecutor-candidates-will-lead-to-increased-crime-police-department-vacancies

510 McEvoy, Jemima, "Historic Police Exodus in Cities Most Impacted by Racial Justice Unrest, New Data Shows," Forbes, April 29, 2021. https://www.forbes.com/sites/jemimamcevoy/2021/04/29/historic-police-exodus-in-cities-most-impacted-by-racial-justice-unrest-new-data-shows/?sh=556f80468cf2

doubling the number of police on the street. We based our calculation not only on our own research from Washington DC but also on the research of many other economists which together provide a remarkably consistent estimate that a 10% increase in policing would reduce crime by 3 to 5%. Using our estimates, as well as those of some more recent papers, the Council of Economic Advisers (CEA) also estimates big benefits (somewhat larger than ours) from an increase in policing. Moreover, what the CEA makes clear is that a dollar spent on policing is more effective at reducing crime than a dollar spent on imprisoning.[511]

The American public fully rejects the Soros agenda on policing. According to polling from Rasmussen Reports in the months after the death of George Floyd (the peak of the "defund the police" madness), 61 percent of all Americans believed that violent crime is likely to go up in communities that defund the police. Only 12 percent thought violent crime was more likely to go down, while 20 percent predicted it will remain about the same. Sixty-six percent opposed reducing the police budget in their communities, while only two in ten supported defunding police where they live.[512]

Many of the cities that hopped on the "defund the police" bandwagon have already reversed course after they were mugged by reality.

Minneapolis was the location of George Floyd's death, and Mayor Jacob Frey cut $8 million from the police department and diverted $2 million of it to "crime prevention programs and mental health crisis response teams." Violent crime increased 21 percent in Minneapolis in 2020, and Frey acknowledged that policy played a role. "When you make big, overarching statements that we're going to defund or abolish and dismantle the police department and get rid of all the officers, there's an impact to that" he said at a news conference before requesting federal and state help to reduce crime in his city. A year after Floyd's death, he proposed a timeline to refund the police by the end of 2023.[513]

511   Tabarrok, Alex, "Underpoliced and Overprisoned, Revisited," Marginal Revolution, June 11, 2020. https://marginalrevolution.com/marginalrevolution/2020/06/underpoliced-and-overprisoned-revisited.html

512   Palumbo,"Poll: Only 2 in 10 Support 'Defund the Police,'" Bongino, July 21, 2020. https://bongino.com/poll-only-2-in-10-voters-support-defund-the-police/

513   Slisco, Aila, "A Year after George Floyd's Death, Minneapolis Mayor Wants to Re-Fund Police," *Newsweek*,

As the *Daily Wire*'s Tim Pearce documented, Minneapolis was hardly the only one:

> In Los Angeles, the spike in crime has been more pronounced. Last year [2020], violent crime in the city rose 36% as elected officials stripped the local police department of $150 million, roughly 8% of the department's funding. The number of murders across the city surged to a decade-high of 350.
>
> Despite Democratic Mayor Eric Garcetti's and the L.A. city council's earlier commitment to cut back police funding, city leaders reversed course last week [May 2021]. The city council approved additional funding for the police department to hire 250 officers, essentially restoring the cuts that the city council approved last year.
>
> In New York City, Mayor Bill de Blasio announced earlier this month [May] that the city is building a new police precinct in Southeast Queens to combat rising crime. The announcement of additional law enforcement comes after de Blasio pledged to cut $1 billion from the New York City Police Department's budget.
>
> From January to April, New York City experienced a more than 50% jump in the number of shootings over the same time last year. The spike comes after last year when shootings jumped 97% and the murders across the city increased 45% in 2019.[514]

Unfortunately, ideology has trumped reality in the majority of cities that defunded their police forces. Those that haven't reversed course include Seattle, Milwaukee, Philadelphia, Baltimore, and a dozen other cities.

May 25, 2021. https://www.newsweek.com/year-after-george-floyds-death-minneapolis-mayor-wants-re-fund-po-lice-1594411

514   Pearce, Tim, "Refund the Police? Major Cities Are Backtracking on Police Cuts After Explosion of Violent Crime," *Daily Wire*, May 25, 2021. https://www.dailywire.com/news/refund-the-police-major-cities-are-back-tracking-on-police-cuts-after-explosion-of-violent-crime

The International Influence of George Soros: Europe

As wide reaching as George Soros' influence is in America, it's still a relatively recent venture for him. As outlined in earlier chapters, Soros' first ventures into political influence were all in Europe, specifically former Soviet states (and then post-Soviet Russia). Soros began his campaign of influence in Europe, and it has remained a main focus of his alongside America.

The Balkans have been another common target for Soros. Similar to what he's done with former Soviet states (and there's some overlap here), he's been able to exploit similarly corruption-prone nations for his own benefit, playing kingmaker under the guise of "fighting corruption" then continuing to wield influence. The OSF moved in as then Yugoslavia was disintegrating in 1991, and has continued holding influence in Serbia and Kosovo.

Soros' tactics remain consistent. In Albania, he faced accusations by then president Ilir Meta of being behind a conspiracy to control the country by interfering in local elections in 2019, much like he's doing in the U.S.[515] Soros had already scored an earlier victory in the nation following a reform campaign that began in 2016 that was funded and aided by Soros-backed "experts." As a result of the campaign, Albania was left without courts, allowing the ruling socialist government to pass laws with no checks and balances while packing the prosecution office with allies.[516] Meta was later

---

515 Dyer, Chris, "Albania's President Claims Billionaire George Soros Is behind a 'Conspiracy' to Seize Control of His Country by Interfering in Local Elections," *The Daily Mail*, July 2, 2019. https://www.dailymail.co.uk/news/article-7207307/Albanias-president-claimed-billionaire-George-Soros-conspiracy-seize-control.html
516 Wood, Todd L., "George Soros's Misguided Agenda Spells Misery for Albania Reform," *The Washington Times*, August 23, 2018. https://www.washingtontimes.com/news/2018/aug/23/george-soros-misguided-agenda-spells-misery-for-al/

impeached in June 2021 after fifty lawmakers from the governing Socialist Party called for an investigation into whether he violated the constitution.

The Albanian parliament is controlled by Edi Rama (who has been prime minister since 2013), who has had a relationship with Soros since the 1990s.[517] Conservative writer Evi Kokalari recalls that "After the Berlin Wall fell, a group of Albanians that included me, Edi Rama, who is now Albania's Prime Minister, and the son of the head of George Soros's Foundation in Albania associated closely in Paris. From this experience I can say that Soros found the perfect opportunity to play puppet master with Rama as his instrument."[518]

Soros had an American ally in Albania in Donald Lu, who served as an ambassador there from 2015-2018 and championed the Soros agenda on open borders, drug legalization, and other liberal policies. Lu later assumed office as U.S. Ambassador to Kyrgyzstan, another country Soros has long been active in. A senior U.S. government source told the *Washington Examiner*'s Todd Wood that Lu aims to redirect U.S. aid money in Kyrgyzstan away from counterterrorism efforts and into Soros-aligned causes such as "building civil society," democratic mobilization, and supposed rule-of-law projects. Soros also has a Kyrgyzstan equivalent of Central European University in the American University of Central Asia.

In Bulgaria, a banned book called *Robbers of Democracy* alleged that Soros-backed NGOs aided the 2013 protests that led to the Center-Right government resigning, which was replaced by a "caretaker cabinet" led by former Communist Party member Marin Raykov. The book also alleges that the Yes Bulgaria Party (formed in 2017) is a Soros project aimed at seizing power.[519] Distribution of the book was halted following a complaint from Yes Bulgaria. The Soros-funded Organized Crime and Corruption Reporting Project (OCCRP) is one of the only publications reporting on the ban, and it did so approvingly. Every article mentioning Soros on the OCCRP's website plays defense for the billionaire.[520]

517 "'He Told Me What You Are Doing,' Prime Minister Rama Tells How He Got to Know George Soros and the Relationship He Has with Him," *Sot*, December 25, 2020. https://sot.com.al/english/politike/me-cfare-merresh-me-tha-kryeministri-rama-tregon-si-e-ka-njohur-george-

518 Kokalari, Evi, "How George Soros Stole Our Election: A Cautionary Tale from an Albanian Patriot," *Revolver*, November 30, 2020. https://www.revolver.news/2020/11/how-george-soros-stole-our-election-a-cautionary-tale-from-an-albanian-patriot/

519 Cheresheva, Mariya, "Bulgarian Activists, Journalists, Named 'Foreign Mercenaries,'" *BalkanInsight*, March 14, 2017. https://balkaninsight.com/2017/03/14/free-book-accuses-civil-society-of-robbing-bulgaria-s-democra-cy-03-14-2017/

520 Yancey-Bragg, N'Dea Akei, "Bulgaria Bans Book That Attacks Government Critics," OCCRP, March 16, 2017. https://www.occrp.org/en/component/content/article?id=6203:bulgaria-bans-book-that-attacks-government-critics

In Ukraine (among much other political influencing outlined in an earlier chapter), Soros backed the 2014 Maidan protests that eventually led to his ally Petro Poroshenko getting elected, who awarded Soros the Order of Freedom the next year. Soros praised the protesters, whom he described as the "cream of society" for ushing in a "New Ukraine."[521] Allegedly hacked documents from 2015 reveal Soros appointing himself the "self-appointed advocate of the Ukraine" and outline his involvement with the Obama State Department and Treasury to push for weapons and billions in assistance for Ukraine under Poroshenko.[522]

In Azerbaijan, the East-West Management Institute, which is similar to Soros' OSF, promotes "justice" and "civic engagement." The group was cofounded by Soros[523] and is run by Delina Fico, who oversees most of Soros' funds in the country. Fico was once a romantic partner of Edi Rama, and has a decade-long relationship with Azay Guliyev, who was appointed as the special coordinator overseeing election observance in Albania's parliamentary elections this year (in which Rama's party won a majority of seats).[524]

And the list goes on and on.

While Soros meddles in individual countries, his eyes are on Europe as a whole, with the health of the European Union as his central focus. A longtime supporter of the Union, Soros believes that it "lost its way" since the 2008 financial crisis.[525] After 2008, the eurozone (EU nations that use the euro) was transformed into a "creditor/debtor relationship," he argues, which enabled crippling austerity measures. He wants it to be a "voluntary association of like-minded states" willing to surrender part of their sovereignty for the common good.[526]

Soros wants the EU to be "radically reinvented." That would include a shared migration policy consistent with Soros' mass immigration agenda. "We still don't have a European migration policy," Soros complained before expressing frustration that "Each country pursues what it perceives to be in its national interest" as opposed to acting in his best interest.[527]

521 Soros, George, *In Defense of Open Society*, pages 136–137.
522 Wood, "George Soros's Snake Oil Bad Medicine for Struggling Ukraine," *Washington Times*, May 24, 2018. https://www.washingtontimes.com/news/2018/may/24/george-soros-snake-oil-bad-medicine-for-struggling/
523 Soros, George, "Underwriting Democracy," page 7.
524 "Gruaja e ministrit Çuçi, 300 mijë USD për azerin që koordinon punën e OSBE në zgjedhjet shqiptare," *Arberia News*, April 22, 2021. http://arberianews.net/264793-2/
525 Soros, George, *In Defense of Open Society*, page 151.
526 Soros, George, *In Defense of Open Society*, page 144.
527 Soros, George, *In Defense of Open Society*, pages 145 and 147

Soros told the European Council on Foreign Relations at an annual 2018 council meeting that the European Union was enduring an "existential crisis" and that member states must set aside "national interests" in the "interest of preserving" the crisis-hit union. Soros said that he regarded the European Union as "the embodiment of the idea of the Open Society," a voluntary association of equal states that banded together and sacrificed a little sovereignty for the "common good." Soros called reclamation of national sovereignty "territorial disintegration" exemplified by Brexit. (Soros had also pumped half a million pounds into a Brexit reversal campaign, backing a secret plot to overturn the final withdrawal deal.)[528] At the end of the keynote speech, Soros lobbied for an "upsurge of grassroots pro-European initiatives" that he pledged Open Society Foundations would do everything in its power to support.[529]

It became crucial for the open borders advocate to keep Italy—a founding member of the European Union's earliest predecessor and keystone to the globalist project—in the bloc. Penning an opinion piece for Italian newspaper *Corriere della Sera* on the country's elections, Soros wrote that "Italy is becoming the most pressing challenge to the sustainability of the Union." On how the European Union should respond to Italy's new populist government, Soros conceded that "in Europe, there is a clear tendency to use the opportunity to teach Italy a lesson…If the EU follows this line [of punishment], it will dig its own grave."[530]

To punish the country would cause "a negative reaction by the Italian electorate, which at that point would reelect the League and the 5-Star Movement with an even larger majority," Soros admitted following the March 2018 general election that witnessed Italians reject the establishment Democratic Party and vote for the populist 5-Star Movement and the nationalist Lega Nord (Northern League). Both parties promised to serve the interests of Italy's citizens and deport half a million illegal migrants who have been ferried into the country in recent years, a move opposed by the European Union's mass-migration-supporting leadership.

---

528   Timothy, Nick et al., "George Soros, the Man Who 'Broke the Bank of England,' Backing Secret Plot to Thwart Brexit," *Telegraph*, February 8, 2018. https://www.telegraph.co.uk/politics/2018/02/07/george-soros-man-broke-bank-england-backing-secret-plot-thwart/

529   Soros, George, "How to Save Europe," European Council *on* Foreign Relations, May 29, 2018. https://ecfr.eu/article/commentary_how_to_save_europe/

530   Soros, George, "George Soros: 'Europe Will Pay You for the Unfair Burden Suffered by Refugees,'" *Corriere*, June 2, 2018. https://www.corriere.it/politica/18_giugno_02/george-soros-l-europa-vi-paghi-l-onere-ingiusto-subito-rifugiati-85732ffa-66a5-11e8-a1d6-396872be4e4c.shtml

Soros' "concern" over the new Italian government meant the populists were on the right track. "Soros worried by the Italian government? So it means we are going in the right direction," League party deputy Claudio Borghi Aquilini said.[531]

Soros claims he only ever wanted the allocation of refugees within Europe to be voluntary, but many migrants simply left the country they were resettled in for other countries in Europe. [532] A large motivating factor for Brexit was refugees and economic migrants posing as such traveling through Europe and multiple safe countries to get to the England. Some refugees established a camp known as the "jungle" in Calais, France. They would wait for cars planning to cross the channel to England and would hop in the trunk or cling onto trucks and the like to try to get there.

Organizations that favor flooding Europe with migrants and refugees from the third world are a favorite of Soros. He's given the Asylum Protection Center in Serbia $150k, Spanish Coordinadora De Barros $138k to provide legal and psychosocial support to migrants and refugees, the Danish Institute for International Studies $50k to research migrants from West and North Africa, the Green Forum of Migrants $116k, the Italian Istituto Affari Internazionali $230k to "foster dialogue with policymakers" about new approaches to refugees and migrants, and the Brussels-based Migration Policy Institute $356k to develop proposals for asylum policy in Europe.[533]

Soros seems to be cognizant of this contradiction, which he hedges by claiming that he wants the EU to protect external borders but keep them open for lawful migrants. "Member states, in turn, must not close their internal borders," he said, rejecting the idea of a "Fortress Europe." In other words, Soros claims to believe that EU nations should be able to reject the initial resettlement of refugees—but not if those refugees resettle in another EU country first and then decide to move to the country who didn't want them in the first place.[534]

Soros says he personally regards the European Union to be the embodiment of an open society, but now views it as being in a state of existential crisis. Soros complains that "subsequent generations" have

---

531 Friedman, Victoria, "Italian Populist: We're Going in the 'Right Direction' if Soros is Worried," Brietbart, June 4, 2018. https://www.breitbart.com/europe/2018/06/04/populist-deputy-right-direction-soros-worried-italy/

532 Soros, George, *In Defense of Open Society*, page 152.

533 "Europe Becomes Soros's Playground—Part VII," *V4 Agency*, May 29, 2020. https://v4na.com/en/v4na-map-europe-becomes-soros-s-playground-part-vii

534 Soros, George, *In Defense of Open Society*, page 153.

come to view the EU as an enemy that deprives them of a "secure and promising future." Soros hopes Brexit is used as a catalyst for far-reaching reforms to prevent other nations from wanting to leave.[535]

Despite his opposition to Brexit, Soros was up to his old tricks once again in the United Kingdom leading up to the Brexit vote, selling $10 billion worth of S&P 500 futures in the days before the vote, and then an addition $3 billion in the last hour of trading before the vote was cast, making him hundreds of millions overnight as markets initially plunged on the surprise success of the referendum.[536]

Ironically, Soros says that he's "learned that democracy cannot be imposed from the outside, it needs to be asserted and defended by the people themselves."[537] For someone making that observation, he sure does a lot of meddling from the outside.

EUROPEAN PARLIAMENT

Soros maintains numerous relationships with politicians in Europe, including country leaders and members of the European Commission and European Parliament.

In 2018, a 177-page document numbering hundreds of MEPs who were judged by Soros and his network as reliable allies was leaked. The document was assembled by "KumquatConsult" for the Open Society European Policy Institute and was titled "Reliable Allies in the European Parliament (2014–2019)."

The document opens:

> This mapping provides the Open Society European Policy Institute and the Open Society network intelligence on Members of the 8th European Parliament likely to support Open Society values during the 2014–2019 legislature.
>
> It spans 11 committees and 26 delegations, as well as the European Parliament's highest decision-making bodies: 226 MEPs who are proven or likely Open Society allies.

---

535 Soros, George, *In Defense of Open Society*, pages 142–143 and 145.
536 Hayward, John, "Matthew Tyrmand: George Soros Made Billions from Brexit, But True Calling Is to 'Engineer the Open Society, Borderless Utopia,'" Breitbart, June 29, 2016. https://www.breitbart.com/radio/2016/06/29/matthew-tyrmand-soros-made-billions-brexit-true-calling-engineer-open-society-borderless-utopia/
537 Soros, George, *In Defense of Open Society*, page 149.

The presence of an MEP in this mapping indicates that they are likely to support Open Society's work. They should be approached with an open mind: although they will most likely want to work on areas they're already interested in, they could also welcome hearing about new issues.

Beyond discussing individual topics, Open Society should seek to build lasting and trustworthy relationships with these European lawmakers.[538]

The extent of Soros' influence over European Parliament is overwhelming.

The document begins with European Parliament bodies, their bodies of work, and potential allies within them. Among the European Parliament bodies, their function, and the number of allies Soros and his network have in each is as follows:

- Conference of Presidents: Parliament's highest political decision body. Six Soros allies.

- Bureau of European Parliament: Responsible for running European Parliament. Thirteen supporters, including the president of European Parliament, and eight vice presidents

- Committee on Foreign Affairs: Responsible for promotion, implementation, and monitoring of EU foreign policy. Over sixty allies, including the committee chair and two vice chairs.

- Subcommittee on Human Rights: Assists Committee on Foreign Affairs on issues "concerning democracy, the rule of law, and human rights." Thirty-seven supporters, including the committee chair and three vice chairs.

---

538 "Leaked Document Reveals Soros' Potential Allies at the European Parliament," *European Post*, August 18, 2016. http://europeanpost.co/leaked-document-reveals-soros-potential-allies-at-the-european-parliament/

- Subcommittee on Security and Defense: Assists Committee on Foreign Affairs on "common foreign and security policy." Twenty-four supporters, including two vice chairs.

- Committee on Development: Responsible for promotion, implementation, and monitoring of the development and corporation policy of the EU. Thirty-one supporters, including the chair and two vice chairs.

- Committee on International Trade: Responsible for "matters relating to the establishment, implementation and monitoring of the Union's common commercial policy and its external economic relations." Forty-four supporters, including the chair and two vice chairs.

- Committee on Economic and Monetary Affairs: Responsible for economic and monetary policies of the EU, rules on competition, facilitating the free movement of capital, boosting exports, tax provisions, regulation and supervision of financial services, and the relevant financial activities of the European Investment Bank. Sixty-plus supporters, including the chair and vice chair.

- Committee on Employment and Social Affairs: Responsible for employment policy, workers' rights, health and safety measures in the workplace, the European Social Fund, labor market discrimination (except based on sex), vocational training policy, and more. Fifty-five supporters, including the chair and two vice chairs.

- Committee on Regional Development: Responsible for the European Regional Development Fund, Cohesion fund, assessment of EU policies on economic and social cohesion, coordination, interregional cooperation, and more. Thirty-three supporters, including the chair and two vice chairs.

- Committee on Legal Affairs: Responsible for "interpretation, application and monitoring of Union law and compliance of Union acts with primary law," measuring concerning judicial and administration cooperation in civil matters, ethical questions relating to new technologies, the organization and statute of the Court of Justice of the European Union, and the Office for Harmonisation in the Internal Market. Twenty-eight supporters, including three vice chairs.

- Committee on Civil Liberties, Justice and Home Affairs: Responsible for protection of human rights within the EU, measures needed to combat discrimination, legislation "in processing of personal data," and more. Seventy-two supporters, including three vice chairs.

- Committee on Women's Rights and Gender Equality: Responsible for the definition, promotion and protection of women's rights, equal opportunities policies, implementation and further development of "gender mainstreaming in all policy sectors," and encouraging women's rights. Thirty-five supporters, including the chair and vice chair.

The EU is represented globally through over 140 delegates and offices around the world.

Soros boasts six allies in the delegation to Albania, thirteen to Bosnia and Herzegovina and Kosovo, eight to the former Yugoslav Republic of Macedonia, ten to Moldova, twelve to Montenegro, eleven to Serbia, fourteen to Turkey, four to Belarus, sixteen to Russia, thirteen to South Caucasus countries, seven to Ukraine, twenty-seven to EuroNest, eighteen to the Union for the Mediterranean, ten to Israel, nineteen to the Palestinian Legislative Council, thirteen to the Maghreb countries, fourteen to the Mashreq countries, twelve to the Arab Peninsula, five to Iraq, five to Afghanistan, seven to Central Asia, fifteen to Southeast Asia and ASEAN countries, fifteen to India, sixteen to South Africa, eight to the Pan-African Parliament, and forty-two to African, Caribbean, and Pacific countries.

The EU political parties that Soros boasts the most allies in include the center-right European People's Party (nineteen allies),

Progressive Alliance of Socialists and Democrats (thirty-nine), European Conservatives and Reformists (two), Alliance of Liberals and Democrats for Europe (twenty), The Left in the European Parliament (nineteen), and Greens/EFA (fourteen). The Alliance of Liberals and Democrats for Europe was succeeded by Renew Europe in 2019.

EUROPEAN COURT OF HUMAN RIGHTS

In Europe, Soros influences the legal system through the European Court of Human Rights (ECHR). The ECHR is the highest judicial body in Europe, and is thus the "final word" legally. Each judge is elected for a nonrenewable nine-year term.

French constitutional lawyer Grégor Puppinck reviewed the CVs of over a hundred justices that worked with the ECHR from 2009 to 2019 to see which NGOs they were affiliated with. After, he published a report outlining Soros' network of NGOs and its infiltration of the ECLJ. Overall, twelve judges (out of forty-seven) were found to have collaborated to varying degrees with the Open Society Foundations and NGOs associated with them.[539]

The collaborators are a mix of judges who directly worked for the OSF and those who worked for NGOs heavily supported by Soros. Most NGO-linked judges are from Eastern Europe, and the causes they support include liberalization of drug policy, legalization of prostitution and abortion, and the rights of refugees and sexual minorities.

The report found that three ECHR justices have collaborated with Amnesty International, which Soros funds. Five judges have worked with the International Commission of Jurists (ICJ), which received $1.9 million from Soros from 2017 to 2018. The current ICJ secretary general, Saman Zia-Zarifi, was deputy director for the Asia division of the Soros-funded Human Rights Watch, and then served as Amnesty International's director for Asia and the Pacific from 2008 to 2012. Seven of the judges have collaborated with the Helsinki Committee. Soros gave the Bulgarian Helsinki Committee $460k in 2016 and $320k in 2018, while he gave the Hungarian Helsinki Committee $610k in 2016 and $50k in 2018.

---

539 Puppinck, Grégor, and Delphine Loiseau, "NGOs and the Judges of the ECHR 2009-2019," European Centre for Law & Justice, February 2020. https://static.eclj.org/pdf/ECLJ+Report%2C+NGOs+and+the+Judges+of+the+EC HR%2C+2009+-+2019%2C+February+2020.pdf?

As for advancing the Soros agenda through the courts, the report explains that:

> The favorite mode of action of NGOs before the Court is through third-party interventions, also called amicus curiae (friend of the court). This procedure is a practice by which a private or legal person submits to the attention of the Court elements of assessment on a case in which it is not a party to the initial proceedings. The author of the third intervention then becomes a "third party" in the case. This procedure is very beneficial, even if the neutrality and the exteriority of the participants are often only a facade. Indeed, the ECHR often has to judge complex and important questions with strong social consequences.
>
> The Court is then placed above national authorities, even legislative ones. The intervening NGOs then have the role of expert, of intermediary body, but also of lobby. In addition to factual information, both sociological and legal, NGOs can also present the Court with a plurality of ideological or philosophical approaches to the issue in question, provided that NGOs of various tendencies are involved. They thus enrich the procedure. By intervening in a case, the objective of NGOs is to enlighten the Court and in doing so to convince it to adopt its own position, and thus to contribute to the development of its case-law, and through it, of that of the European law.[540]

Soros has also benefitted from his influence here more directly.

When Hungary began cracking down on Soros, it was the ECHR that Soros appealed to. In a press release in 2018, the Open Society Foundations called on the body to "act against Hungary over its so-called Stop Soros laws, which criminalize and tax the work of independent civil society groups, under the pretext of controlling migration."[541] The European Court of Justice ended up taking on cases

540   Ibid.
541   "Open Society Foundations Call on European Court of Human Rights to Defend Hungarian Democracy," Open Society Foundations, September 24, 2018. https://www.opensocietyfoundations.org/newsroom/open-society-foundations-call-european-court-human-rights-defend-hungarian-democracy

related to Hungary's anti-NGO laws, and laws against foreign funding of universities.

By 2020, Soros got what he wanted, with the European Court of Justice striking down Hungary's anti-NGO law in June and the ban on foreign-funded universities in October, ruling that it was incompatible with EU law. [542]

As is usually the case, Soros' influence pays off for him.

This isn't a problem with just the courts, either—former commissioner for human rights of the Council of Europe (2012–2018) Nils Muižnieks was also director of programs for the OSF of Latvia until 2012.[543]

Despite the evidence presented, the ECLJ's report was initially dismissed. According to the Hungarian *V4 News*:

> Concerns about conflict of interest within the ECHR seem to be well-founded. In May, 150 European lawyers and jurists issued a joint appeal to ECHR to remedy this situation, demanding that the judges, among others, should be required to publish declarations of interest.
>
> However, the European Court of Human Rights appears to have friends in key positions. In May European Commission Vice President Vera Jourova stressed that "the Commission has no doubt as regards the integrity and independence of the European Court of Human Rights."[544]

The ECHR responded to the ECLJ report two months after its publication…by promoting its most controversial judge, Bulgarian Yonko Grozev, to the position of "section president." There has been no attempt to minimize the ECLJ's findings—a tacit admission of their legitimacy.[545]

Grozev spent his career as a lawyer and activist with Soros-affiliated NGOs and was himself an executive with the Open Society

---

542　"Open Society Welcomes Court of Justice of EU Ruling on Hungary Anti-NGO Law," Open Society Foundations, June 18, 2020. https://www.opensocietyfoundations.org/newsroom/open-society-welcomes-court-of-justice-of-eu-ruling-on-hungary-anti-ngo-law

543　Puppinck and Loiseau, "NGOs and the Judges of the ECHR 2009-2019."

544　"Soros Densely Entrenched in European Court of Human Rights," *V4 Agency*, July 28, 2020. https://v4na.com/en/masszivan-beagyazta-magat-soros-az-emberi-jogok-europai-birosagaba/

545　Puppinck, "Soros's Hold on the European Court of Human Rights: the ECHR Persists and Signs," ECLJ, May 2020. https://eclj.org/geopolitics/echr/emprise-de-soros-sur-la-cour-europeenne-des-droits-de-lhomme--la-cedh-persiste-et-signe-

Foundations until he joined the court in 2015. There was already controversy surrounding his nomination back in 2014 because three members of the Bulgarian selection committee were his NGO fellows. He became a judge despite having no experience as a magistrate (which the majority of ECHR justices do).[546]

As section president, Grozev heads one of five sections of the Court, and will sit in on the most important cases. He is the judge of deontology (right and wrong) in his section and has authority to decide on a case-by-case basis whether to invite, allow, or refuse the intervention of NGOs he's linked to in cases.[547]

As the ECLJ notes:

> As a judge, Grozev was seized of cases which he had brought before the ECHR himself as a lawyer, or which had been brought by his former NGOs. While in 9 of these cases he renounced sitting as a judge as was his duty, he still participated in the judgment of at least 10 other cases brought or supported by NGOs which he himself had founded or directed until recently.

> Such conduct constitutes a serious and repeated breach of a judge's basic ethical obligations. In any State governed by the rule of law, the author of such breaches would be liable to severe disciplinary sanctions. Moreover, following the publication of the report, the Bulgarian Minister of Justice publicly raised the possibility of Yonko Grozev's dismissal, while pointing out that it was for the ECHR to decide. Yonko Grozev defended himself by attacking the ECLJ and declaring it impossible to dismiss him, as all the judges referred to in the report would then have to be removed from office. It would thus be as if he were protected by the other judges involved.[548]

As evidenced by his subsequent appointment as section president, his argument clearly resonated. Four of the nine judges of the section to which Groza belongs were implicated in the ECLJ report.

---

546 Ibid.
547 Ibid.
548 Ibid.

Court rules state that a judge can't participate in a case if "his or her independence or impartiality may legitimately be questioned." Despite Soros' NGOs long-standing support for assisted suicide and euthanasia, Grozev was still allowed to decide on a case of an unnamed Polish man hospitalized in a vegetative state, effectively sentencing him to death. The family of the man had initially lost their case to keep him alive when British High Court Judge Sir Jonathan Cohen ruled in favor of the University Hospitals Plymouth NHS Trust (he was being treated in the U.K.) to "lawfully discontinue" his treatment. Appeals to the ECHR were unsuccessful, and Grozev may have made his decision without even looking at the patient's case file.[549] After discovering Grozev's ties to Soros, the Polish man's family wrote to the president of the Court Mr. Robert Spano to request a review of the case, which was officially rejected on January 19, 2020, with the allegations simply being dismissed as "unfounded." The Polish patient died a week later.[550]

Not until over a year after the ECLJ's report did the Council of Europe (of which the ECHR is its best-known body) concede that there was a problem. Ambassadors of the forty-seven member states of the Council of Europe adopted an official text admitting the credibility of the ECLJ's report on NGOs influencing the ECHR, and announced that they'd reevaluate the effectiveness of their current system of selection by the end of 2024.[551]

In April 2021, the Parliamentary Assembly of the Council of Europe elected a new Belgian judge to the ECHR, having three picks to choose from, one of which was backed by Soros. For the first time in a while, the Soros judge wasn't elected.[552]

Unfortunately, Soros has already made his mark.

549 Puppinck, "A 'Soros-Judge' Abandons a Polish Patient to His Death," ECHR, January 2021. https://eclj.org/euthanasia/echr/echr---a-soros-judge-abandons-a-polish-patient-to-his-death

550 "RS Dies of Starvation, Condemned to Death by a Soros Judge," *Daily Compass*, January 19, 2021. https://newdailycompass.com/en/rs-dies-of-starvation-condemned-to-death-by-a-soros-judge

551 Puppinck, "The Council of Europe Concedes the Veracity of the Report on Ngos and the Judges of the Echr & Rejects the New "Soros-Judge" Candidate," ECLJ, April 2021. https://eclj.org/geopolitics/echr/le-conseil-de-leurope-admet-la-veracite-du-rapport-sur-les-ong-et-les-juges-de-la-cedh-et-rejette-la-candidature-dune-nouvelle--juge-soros-

552 Ibid.

The International Influence of George Soros: Asia, Africa, South America, and the Middle East

The rest of the world outside America and Europe is on Soros' radar too.

Soros maintains influence internationally outside his main two territories and his work there has largely flown under the radar. Outside of America and Europe, Soros is most active in the Middle East, specifically to back pro-Palestinian and anti-Israel causes, but also maintains influence in Latin America, Asia, and Africa.

ASIA

Most countries in Central Asia have strict regulations that make it nearly impossible for NGOs to receive foreign funding. Despite that, Soros and his network manage to circumvent the system to expand their sphere of influence in the region. The OSF has only four offices and foundations in the Asia Pacific region.[553]

Soros avoids donating directly to NGOs, and instead supports programs through American and European organizations that have an impact in Central Asia. His biggest component of this influence-by-proxy strategy is the American University of Central Asia (in Kyrgyzstan), to which he awarded $1.5 million in 2018. [554]

---

[553] "Asia Pacific," Open Society Foundations. https://www.opensocietyfoundations.org/what-we-do/regions/asia-pacific

[554] "V4NA Map Exposes Soros Dependents' Chicanery in Asia—Part II," *V4 Agency*, May 18, 2020. https://v4na.com/en/v4na-map-exposes-soros-dependents-chicanery-in-asia-part-ii

Soros has also funded his Central European University to provide a scholarship to twenty-five people to participate in a course designed to develop a network of researchers and think tanks in Moldova, Armenia, and Kyrgyzstan.[555]

The Soros network is most involved in Georgia in that region. As mentioned earlier, back in 2003, NGOs including Soros' played a large role in the Rose Revolution.[556]

In Southeast Asia, Soros' influence mainly centers around LGBT rights. Soros gave the Los Angeles LGBT Center $200k to train LGBT activists in East Asia. The Korean Beyond the Rainbow Foundation got $240k from Soros to advance equal treatment, Taiwan Tongzhi Hotline Association got $150k to support LGBT policy advocacy, Bangladesh Legal Aid Services Trust got $300k to defend sexual and reproductive rights for women, while Taiwanese Shih Hsin University got $225k to provide education opportunities to gender equality advocates.[557]

Back in the 1990s, like he did previously in England, Soros made massive profits in Thailand with a $1 billion short position against the baht. The 1997 Asian financial crisis began in Thailand and then spread to South Korea, Hong Kong, China, Indonesia, the Philippines, Malaysia, and Singapore. The Thai baht was once pegged to the U.S. dollar, but the peg was removed in July because the government lacked the foreign currency reserves to support the peg, sparking immediate capital flight and a chain reaction throughout Asia. The value of the baht immediately fell to 28.8 baht per U.S. dollar.[558]

After an unsuccessful attempt to prop up the value of the baht by purchasing more baht with dollars in the forex market and raising interest rates, the Bank of Thailand would eventually collapse.

Soros commented on the trade "by selling the Thai baht short in January 1997, the Quantum Fund managed by my investment company sent a market signal that the baht may be overvalued. Had the authorities responded to the depletion of their reserves, the adjustment would have occurred sooner and been less painful. But the authorities allowed their reserves to run down; the break, when it came, was catastrophic."[559]

---

555   Ibid.
556   "Georgians Overthrow a Dictator (Rose Revolution), 2003," Global Nonviolent Action Database. https://nvdatabase.swarthmore.edu/content/georgians-overthrow-dictator-rose-revolution-2003
557   "Soros Network Expands Unscrupulously in Southeast Asia—Part IV," *V4 Agency*, May 21, 2020. https://v4na.com/en/v4na-map-soros-network-expands-unscrupulously-in-southeast-asia-part-iv
558   Hargreaves, Robert, "Here's How George Soros Broke the Bank of Thailand." *Business Insider*, September 6, 2016. https://www.businessinsider.com/how-george-soros-broke-the-bank-of-thailand-2016-9
559   Paul Blustein, "The Chastening: Inside the Crisis that Rocked the Global Financial System," PublicAffairs, 2003, page 62.

It's unclear exactly how much Soros pocketed from the trade, but the value of the baht continued falling from the exchange rate of 28.8 baht per USD after the peg was removed to 48.8 baht per USD by December, the lowest rate ever since records started being kept in 1969,[560] and a nearly 70 percent devaluation since the initial devaluation. Due to the leveraged nature of his trade, it's likely Soros' profits on the baht trade exceeded $1 billion.

Elsewhere, Soros faced allegations from Malaysian Prime Minister Mahathir Mohamad of ruining his country's economy with "massive currency speculation"—and also of "being a moron." That came after Malaysia's currency (the ringgit) plunged 20 percent against the U.S. dollar in the two months that followed Thailand removing its peg.[561] At the time, the chief investment strategist for Soros Fund Management claimed that they initially bet against the ringgit but changed their mind and went long instead. They provided no evidence for this, or any indication of how big their position was.[562]

Fast-forward to 2013 and Soros netted another $1 billion betting against the yen, betting that massive monetary stimulus would devalue it.[563]

AFRICA

In 2018 Soros awarded a total of 288 grants to organizations throughout Africa. Similar to Soros' influence in Asia, most influence in Africa related to LGBT causes. The OSF has twelve offices and foundations in the continent.[564]

The biggest grant of $6 million went to the Ethiopia Education Initiatives. Other spending went toward migrant and refugee related causes. That included $410k to support 220 people living in the Kakuma refugee camp via Jesuit Worldwide Learning, $94k to the Dutch Lighthouse Reports Foundation to help establish a journalistic network covering migration policy, and $413k on four fellowships in Africa to train people in "human rights."[565]

560 Laplamwanit, Narisa, "A Good Look at the Thai Financial Crisis in 1997–98," Columbia University, Fall 1999. http://www.columbia.edu/cu/thai/html/financial97_98.html
561 Gargan, Edward A., "Premier of Malaysia Spars with Currency Dealer," *New York Times*, September 22, 1997. https://www.nytimes.com/1997/09/22/world/premier-of-malaysia-spars-with-currency-dealer.html
562 Ip, Greg, and Darren McDermott, "Soros Says Funds Didn't Cause Malaysia's Currency Crisis," *The Wall Street Journal*, September 5, 1997. https://www.wsj.com/articles/SB87340954838461500
563 Neate, Rupert, "George Soros Makes $1.2bn Betting Against Yen," *The Guardian*, February 15, 2013. https://www.theguardian.com/business/2013/feb/15/george-soros-bet-against-yen
564 "Africa," Open Society Foundations. https://www.opensocietyfoundations.org/what-we-do/regions/africa
565 "Soros Network Gains Ground in Africa—Part V," *V4 Agency*, May 23, 2020. https://v4na.com/en/v4na-map-soros-network-gains-ground-in-africa-part-v

Over 195 grants have gone to causes in North Africa and the Middle East region, also mostly to migrant-and-refugee-supportive causes. Soros gave Bard College $270k to support learning initiatives for refugees in Germany, Jordan, and Palestine. He also helped fund Mideast Youth launch an online campaign about migrant issues with $150k.[566]

The South African organization Gender Dynamix, a "public benefit organization to focus solely on trans and gender diverse communities," received $40k. Soros gave $50k to the Team No Sleep Foundation to help "LGBTQ refugees" in Nairobi. The University of Pretoria got $240k to train professionals in "sexual and reproductive rights."[567]

Soros' most significant contribution in South Africa is to the South African National Editors' Forum (SANEF), which tried to play off the news of their Soros funding by pretending that it somehow doesn't affect its behavior at all. SANEF's executive director said in light of the funding revelation: "We do get funding from George Soros, we got a specific amount of money to look at election issues and we ran a whole lot of election training workshops. Obviously, we get money from a whole lot of different sources including our own members and from the media companies. To say that we are getting from Soros and therefore being controlled by him is not correct."[568] SANEF is composed of editors, senior journalists, and journalism trainers, and they are engaged in research and writing policy submissions, as well as training journalists and have outsized influence in South Africa.

Soros is accused of plotting to oust the president of Equatorial Guinea Teodoro Obiang Nguema Mbasogo by British mercenary Simon Mann, who himself was the leader of a failed attempt by British financiers to overthrow the government in 2004. He alleges that he warned Mbasogo of the plot in 2011.[569]

566 "Soros Feeds Pro-Migration Organizations—Part III," *V4 Agency*, May 19, 2020. https://v4na.com/en/v4na-map-soros-feeds-pro-migration-organisations-part-iii
567 "Soros Network Gains Ground in Africa—Part V."
568 "SANEF Responds to Journalist Piet Rampedi's Allegations," SABC News, July 21, 2019. https://www.sabcnews.com/sabcnews/sanef-responds-to-journalist-piet-rampedis-allegations/
569 "George Soros 'Plotted to Oust Equatorial Guinea's Leader,'" BBC, June 27, 2017. https://www.bbc.com/news/world-africa-40420872

SOUTH AMERICA

Soros gave a total of 312 grants to Latin American or Caribbean organizations and programs in 2018, with most of his activity centered in Brazil and Columbia.[570] The majority of funding is aimed at protecting "migrants" and "refugees," both terms often acting as synonyms for illegal aliens.

The largest grant went to the Columbian organization Centro de Estudios de Derecho, Justicia y Sociedad (Dejusticia), a borderline socialist organization that deals with "environmental justice," "economic justice," and "transitional justice," among other buzzwords.[571]

Brazilian pro-choice Anis - Instituto de Bioetica, Direitos Humanos e Genero got $70k. Brazilian Associação Direitos Humanos em Rede got $349k, which was spent on human rights issues in Brazil and strengthening protections for migrants and refugees.[572]

Columbia-based Fundacion Servicio de los Jesuitas para los Refugiados got $176k to spend on legal protections for migrants, U.S.-headquartered Political Research Associates, Inc. got $46k to promote LGBT communities in Haiti, and the NGO Migrar es Vivir A.C. got $55k to provide family reunification counseling to those deported back to Mexico.[573]

Despite Brazil facing one of the highest murder rates in the world, so-called police reform is apparently a priority. Instituto Sou da Paz got $108k, which was spent on a program to "to improve both the state's and police's capacity to respond to protests with a human rights perspective."

Soros also made an attempt at thwarting the presidential candidacy of the current right-wing nationalist Brazilian President Jair Bolsonaro by awarding a $25k grant to the organization J T V Faria Producao de Conteudo - ME, to help produce a web series to educate viewers about Brazil's electoral system. He also gave Instituto Update $15k to produce podcasts to supposedly combat election disinformation.[574]

Soros failed in his goal of defeating Bolsonaro—and on the first day of Bolsonaro's presidency, he began cracking down on NGOs, mandating that the office of the government secretary "supervise,

570 "George Soros's Network Ensnares South America," *V4 Agency*, May 25, 2020. http://v4na.com/en/v4na-ter-kep-del-amerikat-is-behalozta-soros-gyorgy/
571 Ibid.
572 Ibid.
573 Ibid.
574 Ibid.

coordinate, monitor and accompany that activities and actions of international organizations and non-governmental organizations in the national territory." Bolsonaro tweeted that Brazilians are "exploited and manipulated by NGOs. We will live together and integrate these citizens and value all Brazilians."[575]

THE MIDDLE EAST

At seemingly any left-wing political rally you can see some hysteric backing the Palestinian cause, and Soros inevitably shares their view.

Of the state of Israel, Soros has said "I don't deny Jews their right to a national existence, but I don't want to be part of it." Soros has characterized the founding of Israel as a pathological reaction of Jews "obsessed with emulating their Nazi oppressors" in a "process of victims turning persecutors."[576] It would be social suicide even for someone in Soros' circles to openly speak out against the statehood of Israel—though comparing Israelis to Nazis comes close.

Soros has blamed anti-Semitism on Israel, stating in 2003 that "There is a resurgence is anti-Semitism in Europe. The policies of the Bush administration and the Sharon administration contribute to that…It's not specifically anti-Semitism, but it does manifest itself as anti-Semitism as well. I'm critical of those policies…If we change that direction, then anti-Semitism will also diminish."[577] Ariel Sharon was Israel's prime minister from 2001 to 2006 and he belonged to the right-wing Zionist party Likud.

Of his own Jewish ethnicity, Soros said "I am proud of being a Jew—although I must admit it took me practically a lifetime to get there. I have suffered from the low self-esteem that is the bane of the assimilationist Jew. This is a heavy load that I could shed only when I recognized my success. I identify being a Jew with being a minority."[578]

Soros criticized the U.S. in 2007 for refusing to recognize the "democratically elected" terrorist Hamas government, or support Hamas in a future unity government with the West Bank. He's also complained about the influence groups like AIPAC have on U.S. foreign policy, pretending to care about Israel when making the case

575   Barnes, Luke, "Brazil's New President Has Already Started Targeting NGOs," *ThinkProgress*, Jan 3, 2019. https://archive.thinkprogress.org/jair-bolsonaro-enacts-sweeping-new-powers-over-ngos-in-brazil-5e955332ed33/
576   Horowitz and Poe, *The Shadow Party*, page 83.
577   Porter, Anna, *Buying a Better World: George Soros and Billionaire Philanthropy*, TAP Books, 2015, page 33.
578   Soros, George. *Soros on Soros*, page 242.

against them, claiming that "far from guaranteeing Israel's existence, AIPAC has endangered it."[579]

Archaeologist and historian Alexander H. Joffe compiled a comprehensive overview of Soros' sphere of influence in the Middle East, particularly when it comes to the Arab-Israeli conflict. It's documented in his 2013 paper "Bad Investment," which was published by NGO Monitor.[580]

The web of NGOs that Soros funds in the Middle East support an anti-Israel strategy that focus on three categories of strategies; 1) delegitimizing Israel as an apartheid state, 2) funding organizations aimed at weakening U.S. support for Israel, and 3) funding fringe Israeli organizations to make it appear as if their radical views are held by Israelis themselves.

Human Rights Watch has received over $100 million from Soros. HRW was cofounded in 1981 by Aryeh Neier, who served as its executive director until 1993 when he joined the Open Society Institute. In 2009, nearly a third of HRW's reporting and commentary was critical of Israel, a country that accounts for 0.11 percent of the world's population.[581]

Soros funds the lobbying organization J Street, which, as you'll learn in the next chapter, the organization didn't want the public to know about. The group is a self-proclaimed alternative to AIPAC and was designed to launch other progressive Jewish organizations.[582]

The CFO of Soros Fund Management Abbas Zuaiter sits on the board of the Institute of Middle East Understanding. The group attacks Israel by accusing its people of violence, amplifying biased news reports, and promoting the boycott, divest, and sanction (BDS) movement against Israel. As part of his support for BDS, Soros divested his stake from the Israeli company SodaStream.[583]

The OSF funded the Middle East and North Africa Initiative by funneling grants through the Jordan-based Arab Regional Office, which appears to be the OSF's primary clearinghouse for grants in the region and keeps a low profile.[584]

579　Soros, George, "On Israel, America and AIPAC," *The New York Review of Books*, April 12, 2007. https://www.georgesoros.com/2007/04/12/on_israel_america_and_aipac/
580　Joffe, Alexander H., and Gerald Steinberg, "Bad Investment: The Philanthropy of George Soros and the Arab-Israeli Conflict," NGO Monitor, May 1, 2013. https://www.ngomonitor.org/books/bad_investment_the_philanthropy_of_george_soros_and_the_arab_israeli_conflict/
581　Ibid.
582　Ibid.
583　"Soros Fund Drops Shares in Israel's SodaStream," BDS Movement, August 3, 2014. https://bdsmovement.net/news/soros-fund-drops-shares-israel%E2%80%99s-sodastream
584　Ibid.

The OSF also has a "Open Society Justice Initiative" under its umbrella. The Justice Initiative has consultative status with the UN's Economic and Social Council. The Initiative is able to file complaints with the European Social Charter Committee and the Council of Europe. It has been involved in several cases regarding Israel, mainly at the request of a Palestinian advocacy group called Adalah.[585]

The number of questionable organizations that Soros backs in the region far outnumber any that could be considered mainstream. Most organizations on this list claim to receive funding from the OSF, but the funding doesn't appear in any OSF Forms 990 (the IRS form that provides public information about nonprofit activities). That indicates that the donations were funneled by the OSF through another entity before reaching their destination.[586]

The organizations include:[587]

- Adalah, The Legal Center for Arab Rights in Israel: Promotes the image of Israel as a racist, colonial apartheid state. Regularly participates in international forums to condemn Israel for alleged human rights abuses.

- Al-Haq: A leader in bringing lawsuits against Israel in domestic and international courts, and backer of the BDS movement. Its executive director Shawan Jabarin was formally an activist for the terrorist-designated Popular Front for the Liberation of Palestine, and he's been denied visas by both Israel and Jordan as a result. Because of that fact, it's questionable if the OSF's donations to Al-Haq are even legal.

- Al-Mezan: Accuses Israel of war crimes and committing massacres and has worked in partner with Al-Haq. The organization's chairman Dr. Kamal Al-Sharafi is also a former member of the Popular Front for the Liberation of Palestine, also raising questions about the legality of donations.

585　Ibid.
586　Ibid.
587　Ibid.

- B'Tselem: Outspoken in criticism of Israel's security policies. The organization has been criticized for exaggerating Palestinian casualties from military operations, and for supporting the BDS movement. In the past, B'Tselem has misrepresented staged events in which Palestinians lied about being attacked by Israelis as real.

- Breaking the Silence: Accuses the Israeli military of war crimes, and lobbies in the U.S. and Europe against Israeli policy.

- Gisha: Regularly brings lawsuits in Israeli courts against Israeli security measures. Executive director Sari Bashi has accused Israel of wanting to ethnically cleanse the West Bank.

- Ir Amim: Strongly criticizes Israel's separation barrier, which was constructed following a surge in Palestinian terrorism. The construction of the barrier immediately cut deaths from Palestinian terrorism in half, and it continued falling from there.[588]

- Mada al-Carmel Arab Center for Applied Social Research: Characterizes the concept of Israel as a Jewish state as a "threat" and source of "continuing injustice." It calls for international boycotts against Israel and a one state solution that would eliminate Israel.

- Mossawa Center: Supports international BDS efforts and proposed a constitution for Israel to strip it of its Jewish identity.

- Palestinian Center for Human Rights: Regularly accuses Israel of being an apartheid state guilty of war crimes, and published exaggerated statistics on deaths of Palestinian civilians.

---

588   Palumbo, "These Three Charts Prove That Walls Work," Bongino, January 11, 2019. https://bongino.com/these-three-charts-prove-that-walls-work/

- Yesh Din—Volunteers for Human Rights: Harshly criticizes the Israeli military and regularly files lawsuits in response to their actions. The organization's legal adviser Michael Sfard has appeared as a paid witness on behalf of the Palestine Libertarian Organization in a lawsuit filed in U.S. federal court. The suit was brought by a victim of a Palestinian terror attack, and the PLO thought Sfard's expertise would help it escape liability from the crime.

Among the other controversial recipients who engage in similar behavior to those listed above, include Amnesty International, Avaaz, the Center for Constitutional Rights, Crimes of War Project, National Iranian American Council, New America Foundation, and the US/Middle East Project.

Quite understandably, Soros has been vilified in Israel. Former Prime Minister Benjamin Netanyahu has publicly branded Soros as "anti-Israel," and Israel's Foreign Ministry has accused Soros of undermining Israel's "democratically elected governments" and funding organizations that "defame the Jewish state and seek to deny it the right to defend itself."

And in response to those criticisms, Netanyahu, the former Jewish leader of the Jewish state of Israel, has been accused of anti-Semitism. [589]

---

589 Epstein, Nadine, "The Vilification of George Soros in Israel," *Moment Magazine*, Winter 2019. https://moment-mag.com/the-vilification-of-george-soros-in-israel/

The Leaked George Soros Documents Revelations

In the summer of 2016, a website purporting to be "launched by the American hacktivists who respect and appreciate freedom of speech, human rights and government of the people" called DC Leaks leaked a massive trove of 2,576 files from multiple departments of Soros' organizations around the world using a server that anonymized the identity of the registrants. The website went live one day after Clinton declared victory in several Democratic primaries.

"Soros is an oligarch sponsoring the Democratic party, Hillary Clinton, hundreds of politicians all over the world," the hackers posted on the website upon the leak. "These documents shed light on one of the most influential networks operating worldwide."[590] The section of the DC Leaks webpage dealing with Soros went offline for unknown reasons, while the rest of the site was operational. Twitter immediately suspended the "DC Leaks" account around the same time with no explanation following the damaging document drop.

The documents detail the ins and outs of Soros groups and span 2008–2016. Neither the contents nor existence of them received any coverage from the *New York Times*, CNN, the *Washington Post*, CBS News, or any other major news source except Fox News. The establishment media kept curious readers in the dark, turning a collective blind eye, though that's unsurprising given what you gleaned from the chapter about Soros' countless connections to mainstream news publications (including those named above).

---

590   Hattem, Julian, "Thousands of Soros Docs Released by Alleged Russian-backed Hackers," *The Hill*, August 15, 2016. https://thehill.com/policy/national-security/291486-thousands-of-soros-docs-released-by-alleged-russia-backed-hackers

A Soros spokesperson called the release of the documents "a symptom of an aggressive assault on civil society and human rights activists that is taking place globally."[591] The representative said that some of the documents reflect "big-picture strategies" over several years from within the Open Society Foundations network. The OSF statement postured the widespread accusations of "backdoor bankrolling" as "an effort to work with civil society and governments to boost democratic practice and strengthen human rights."

Included in the dump of files are drafts of fact sheets, calendars, memos, funding reports, and similar material as expected from non-profits. But some documents in particular raised eyebrows, further revealing Soros' sphere of influence and meddling practices.

SOROS ADVOCATED REGULATING THE INTERNET TO FAVOR HIS CAUSES

Among the documents leaked was a thirty-four-page internal proposed strategy from the Open Society Justice Initiative (OSJI) that advocates for international regulation of "what information is taken off the Internet and what may remain" and policing the web to favor "open society" supporters.[592] According to the organization's website, the OSJI's team of human rights lawyers "uses law to protect and empower people around the world, supporting the values and work of the Open Society Foundations."[593]

The document, titled "2014 Proposed Strategy," argues that international regulation of the internet is needed to protect freedom of expression. In other words, Soros wants to stifle free expression on the internet on the basis that it will protect freedom of expression on the internet.

> "The internet has been a key tool for promoting freedom of expression and open societies—as in the Arab Spring—and is a potential safeguard against monopoly control of information in such places as China and Central Asia," the nineteenth page of the

---

591 Hasson, Peter. "Open Society Foundations Claims Secret Payments to Foreign Gov Officials Were to 'Boost Democratic Practice.'" *Daily Caller*, August 26, 2016. https://dailycaller.com/2016/08/26/soros-group-claims-secret-payments-to-foreign-officials-were-to-boost-democratic-practice/

592 Hasson, "Leaked Soros Document calls for Regulating Internet to Favor 'Open Society' Supporters," *Daily Caller*, August 29, 2016. https://dailycaller.com/2016/08/29/leaked-soros-document-calls-for-regulating-internet-to-favor-open-society-supporters/

593 "Open Society Justice Initiative," Open Society Foundations. https://www.opensocietyfoundations.org/who-we-are/programs/open-society-justice-initiative

OSJI document reads. "But it is also presenting under addressed challenges, including lack of regulation of private operators that are able to decide, without due process procedures, what information is taken off the Internet and what may remain. A 'race to the bottom' results from the agendas of undemocratic governments that seek to impose their hostility to free speech on the general online environment. We seek to ensure that, from among the norms emerging in different parts of the world, those most supportive of open society gain sway."

One proposed program concept and initiative is to "Promote—by advocating for the adoption of nuanced legal norms, and litigation—an appropriate balance between privacy and free expression/transparency values in areas of particular interest to the OSF and the Justice Initiative, including online public interest speech, access to ethnic data, public health statistics, corporate beneficial ownership, asset declarations of public officials, and rights of NGOs to keep information private."[594]

OSJI argues throughout the document that private actors on the internet must be brought under international control in order to prevent them from suppressing each other's freedom of expression and speech. One of the organization's goals is to establish soft law and judicial precedents "safeguarding online free expression," including protection against blocking of online content, intermediary liability, and user standing.[595]

THE SOROS FIGHT AGAINST POPULIST MOVEMENTS IN EUROPE

The rise of the populist movement in Europe prompted a reaction from Soros. He lost ground following populist victories in Hungary, Italy, the Czech Republic, and Austria, where citizens voted to reject mass migration and an "ever closer union" with the European Union.

Soros attempted to sway electoral outcomes in support of his open borders worldview as populist candidates opposed to mass migration represented a direct threat to his philosophy. To resolve the

---

594 Hasson, "Leaked Soros Document calls for Regulating Internet to Favor 'Open Society' Supporters."
595 Ibid.

refugee crisis plaguing Europe, he suggested no defined quotas for the number of migrants that nations should accept. He detailed his comprehensive plan in 2015 to "solve the asylum chaos," instructing the EU to accept at least one million asylum-seekers per year for the foreseeable future.[596]

Leaked OSF documents reveal how Soros worked to defeat populist candidates. "The next EU elections might also bring more populists and extremists into the European Parliament, which could undermine all our achievements to date," an internal document, marked "confidential," from 2013 warned.[597] His efforts would be unsuccessful, as this predates the wave of aforementioned populist victories.

Another document revealed the extent of the OSF's financial backing in the 2014 European Parliamentary elections. In total, over $6 million was awarded to ninety different organizations to influence electoral outcomes as Soros continued to intervene behind the scenes. The stretch of elections across Europe served as referenda on nationalism, which Soros is a zealous opponent of, and globalism, which the open society figurehead favors.[598]

The projects that Soros funded to fight the rise of right-wing populism in Europe included $35,000 to the Athena Institute for the purpose of "Analyzing and reporting the 2014 European elections and countering extremist and populist political voices in Hungary." Soros paid another $49,930 to the Institute for European Policy for a "Naming and shaming populism [in European Parliament] campaign" in the Czech Republic, Hungary, and Slovakia.[599]

Over $27k was given to the Public Diplomacy Council of Catalonia for a workshop to influence "leading journalists and media practitioners from Europe" to change coverage to prevent "populist, xenophobic and Eurosceptic movements." The workshop's stated objective was to "trigger a change of attitude amongst journalists and media practitioners so that they will report about the EU in a way that does not directly promote the cause of these movements."[600]

596   Soros, George, "Opinion: George Soros: Here's My Plan to Solve the Asylum Chaos," Market Watch, September 29, 2015. https://www.marketwatch.com/story/george-soros-heres-my-plan-to-solve-the-asylum-chaos-2015-09-29

597   Hasson, "Leaked Docs Show How Soros Spends Big to Keep Populists Out of Power in Europe," Daily Caller. April 5, 2017. https://dailycaller.com/2017/04/05/leaked-docs-show-how-soros-spends-big-to-keep-populists-out-of-power-in-europe/

598   Open Society Initiative for Europe, "List of European Elections 2014 Projects," Scribd, 2014. https://www.scribd.com/document/343846323/European-Election-Portfolio-Review-Annex-i-Ee14-Project-List-of-All-Elections-Related-Grants-3?secret_password=m3V6G7QksxsGSFvjnXa4#fullscreen&from_embed

599   Ibid.

600   Ibid.

Instead of publicly financially supporting EU candidates, Soros opted to fund organizations that opposed populism and clashed with the OSF worldview.

For example, a $46,840 grant to the Center for Peace Studies, intended to "stimulate public support and election turnout among ambivalent voters in order to prevent the election of xenophobic, racist, and other radical political options representing Croatia at the EU level."[601] The term "xenophobia" was synonymous with supporting restrictions on immigration and the OSF's derogatory word choice to vilify opposition to uncapped mass migration.

$100,000 went to UNITED for Intercultural Action to "counter the election [of European Members of Parliament] from populist and far-right parties in Europe." UNITED teamed up with the European Network Against Racism and Hope not Hate to push back against populist candidates in all twenty-eight (now twenty-seven) member states of the European Union, while focusing on several nations. Local groups in the handful of targeted countries were to be formed to organize meetings and door-to-door campaigns ahead of the European Parliament elections to "encourage voters to register and vote" and to coax the constituents to "vote for non-extremist candidates."[602]

Another document reveals that the Netherlands are one of the OSF's five "priority countries," with no information on what the other four are. "Dutch society has changed rapidly in the last two decades. Multiculturalism has been seriously questioned and the Muslim communities have been on the focus of heated debates," the document reads.[603]

In particular, the OSF feared the rise of the right-wing Party for Freedom (PPV), which was (and still is) the third largest party in Dutch Parliament at the time and had five seats in European Parliament. The PPV "will have a very good result in the European Parliament elections, and because it is one of the drivers of anti-European and anti-migration discourse in the EU," polling predicted. Two months before European Parliament's election in May 2014, the OSF said, "The outcome of the European Parliament elections in May 2014 and how well the PPV, the populist party of Geert Wilders, does will help to determine [the OSF's] next steps in the Netherlands."[604]

601　Ibid.
602　Ibid.
603　Open Society Initiative for Europe, "Portfolio Review Document: OSIFE in The Netherlands," Scribd, March 14, 2014. https://www.scribd.com/document/343964471/Portfolio-Review-Materials-From-Reviews-With-Chris-Stone-open-Society-Initiative-for-Europe-Osife-Osife-in-the-Netherlands-March-14-2014-Osife-Nether?secret_password=DZdLAFvLHTn4MK9XX9y5
604　Ibid.

Domestically, Soros gave liberal think tank Center for American Progress (CAP) $200,000 to conduct "high-quality opposition research" to "combat Islamophobia" in the form of funding opposition research on critics of radical Islam and trying to discredit the Israeli government.[605]

The 2011 OSF document "Extreme Polarization and Breakdown in Civil Discourse," framed the OSF's fight against "anti-Muslim xenophobia" as an initiative "to promote tolerance." The OSF named prominent critics of radical Islam such as conservative blogger Pamela Geller, activist Frank Gaffney, who was hailed by the Israeli ambassador to the United States as "a steadfast friend of Israel, and Jihad Watch director Robert Spencer as targets for opposition researchers working on the project, called the Examining Anti-Muslim Bigotry Project, operated by CAP.[606]

CAP's first self-outlined steps were to interview and engage journalists, researchers, academics, and leaders in "the anti-hate movement who are researching and writing on Islamophobia" and to develop "a roster of knowledgeable and credible experts to whom journalists and policymakers can turn for information." CAP also explored the interactions of conservative think tanks, pundits, and politicians that were part of the so-called Islamophobia movement. In addition, CAP planned to "research and track" the activities of conservative writer and the Freedom Center's eponymous founder David Horowitz, historian and Middle East Forum president Daniel Pipes, and current Representative Liz Cheney, the elder daughter of former vice president Dick Cheney.[607]

"We need a clearer understanding of what by all indications is a well-orchestrated and well financed system by which right-wing think tanks, pundits, and politicians are able to introduce false narratives and flawed research into the media cycle and use their misinformation to manipulate public opinion and thwart progressive counterterrorism policies," the 2011 memo states. "Just as critically, CAP will approach its work with an appreciation of the connections between the Islamophobia movement and related forms of xenophobia."[608]

605 Fredericks, Bob, "Hackers Reveal Soros Funds Research on Critics of Islam," *New York Post*, August 17, 2016. https://nypost.com/2016/08/17/hackers-reveal-soros-funds-research-on-critics-of-islam/

606 Ross, Chuck, "Memo: Soros Group Funded 'Opposition Research' On Critics of Radical Islam," *Daily Caller*, August 14, 2016. https://dailycaller.com/2016/08/14/memo-soros-group-funded-opposition-research-on-critics-of-radical-islam/

607 Ibid.

608 Ibid.

UKRAINE

Documents revealed the extent to which Soros aided Hillary Clinton in 2016, which fortunately ended with her humiliating loss regardless. Those documents also shine new light on how Soros wanted to reshape Ukraine's government to his liking, hoping that his business empire would find fertile ground within the former Soviet state.[609]

As Trump ascended on the campaign trail in spring 2016, Soros' network reached out to the top of the State Department to hedge his big bet that Hillary would win the presidency.

Soros and his minions reached out to then Assistant Secretary of State Victoria Nuland by phone and email to request meetings, according to the department memos obtained under the Freedom of Information Act by conservative group Citizens United. In one email dated May 25, 2016, Soros Fund Management's Chris Canavan, who was the director of Global Policy Development, sent Nuland a briefing with the subject line "Russia sovereign bond issue."

"Toria, here is my take on Russia's foray into the bond markets this week, based on the market chatter I've been able to pick up," Canavan wrote in a heavily redacted email that conceals most of his specific advice to Nuland.[610] *For context,* Russian president Vladimir Putin's regime had threatened Soros' bold vision for Ukraine.

Canavan worked on the for-profit side of the Soros empire. Nuland's nickname relationship with the top Secretary of State official responsible for Russia and Ukraine policy and Canavan's election-year contacts at the federal department spoke volumes about the access to the Obama administration that Soros was afforded (despite Soros' aforementioned personal complaints about not being able to influence Obama enough).

Six days later, an official from Soros' OSF rang the same bell and reached out to Nuland to discuss European migration policy, which she did in an arranged call with Soros. This OSF official said of the meeting in an email to Nuland's aide: "Many thanks for sorting today's call on such short notice—much appreciated. During the call, Mr. Soros promised A/S Nuland he would send her his draft article on migration policy for the *New York Review of Books.*"[611]

609 Solomon, "George Soros's 2016 Access to State Exposes 'Big Money' Hypocrisy of Democrats," *The Hill,* August 7, 2019. https://thehill.com/opinion/white-house/456619-george-soross-secret-2016-access-to-state-exposes-big-money-hypocrisy-of-democrats

610 U.S. Department of State, "Soros Nuland Russia Bond Market," Scribd, November 7, 2018. https://www.scribd.com/document/421082234/SorosNulandRussia-Bond-Market

611 Ibid.

A week later, after meeting in Brussels with a top European Union official, Soros' team reached out yet again to Nuland to discuss the "EU visa liberalization for Ukraine and Georgia," wanting the U.S. to intervene to get the EU to ease visa rules to help Ukraine as the country advanced reforms favored by Soros.[612] Johannes Hahn, the European Commissioner for Neighborhood Policy and Enlargement Negotiations, was referenced in the emails as the person Soros met with in Brussels. Soros told Hahn that Ukrainian civil society is "concerned that without reciprocity from the EU for steps Ukraine has taken to put in place sensitive anti-corruption and anti-discrimination legislation and institutions it will not be possible to continue to use the leverage of EU instruments and policies to maintain pressure for reforms in the future." He urged Hahn to advocate with member states to move ahead with visa liberalization for Ukraine. On scores of occasions, Hahn was a featured speaker at roundtables and other events hosted by the Atlantic Council think tank, which is financed by Soros' OSF.[613]

Nuland replied to the pressure: "We are working it. Not sure whether intervention by GS [George Soros] would help." Nuland also alerted Jeff Goldstein, who was Soros' top policy analyst on Eurasia at the foundation, to a key piece of intelligence: One of the European Union countries "has changed its mind" and she was "happy to discuss this further."[614]

Emails showed that Goldstein kept Nuland as well as CIA officer and alleged Ukraine whistleblower Eric Ciaramella, who was also included in the communications loop between Soros and the State Department, regularly updated on Ukraine policy and on Soros' personal Ukraine activities.[615]

The emails informed Ciaramella and a handful of other Obama administration foreign policy officials about Soros' whereabouts, the contents of Soros' private meetings about Ukraine, and a future meeting Soros was holding with the prime minister of Ukraine.[616]

Goldstein wrote June 9, 2016, to Nuland and Ciaramella: "[George Soros] is also meeting [Georgian] President [Giorgi] Mar-

---

612 Ibid.
613 Klein, Aaron, "Emails: Open Society Kept Alleged 'Whistleblower' Eric Ciaramella Updated on George Soros's Persona Ukraine Activities," Breitbart, November 17, 2019. https://www.breitbart.com/politics/2019/11/17/emails-open-society-kept-alleged-whistleblower-eric-ciaramella-updated-on-george-soross-personal-ukraine-activities/
614 U.S. Department of State, "Soros Nuland Ukraine Visa Memos June 2016," Scribd, June 10, 2016. https://www.scribd.com/document/421081036/SorosNulandUkraineVisaMemosJune2016
615 Klein, "Emails: Open Society Kept Alleged 'Whistleblower' Eric Ciaramella Updated on George Soros's Persona Ukraine Activities."
616 Ibid.

gvelashvili today and speaking with [Ukrainian] PM [Volodymyr] Groyman." CC'd were three other State Department officials involved in European affairs, including Alexander Kasanof, who worked at the U.S. embassy in Kiev.[617]

"I'm sure you've been working this issue hard; if you have any thoughts on how this is likely to play out or where particular problems lie I'd appreciate [it] if you could let us know," Goldstein's email concluded. Nuland answered that she would be happy to discuss the issues by phone. Goldstein set up a phone call and wrote that Soros specifically asked that an employee from the billionaire's "personal office" join the call with Nuland.[618]

According to investigative journalist John Solomon, who noted in an op-ed for *The Hill* that it's ironic that Soros, a mastermind of political persuasion, is emblematic of the very financial influence and deep state access that Democrats campaign to destroy:

> People close to Soros told me in interviews that he often had contact with government officials during the Obama years, including a 2010 meeting with Clinton at State. But they acknowledged the flurry with Nuland in spring 2016 was unusual both for its frequency and its intensity.
>
> They said the exchanges were driven by Soros' concerns about Ukraine's future, not politics or business. "George Soros is the founder of an organization that gives away a billion dollars a year to promote democracy and human rights around the world. It is for that reason that people at the State Department speak to him, not because he is a political donor," top Soros aide Michael Vachon told me.[619]

Of course, in reality Soros' business and political interests are often mixed.

Soros had also turned to John Podesta, then Clinton's campaign chairman, as a prelude to Nuland's enchantment while he sought to influence Ukraine policy. Vachon wrote Podesta in a March 2016 email published by WikiLeaks that was seeking a meeting with him:

---

617 Ibid.
618 Ibid.
619 Solomon, "George Soros's 2016 Access to State Exposes 'Big Money' Hypocrisy of Democrats."

"Both the migration crisis and Ukraine are part of his view of Europe as falling apart, and the U.S. as ultimately not doing enough to prevent the political disintegration of its most important ally."

ILLEGAL IMMIGRATION

In 2010, the OSF attempted to broker an alliance between leftist and libertarian think tanks and organizations with the goal of blocking "comprehensive immigration reform" legislation that would've required the closer tracking of immigrants. While the bill they wanted to block would legalize at least eleven million illegal aliens, they were upset with a provision that would require them and one hundred forty million American citizens to participate in a biometric database for tracking fingerprints. The bill ultimately failed as did the movement for so-called "comprehensive immigration reform."[620]

This came after an off-the-record meeting in November 2019 between the American Civil Liberties Union, Human Rights Campaign, National Immigration Law Center, and Cato Institute.[621]

Another leaked memo stated: "Our goal was to ensure that the privacy rights community and the immigrant rights community, two groups that receive significant support from [Soros] but rarely interface with one another, share information and strategies to avoid the loss of privacy and risk to information security." While so-called "comprehensive immigration reform" would've failed with or without Soros involvement, he did succeed in a related pursuit to convince the Obama administration to boost the number of refugees the U.S. admits annually to one hundred thousand. [622]

A leaked memo between the OSF's top officials and board members from February 2016 revealed the OSF's extensive attempt to influence the Supreme Court for its desired outcome on a case on illegal immigration enforcement. The memo, addressed to the OSF's fourteen advisory board members for U.S. operations, was authored by OSF programs director Ken Zimmerman and deputy director Andrea Batista Schlesinger.[623]

---

620   Hasson, "Leaked Board Documents: Soros Organization Tried to Influence Supreme Court Ruling on Illegal Immigration," *Daily Caller*, August 17, 2016. https://dailycaller.com/2016/08/17/leaked-board-documents-soros-organization-tried-to-buy-supreme-court-ruling-on-illegal-immigration/
621   Takala, Rudy, "Hacked: Soros Worked to Prevent Documentation of Illegals," *Washington Examiner*, August 23, 2016. https://www.washingtonexaminer.com/hacked-soros-worked-to-prevent-documentation-of-illegals
622   Ibid.
623   Hasson, "Leaked Board Documents: Soros Organization Tried to Influence Supreme Court Ruling On Illegal Immigration."

One section of the report documents "new challenges," the *U.S. v. Texas* case among them. The case was regarding the constitutionality of Obama's 2014 Deferred Action for Parents of Americans (DAPA) program. The policy effectively allowed illegal aliens to work in the U.S. without fear of deportation, as it granted deferred status to illegals who have lived in the U.S. since 2010 and have children who are either American citizens or lawful permanent residents. A split four-to-four SCOTUS decision (Antonin Scalia's vacancy was still unfilled) in June 2016 would leave the policy in effect, and Donald Trump would later rescind it.[624]

While the case was still active, the memo stated that "Grantees are seeking to influence the Justices (primarily via a sophisticated amicus briefs and media strategy) in hopes of securing a favorable ruling in U.S. v Texas." The memo adds: "We are also seeking to shore up state and local infrastructure through Emma Lazarus II investments, positioning the field to move swiftly on a large-scale implementation effort in the event of a favorable ruling—efforts complicated by lagging implementation capacity at the federal level."[625]

SECRETLY PAYING STAFFERS OF MOLDOVA'S PRIME MINISTER

Leaked documents revealed that from July 2013 to February 2015, the OSF secretly paid the salaries of three staffers to then Moldovan prime minister Iurie Leancă. Documents detailed that money was funneled through a German nonprofit to evade the law.[626] The document notes "Due to the constraints in the Moldovan legislation, OSF cannot directly pay staff members of PM office. The advisors will be paid as research consultants within a project run by a German think tank—the Institute for European Policies (Institut für Europäische Politik)."

One document dated July 3, 2014, reveals that $141,750 was disbursed to "support the Moldovan Prime Minister Leanca." As the *Daily Caller*'s Peter Hasson reported:

---

624   Ibid.
625   Ibid.
626   Hasson, "Soros Organization Secretly Paid Salaries for Staffers of Moldovan Prime Minister," *Daily Caller*, August 24, 2016. https://dailycaller.com/2016/08/24/soros-organization-secretly-paid-salaries-for-staffers-of-moldovan-prime-minister/

At Leanca's request, OSF began paying salaries to three of his staffers in July 2013: chief of staff Eugen Sturza, economic adviser Valeriu Prohnitchi and political affairs adviser Vlad Kulminski. A fourth staffer, Liliana Vitu, was added to the payroll with the July 2014 proposal. Vitu, it's noted, previously served on the board of OSF's Moldova branch.

The proposal was approved by Leonard Benardo, who is now OSF's regional director of Eurasia.

OSF paid each of the four staffers $33,750 for the eight months of work between July 2014 and February 2015. The Institute for European Policies received a $6,750 administrative fee for channeling the money to the staffers.[627]

The proposal outlines the reason for the payments.

Of Sturza, the proposal states that he "has led and coordinated the work of the office. He put into place the institutional framework which helps the Government to focus on its strategic priorities, including its reforms agenda. He has assigned tasks to advisors to make sure that strategic priorities, as well as operational issues, are efficiently addressed. He ensures the liaison between the PM's office and ministries and departments, as well as the local authorities."

Of Prohnitchi, the proposal notes that she "has provided key contribution to the development, implementation and follow-up of the PM's economic and market reform policies," later adding: "Valeriu has led the work and relations with investors, the IMF, the European Bank for Reconstruction and Development and donor institutions."

Of Kulminski, the proposal states that he "has contributed to strengthening the PM's focus on the strategic task for the country— to draw Moldova close to Europe, while also making this goal acceptable to a wider audience." The proposal also says he contributed "to the elaboration and implementation of policies and actions in many directions, including relations with Russia, the policies of the central government in the Gagauz region, in Taraclia and in Balti. He leads development and communication priorities for these regions, and outreach to the leadership and public there."

627　Ibid.

According to the proposal, Prime Minister Leanca was "very satisfied with the quality of expertise and the support his advisors provided," describing their contribution as "crucial."

MIGRATION

Leaked documents reveal that Soros viewed the European refugee crisis caused by the Syrian Civil War as "new opportunities" to create a "new normal" by pushing mass migration.[628]

A memo dated May 12, 2016, authored by OSF program officer Anna Crowley and program specialist Kate Rosin titled "Migration Governance and Enforcement Portfolio Review" focuses on the OSF's International Migration Initiative's (IMI) attempts to influence migration policy.

In a section with the header "Our Ambitions," they explain that "Our premise for engaging in work related to governance was that, in addition to mitigating the negative effects of enforcement [of immigration laws], we should also be supporting actors in the field proactively seeking to change the policies, rules, and regulations that govern migration." They continue in a later paragraph, "As our aspirations have evolved, our targets have shifted from harm reduction to more proactive solutions-based policy influencing."[629]

They also say that IMI "has had to be selective and opportunistic, particularly at the global level, in supporting leaders in the field to push thinking on migration and better coordinate advocacy and reform efforts. We have supported initiatives, organizations, and networks whose work ties directly to our aims in the corridors."[630]

In the next section, titled "Our Place," they reveal their apparatus to influence policy.

> "Early on, IMI identified a handful of organizations able to engage on migration globally and transnationally, elevating IMI's corridor work beyond the national level. These included key think tanks such as the Migration Policy Institute (MPI) and advo-

---

628   Hasson, "Leaked Soros Memo: Refugee Crisis 'New Normal,' Gives 'New Opportunities' for Global Influence," *Daily Caller,* August 15, 2016. https://dailycaller.com/2016/08/15/leaked-soros-memo-refugee-crisis-new-normal-gives-new-opportunities-for-global-influence/

629   Crowley, Anna, and Kate Rosin, "Migration Governance and Enforcement Portfolio Review," US Archive, May 12, 2016. https://ia601207.us.archive.org/10/items/321383374OpenSocietyFoundationsInternationalMigrationInitiativeMigrationGovernan/321383374-Open-Society-Foundations-International-Migration-Initiative-Migration-Governance-and-Enforcement-Portfolio-Review.pdf

630   Hasson, "Leaked Soros Memo: Refugee Crisis 'New Normal.'"

cacy networks such as the International Detention Coalition (IDC). IMI initially chose not to work in Europe, and therefore did not engage with leading academic policy centers such as Oxford's Centre on Migration, Policy and Society. We also considered supporting global rights watchdogs, such as Human Rights Watch and Amnesty International, to promote migrant rights. However, we saw greater potential for constructive policy engagement through different approaches than those that solely adopted a rights angle."[631]

The OSF says it was the "severity of the migration crisis in Europe" and how it affected the "global state of play" that led to them taking an interest in Europe. "This has created space within this year's international cycle of events to examine protections for undocumented and other vulnerable migrants and to explore possibilities for multi-stakeholder collaboration for support to migrants as well as refugees." It concludes that "the current climate presents new opportunities for reforming migration governance at the global level, whether through the existing multi-lateral system, or by bringing together a range of actors to think more innovatively."[632]

In the final section, titled "Our Work," Crowley and Rosin describe how they've been able to "shape migration policy making and influence regional and global processes affecting the way migration is governed and enforced." They explain,

"For example, MPI-Europe partnered with the European Council on Refugees and Exiles to engage civil society actors in a process to develop new policy proposals and facilitate civil society engagement with policymakers. Similarly, MPI's Transatlantic Council on Migration and the Central America Migration Study Group have provided opportunities for experts, senior political leaders, policymakers, and civil society to come together to catalyze changes to migration policies."[633]

---

631 Crowley and Rosin, "Migration Governance and Enforcement Portfolio Review."
632 Ibid.
633 Ibid.

In that section, they admit to coordinating with foreign governments while attempting to claim impartiality: "While MPI is sometimes criticized for its closeness to governments, flexible funding from OSF has allowed it to maintain some independence from the governments it advises. This is particularly important, as its revenue stream increasingly comes directly from government clients."[634]

ISRAEL AND IRAN

Soros aimed to help build a relationship between the U.S. and Iran at the expense of Israel, two leaked documents exposed. The OSF works closely with the leftist J Street, which Soros has been a donor to since 2008 (and is one of J Street's largest individual donors).

J Street has attempted to deny being funded by Soros, with founder Jeremy Ben-Ami joking in 2020 that the group got tagged as having Soros support "without the benefit of actually getting funded!" When it was confirmed through tax records that the "joke" was actually a statement of fact, J Street did a 180 and claimed they have "always said that [they] would be very pleased to have funding from Mr. Soros."[635]

We learn that the OSF works closely with J Street, but that the OSF doesn't want that being known. "For a variety of reasons we wanted to construct a diversified portfolio of grants dealing with Israel and Palestine, funding both Israeli Jewish and (Palestinian Citizens of Israel) groups as well as building a portfolio of Palestinian grants and in all cases to maintain a low profile and relative distance—particularly on the advocacy front." They cited the previous "toxic atmosphere" when they began doing work in the Middle East, fearing "politically motivated investigations" from pro-Israel entities if their work were exposed to the public.

The documents reveal a web of grants to Palestinian and Israeli human rights groups (all of which are pro-Palestinian) that are part of a larger effort to influence Congress. Following Barack Obama taking office in 2009, the OSF saw an opportunity to weaken the Israel lobby's influence in Washington, and began a project aimed to persuade European and U.S. leaders to "hold Israel accountable" for supposed violations of international law.

---

634   Ibid.
635   Lifhits, Jenna, "Soros Empire Concealed Ties to WH-Linked Liberal Jewish Lobby, Hacked Documents Show," *Washington Examiner,* August 18, 2016. https://www.washingtonexaminer.com/weekly-standard/soros-empire-concealed-ties-to-wh-linked-liberal-jewish-lobby-hacked-documents-show

As Bloomberg's Eli Lake summarizes:

> It started with so much hope after Obama won the 2008 election. "The right-wing so called 'pro-Israel' lobby has lost some credibility by being closely associated with Bush Administration Middle East policies," a 2013 summary of the foundation's "Palestine/Israel International Advocacy Portfolio" said. "As the Obama Administration distances itself from these somehow discredited policies, space for reasonable, unbiased discussions in the policy deliberations, including criticism of Israeli policies, is opening."[636]

Among the organizational funding by the OSF is $100k to Breaking the Silence, an organization that employs former IDF soldiers to push pro-Palestinian narratives. One leaked document explains the reasoning behind funding them: "Our theory of change was based on strengthening the advocacy efforts of civil society organizations and platforms in order to maintain sustained and targeted international advocacy that would oblige the international community (mostly Europe and America) to act and to hold Israel accountable to its obligations under the international law."

Soros also backed Obama's outreach to Iran, a 2014 program summary revealed: "Human rights defense work remains an important priority for the Iran Program. But should not be pursued to the exclusion of all other work, including work on supporting better policy outcomes such as support for a nuclear deal with Iran."

One leaked review of the OSF's Arab Regional Office's work dated September 1, 2015, cited various regional achievements, including increased advocacy by Palestinians in Israel, challenging Israel's "racist" policies, and casting doubt on Israel's reputation as a democracy. "There have been a number of successes in challenging Israel's racist and anti-democratic policies in the international arena and influencing EU-Israel bilateral negotiations," the review states.

We also learn of groups in the region Soros is funding, including the New Israel Fund ($837.5k from 2002 to 2015) and Adalah ($2.7 million).[637]

---

636   Lake, Eli, "A Soros Plan, a Marginalized Israel," Bloomberg, August 16, 2016. https://www.bloomberg.com/opinion/articles/2016-08-16/how-george-soros-threatens-to-make-israel-a-pariah
637   JTA, "Hacked Soros E-mails Reveal Plans to Fight Israel's 'Racist' Policies," The Jerusalem Post, August 15, 2016. https://www.jpost.com/israel-news/politics-and-diplomacy/hacked-soros-e-mails-reveal-plans-to-fight-israels-racist-policies-464149

POPE FRANCIS

When Pope Francis visited the U.S. in 2015, Soros shelled out $650k in an attempt to influence him on "economic and racial justice issues."[638]

One document reveals an agenda for a May 2015 meeting in New York of the U.S. programs division of the OSF. It states that $650k has been allocated toward a grant for Francis' visit. "In order to seize this moment, we will support PICO's organizing activities to engage the Pope on economic and racial justice issues, including using the influence of Cardinal Rodriguez, the Pope's senior advisor, and sending a delegation to visit the Vatican in the spring or summer to allow him to hear directly from low-income Catholics in America." According to the national network's website, PICO— now known as Faith in Action—is a Catholic interfaith organization "working to create innovative solutions to problems facing urban, suburban and rural communities."[639]

The document outlines the purpose for the grant: "The grant will also support FPL's media, framing, and public opinion activities, including conducting a poll to demonstrate that Catholic voters are responsive to the Pope's focus on income inequality, and earning media coverage that drives the message that being 'pro-family' requires addressing growing inequality." FPL is "Faith for Public Life," a group that claims to have "played an important role in changing the narrative about the role of faith in politics, winning major progressive policy victories, and empowering new religious leaders to fight for social justice and the common good." FPL's mission is to "advance just policies at the local, state and federal levels" as an organization of fifty thousand clergy and faith leaders united in the "prophetic pursuit" of justice and equality.[640]

FPL's website states the group has carried out the primary functions of the Soros grant: "In preparation for the Pope's visit to the US, we commissioned extensive opinion research about how Catholics respond to the Pope's prophetic messages and released the poll at the National Press Club." Throughout the papal trip, the FPL said it "coordinated messaging among numerous Catholic groups and did extensive media outreach."[641]

---

638 Pfeiffer, Alex, "Leaked Document Shows Soros Spent $650k To Influence Pope Francis on 'Economic and Racial Justice Issues,'" *Daily Caller,* August 24, 2016. https://dailycaller.com/2016/08/24/leaked-document-shows-soros-spent-650k-to-influence-pope-francis/
639 Ibid.
640 Ibid.
641 Ibid.

The Soros document reads: "By harnessing the Papal visit to lift up the Pope's searing critique of what he calls 'an economy of exclusion and inequality' and his dismissal of 'trickle down' theories, PICO and FPL will work to build a bridge to a larger conversation about bread-and-butter economic concerns and shift national paradigms and priorities in the run-up to the 2016 presidential campaign."[642]

CATHOLIC SPRING

Soros backed a "Catholic Spring" group that played a role in influencing Barack Obama's 2009 Notre Dame speech in an attempt to get Catholic voters to see abortion as just one of many campaign issues as opposed to one that makes or breaks support for a candidate.

His agenda here is "to inspire greater public participation from mainstream and social justice oriented faith communities" on Open Society Foundations priority issues and also to "counter the outsize influence and impact of right-wing religious constituencies," according to the memo.

The nonpartisan Catholics in Alliance for the Common Good (CACG) was founded in 2005 with early backing from Soros. The memo indicates that the group received at least $450k in financial support from Soros between 2006 and 2010. Emails leaked to WikiLeaks from 2012 allegedly belonging to John Podesta reference CACG as being founded to aid a "Catholic Spring" political revolution in the church.

A leaked memo attributed to the OSF's U.S. Programs' Democracy and Power Fund dated September 22, 2009, reads: "CACG has helped to transform Catholic values in the mainstream media and in the public discourse on religion and politics, thereby thwarting previously successful attempts by the conservative movement to use religious faith for partisan advantage." The memo further states that the group played a pivotal role in "critical Catholic moments," such as Obama's aforementioned Notre Dame speech.

The memo praised the "reframing" of the abortion debate, stating "Indeed, this reframing is where the group has showed some of its most successful policy influence within the new Obama administration: the President made this reframing the centerpiece of his much anticipated Notre Dame speech."

---

642   Ibid.

When these memos became public, CACG's executive director Christopher Hale distanced himself from the allegations and claimed that the group is "categorically" pro-life. Hale had previously worked for Obama's 2008 campaign, and again in 2013,[643] and ran for office in 2020 as a pro-life Democrat.[644] CACG also condemned Planned Parenthood when the infamous "baby body parts" videos were released. Other leaked documents reveal that the OSF took part in a $7–8 million damage control effort after those baby body parts videos went public.

The OSF's memo indicates that it sees CACG's public pro-life stance as a benefit, however, because it allows the OSF to stealthily push its own personal agenda on abortion through a pro-life face. The Catholic News Agency explains:

> According to the 2009 Open Society Foundations memo, Catholics in Alliance drew criticisms from pro-abortion rights groups like Catholics for Choice for its efforts to "play down abortion rights and reframe the debate in terms of reducing the number of abortions."

> "We believe that CACG's reframing may actually be one of its strengths," said the memo.

> The Soros network typically supports abortion rights. The memo added: "We will continue to monitor this issue, but at this time feel that CACG's position on choice is not at odds with OSI priorities."

> Catholics in Alliance's politics-related actions also drew praise from the grant maker. "Unlike in 2004, CACG and the progressive faith community in 2008 provided a consistent counterpoint to the religious right-wing's message in key media stories," the memo said. "Importantly, CACG broadened the agenda of Catholic voters."[645]

---

643   Long, Erica, "Pope Francis, Faith, and Presidential Politics," Harvard, September 30, 2014. https://hds.harvard.edu/news/2014/09/30/pope-francis-faith-and-presidential-politics#

644   Roe, Josh, "'Pro-life' Democrat House Candidate Christopher Hale on the Attack vs. Opponent DesJarlais," News Channel 9, September 29, 2020. https://newschannel9.com/news/election/pro-life-democrat-house-candidate-christopher-hale-on-the-attack-vs-opponent-desjarlais

645   Jones, Kevin J., "What the George Soros Network Saw in a 'Catholic Spring' Group," Catholic News Agency, October 20, 2016. https://www.catholicnewsagency.com/news/34780/what-the-george-soros-network-saw-in-a-

The OSF claims that because of CACG's outreach to Catholic voters in 2006 and 2008, it created a situation in which "abortion is not the overriding issue at the ballot box." As proof of its claim, the OSF cited polls showing that majority of evangelical and Catholic voters in 2008 said that the religious should focus on all issues instead of "one of two." The OSF also cited poll results that only 14 percent say abortion is their top issue.

Regardless of CACG's pro-life stance, Soros was still able to use the group as a Trojan horse to cryptically push a pro-choice agenda.

In addition to abortion, the memo praises CACG for its role in immigration reform and in states that have immigration raids. The group planned to offer media and leadership training to Latino faith leaders.

HILLARY CLINTON

Unlike everything prior, this particular leak is out of WikiLeaks, not LeaksDC.

Hacked emails released by WikiLeaks in late October 2016 revealed Hillary Clinton went out of her way to keep Soros pleased.[646] The emails, hacked from the account of Clinton campaign chairman and Soros ally John Podesta, disclosed that Clinton was advised to do fundraisers to satisfy Soros' marching orders. The communications showed that Soros, through top aides, reached out to Podesta on issues ranging from trade to migration to the Supreme Court.

In one email, Hillary's deputy chief of staff Huma Abedin wrote to eventual campaign manager Robby Mook on October 7, 2014, to tell him that Hillary was having dinner with Soros. Abedin told Mook that she believed Soros would ask Hillary to appear at a fundraiser at one of the liberal organizations he funds, America Votes, and wanted advice on how to proceed. "I would only do this for political reasons (ie, to make Soros happy)," Mook replied.

On January 23, 2011, Hillary's staff was forwarded an email by Soros aides in which he asked her to address "a serious situation in Albania which needs urgent attention at senior levels of the US government" and laid out two actions to be "done urgently." One of the actions was to appoint a senior European official mediator, such

catholic-spring-group
646 "'Make Soros Happy' Inside Clinton Team's Mission to Please Billionaire VIP," Fox News, October 27, 2016. https://www.foxnews.com/politics/make-soros-happy-inside-clinton-teams-mission-to-please-billionaire-vip

as "Carl Bildt, Martti Ahtisaari, or Miroslav Lajcak." Hillary, while serving as Secretary of State, received the email the following day. On January 27, European Union special envoy Lajcak was sent to Tirana and met with Albanian leaders for mediation talks. Lajcak said it was up to Albania's leadership "to do what we ask them to do."[647]

"I made it clear that the European future for Albania depends very much on whether the political leaders choose to do what we ask them to do, and do it now," Lajcak said after the negotiations aimed at easing tension and getting the country's European Union membership bid back on track.

The initial message from Open Society Foundations special adviser to the chairman Jonas Rolett was first sent to then State Department official Richard Verma who duly passed the memo along in an email chain including Abedin, Hillary's top foreign affairs adviser Jacob Sullivan, Assistant Secretary of State for European and Eurasian Affairs Philip Gordon, and a recipient named "William J" believed to be William Joseph Burns, who was then Deputy Secretary of State.

"Below message is from George Soros for the Secretary. Understand his organization was sending through other channels as well," read Verma's attached note to the "Unrest in Albania" email.

What followed in the "Dear Hillary" message could only be construed as instructions for the Secretary of State signed by Soros himself. Soros wrote that all of his mediator appointment suggestions "have strong connections to the Balkans" and that his foundation in Tirana was "monitoring the situation closely and can provide independent analysis of the crisis."[648]

Other emails reveal that just hours after conservative Supreme Court Justice Antonin Scalia was reported dead on the morning of February 13, 2016, the Open Society Foundations then president Chris Stone took to emailing Podesta. "Remember our discussion of Wallace Jefferson, [former] Chief Justice in Texas?" Stone asked Podesta in cryptic fashion. As a nod to an unknown previous conversation, Podesta responded, "Yup." Jefferson, a former chief justice on the Texas Supreme Court, was the subject of the email titled "Re: Scalia replacement."[649] Even though Jefferson is a black Republican,

---

647   BBC, "EU Urges Albania to Defuse Political Crisis," BBC, January 27, 2011. https://www.bbc.com/news/world-europe-12296146

648   U.S. Department of State, "Hillary Clinton Email Archive," WikiLeaks, October 30, 2015. https://wikileaks.org/clinton-emails/emailid/24651

649   Podesta, John, "Re: Scalia Replacement," WikiLeaks, February 13, 2016. https://wikileaks.org/podesta-emails/emailid/14273

the floated Clinton nominee's judicial philosophy could've been centrist or left of center on the Supreme Court. Jefferson possessed attractiveness to the Left as a minority appointment and the moderate force would have brought racial diversity to the court.

Most Soros-related communication with Podesta came through Michael Vachon, a Soros adviser and spokesman. Emails were usually to schedule phone calls and meetings and notify him of Soros' policy positions. Many of the messages were brief or mysterious. On February 23, 2015, Vachon wrote that he needed to tell Podesta something "separately, important, timely but certainly not urgent." Another message dated January 13, 2009, showed Vachon thanking Podesta for meeting with Soros the previous day. "He found it extremely useful," Vachon wrote.

Soros directly invited Podesta to his house in January 2015 to watch a short documentary based on Soros' essays about Ukraine, and again later that July to watch a film about climate change. A Soros-authored piece titled "Recapitalize the Banking System" was also sent Podesta's way back in October 2008.

On March 7, 2017, Vachon sent Podesta a "TPP and Malaysia's Corruption Crisis" memo criticizing Obama for making "visible compromises" in his efforts to get the Trans-Pacific Partnership completed, and wanted Podesta to speak about it with Soros and his son during a dinner later that month. Six days later, Vachon said that Soros would be more interested in discussing policy than "the campaign per se" during the dinner. Vachon wrote: "In a separate email I will send you George's latest thinking on the migration crisis, which he is spending a lot of time on. His other big preoccupation these days is Ukraine."

Post-Soros

George Soros is ninety-one years old as of writing, and the average person who reaches that age has about four years of life left.[650]

Time itself is set to end Soros' reign as the world's biggest living influencer of politics, but his agenda and its backing will survive him. Even if those who succeed him are only half as effective, there's a lot they can accomplish toward any cause with a war chest that nears $20 billion.

Soros explained in an essay titled "My Philanthropy" published in the *New York Review of Books* in 2011 two concerns for his efforts: what happens to the OSF when its president and him are no longer alive, and what more they could accomplish in their lifetimes.

"When I established the Open Society Foundations, I did not want them to survive me. The fate of other institutions has taught me that they tend to stray very far from the founders' intentions." Soros noted. "But as the Open Society Foundations took on a more substantial form, I changed my mind. I came to realize that terminating the foundations' network at the time of my death would be an act of excessive selfishness. A number of very capable people are devoting their lives to the work of the Open Society Foundations; I have no right to pull the rug out from under them," he continued.[651]

His desire to influence from beyond the grave is why he decided to set up the School of Public Policy at Central European University. "Our main difficulty has been in keeping our network of national foundations and "legacy" programs from going stale because that

---

650 "Actuarial Life Table," Social Security Administration. https://www.ssa.gov/oact/STATS/table4c6.html
651 Soros, George, *In Defense of Open Society*, page 82

requires almost as much effort as starting new ones; yet my bias has been to focus on the cutting edge. That is where I look for relief from the School of Public Policy. It should explore new frontiers; therefore it should be able to keep the continuing programs up to date even in my absence."

He continues:

> Having decided that the Open Society Foundations should survive me, I have done my best to prepare them for my absence. But it would contradict my belief that all human constructs are flawed if I had fully succeeded. Therefore, I bequeath my successors the task of revising any of the arrangements I shall have left behind in the same spirit in which I have made them.

Soros has since done some estate planning to further that goal.

Near the end of 2017, Soros transferred nearly $18 billion (80 percent of his net worth) to Open Society Foundations, which now holds most of his wealth. The donation made the OSF the second-largest private foundation in the U.S. by asset size (with only the Bill and Melinda Gates Foundation being larger).[652]

The infrastructure that Soros created will always exist, and a large motivating factor for me writing this book is to create a directory to help people identify it. In some cases, it'll be even more obvious than before that Soros is the one pulling the strings, albeit posthumously. Soros himself says that after his passing, he wants his "Open Society University Network" to be rebranded the "Soros University Network."[653]

Soros acknowledges that "what will be missing when I am gone is the entrepreneurial and innovative spirit that has characterized us....The governing board that will succeed me will not be able to follow my example; it will be weighed down by fiduciary responsibilities. Some of its members will try to be faithful to the founder's intentions; others will be more risk averse."[654]

---

652   Tucker, Higgins. "George Soros Just Gave Almost 80 Percent of His Wealth to Charity." CNBC, October 17, 2017. https://www.cnbc.com/2017/10/17/philanthropist-george-soros-donates-most-of-his-net-worth-to-charity.html
653   Soros, George, *In Defense of Open Society*, pages 108–109.
654   Ibid., page 83.

Soros acknowledges that his "conceptual framework" is the product of both his "inflated ego and the source of the systemic reforms I advocate."[655]

Fearing that the current structure of the OSF would be unmanageable in his absence, Soros allowed the task of reorganization to fall to new management in 2018, which he says are "making good progress." [656]

Soros has the added benefit that his family has been installed in his key spheres of influence, whether it be his second wife Susan Weber at Bard College or his son Alexander Soros at the OSF.

Reflecting on the enemies he's attracted over his lifetime of political influence, Soros remarks "I'm very proud of my enemies. When I look at the list, I feel I must be doing something right. Still, I wish the list would be shorter." He cryptically concludes, "I and my foundations will do our best to shorten it."[657]

In recent years Soros has seemingly been positioning himself to influence for centuries, all from beyond the grave.

All people have to do to stop him is to fight back.

While we haven't seen it yet here in America, Soros has been met with resistance around the globe.

As mentioned earlier, Hungary had led the most aggressive charge in purging its country of Soros' influence, and it's not the only one.

In 2013, before he entered office as Turkey's president, Recep Tayyip Erdoğan accused Soros of supporting protests against him, saying he assigned people the task of "dividing and ruining" nations. When an investigation into the protests was reopened in 2018, Soros' foundation closed its office in Turkey.[658]

The General Prosecutor's Office in Russia banned two branches of the Soros network in 2015. Both were placed on a "stop list" of foreign NGOs whose activities were deemed "undesirable." The office wrote in a statement that "It was found that the activity of the Open Society Foundations and the Open Society Institute Assistance Foundation represents a threat to the foundations of the constitutional system of the Russian Federation and the security of the state."[659]

655   Ibid., page 88.
656   Ibid., page 84.
657   Ibid., page 86.
658   "George Soros's Open Society Foundations to Pull Out of Turkey." *The Guardian*, November 26, 2018. https://www.theguardian.com/business/2018/nov/26/george-soross-open-society-foundation-to-pull-out-of-turkey
659   Ablan, Jennifer. "Russia Bans George Soros Foundation as State Security 'Threat.'" Reuters, November 30, 2015. https://www.reuters.com/article/russia-soros-idUSL1N13P22Y20151130

In 2021, the prosecutor's office announced they'd be banning Bard College as well.[660]

The government of Poland intervened to "stop speculators" when Soros and a group including other billionaires moved to purchase a stake in the nation's second largest radio station before the 2019 parliamentary elections. Poland's antimonopoly watchdog UOKiK ended up blocking the takeover. As is inevitable, Soros' defenders in the media blamed anti-Semitism for the concerns of foreign influence in their media.[661]

Poland has also honored Soros' targets. Poland's president, Andrzej Duda, bestowed Sir Roger Scruton with the Grand Cross of the Order of Merit of the Republic of Poland, the nation's highest award for a non-Pole, for his contributions to Poland's struggle against communism in the 1980s. That came just two months after Scruton was fired by the U.K. government from his position of head of a public housing body after being quoted speaking out against Soros in a British magazine.[662]

In Africa, Kenya's NGOs Co-Ordination Board banned the operations of two NGOs for receiving money from Soros.[663]

Myanmar seized control of the bank accounts of the OSF, and announced it would take legal action against the OSF for allegedly violating restrictions on NGOs.[664]

In India, Delhi's High Court put the OSF on a watch list for funding NGOs and associations not registered under its Foreign Contribution Regulation Act.[665]

Israel's Foreign Ministry issued a statement in 2017 denouncing Soros and backing Hungary's crackdown on him.[666]

In North Macedonia, the Public Revenue Office sent financial inspectors to the OSF after its December 2016 elections. The leader

660 "Russia Bans US NGO Bard College." *American Military News*, June 24, 2021. https://americanmilitarynews. com/2021/06/russia-bans-us-ngo-bard-college/

661 Harper, Jo. "Soros's Polish Media Acquisition Gets Old Dogs Whistling." *Forbes*, February 22, 2019. https://www. forbes.com/sites/joharper/2019/02/22/soros-polish-media-acquisition-gets-old-dogs-whistling/?sh=58d92edd463b

662 "Poland Honors Conservative Philosopher Fired by UK Government Over Soros Rant." *The Times of Israel*, June 6, 2019. https://www.timesofisrael.com/poland-honors-conservative-philosopher-fired-by-uk-government-over-soros-rant/

663 "Two NGOs Banned Over Sh36m From Billionaire Soros." *Business Daily Africa*, November 6, 2017. https:// www.businessdailyafrica.com/bd/economy/two-ngos-banned-over-sh36m-from-billionaire-soros-2176224

664 https://www.irrawaddy.com/news/burma/myanmar-regime-seizes-bank-accounts-soros-open-society-foundation.html

665 "Days Before George Soros Launched Attack Against India, His NGO Open Society Foundations Filed Plea in Delhi Hc Against Modi Government." *OpIndia*, January 30, 2020. https://www.opindia.com/2020/01/george-soros-ngo-open-society-foundations-plea-against-modi-government-watch-list-delhi-hc/

666 Baker, Luke. "Israel Backs Hungary, Says Financier Soros is a Threat." Reuters, July 10, 2017. https://www.reuters. com/article/us-israel-hungary-soros/israel-backs-hungary-says-financier-soros-is-a-threat-idUSKBN19V1J4

of the VMRO-DPMNE political party Nikola Gruevski called for the "desorosoization" of Macedonian civil society, signaling an intense crackdown on groups he has a hand in. That sparked a "Stop Operation Soros" citizens movement.[667]

"I have to admit that the tide has turned against me, but I don't think that I have failed," Soros remarked in 2019.[668]

We'll see about that.

667 "Macedonia Goes After Soros-Funded Civil Society," Monitor: Tracking Civic Space, January 31, 2017. https://monitor.civicus.org/updates/2017/01/31/Maceonia-Soros-funded-civil-society/
668 Martin, Michel and Emma Bowman. "George Soros: Open Societies Are Under Threat." Delmarva Public Media, October 26, 2019. https://www.delmarvapublicradio.net/post/george-soros-open-societies-are-under-threat

Appendix:
Notable Organizations
Funded Directly by
George Soros

Organization	Description
Advancement Project	Created with the objective to "address race and civil rights issues through the legal system and community activism," it strives for a "future where people of color are free," which will be "driven by the genius of ordinary people and their movements."
All of Us or None	Fights for the "formally-and-current-incarcerated" people. Aims to strengthen the voices of those "most affected by mass incarceration" and the so-called "prison industrial complex."
Alliance for Justice	Advocates for a "vibrant democracy that values and protects a just and equitable society" which includes "a government where all voices, regardless of wealth, power, or privilege, are heard and valued."
America Coming Together	Created with the goal of preventing then president George W. Bush from being reelected. Focused on getting out the vote.
America Votes	Works to create "change" at the state level in twenty states. Acts "as a permanent campaign to continually advance progressive causes," including climate change and "improv[ing] election systems and fight[ing] back against efforts to suppress voters."
America's Voice	Established to "win reforms that put 11 million undocumented Americans on a path to full citizenship."

American Bar Association Commission on Immigration Policy	Guides the ABA's "efforts to ensure fair treatment and full due process rights for immigrants, asylum-seekers, and refugees within the United States." Established "projects" in El Paso and San Diego where "indigent immigrants and asylum-seekers" can obtain pro bono immigration legal services.
American Bridge 21st Century	PAC that backs Democratic candidates through "research, video tracking, and rapid response" operations. Serves as an "opposition research hub for the Democratic Party."
American Civil Liberties Union	Works "to defend and preserve the individual rights and liberties guaranteed to every person in this country by the Constitution and laws of the United States." Maintains an emphasis on "achieving full equality for LGBT people, establishing new privacy protections for our digital age of widespread government surveillance, ending mass incarceration, or preserving the right to vote or the right to have an abortion."
American Constitution Society for Law and Policy	Designed to "ensure that fundamental principles of human dignity, individual rights and liberties, genuine equality, and access to justice enjoy their rightful, central place in American law." Members include "law students, lawyers, scholars, judges, policymakers and activists."
American Family Voices	Established to support Al Gore's presidential election and attack President George W. Bush's reelection campaign. Now works to "organiz[e] left-progressive action and funding obscure progressive campaigns."
American Federation of Teachers	Teachers' union "that champions fairness; democracy; economic opportunity; and high-quality public education, health care and public services for our students, their families and our communities." Utilizes "community engagement, organizing, collective bargaining and political activism" to advance its cause.
American Friends Service Committee	Works to "fundamentally transform" the nation and "institutions" so the "world [is] free of violence, inequality, and oppression."

American Immigration Council	Provides legal resources for illegal aliens and promotes "the rights of immigrants in the legal system, such as right to counsel, immigration courts, federal courts, and jurisdictions." Seeks to influence public discussions surrounding illegal immigration by offering "explainers" about programs such as "Deferred Action for Childhood Arrivals (DACA), Deferred Action for Parents of U.S. Citizens and Lawful Permanent Residents (DAPA), the Child Status Protection Act, adjustment of status, waivers and relief from deportation, and employment authorization."
American Independent News Network	Originally launched as a nonprofit news organization known as the Center for Independent Media. Goal was to provide investigative journalism for Minnesota, Colorado, and eventually, Washington, D.C.
American Institute for Social Justice	Provides support to local community organization groups, including "leadership and staff training, technical assistance, research, and project support." Most known for Association of Community Organizations for Reform Now (ACORN), "one of the largest community organizing networks."
American Library Association	Utilizes a "social justice framework" when "provide[ing] leadership for the development, promotion and improvement of library and information services and the profession of librarianship in order to enhance learning and ensure access to information for all." Places an emphasis on "equity, diversity, and inclusion."
The American Prospect	Progressive magazine "devoted to promoting informed discussion on public policy from a progressive perspective." Provides "policy alternatives" while "dispel[ing] myths, challeng[ing] conventional wisdom, and expand[ing] the dialogue
Amnesty International	International NGO aimed at "fight[ing] abuses of human rights worldwide" by "chang[ing] oppressive laws."

Applied Research Center	Research conducted at Florida International University. Emphasis on environment, energy, and information technology that "allows for free-flowing exchange of ideas between the University's applied researchers, academia, government, private sector and industry partners."
Arab American Institute	Promotes "the issues and interest of Arab-Americans nationwide," including the idea "that the US should enhance its ties with Arab countries in all fields: cultural, educational, diplomatic, economic, and security." Also advocates for a Palestinian state.
Aspen Institute	Advocates for "a free, just, and equitable society." Utilizes seminars and conferences "to provoke, further and improve actions taken in the real world."
Association of Community Organizations for Reform Now	Coalition of organizations that "advocated for low- and moderate-income families." Emphasized a need for "neighborhood safety, voter registration, health care, [and] affordable house.'
Ballot Initiative Strategy Center	Encourages Americans to get out the vote by "leverage[ing] ballot measures across the United States" as a means of moving toward "society racial equity."
Bill of Rights Defense Committee	Aims to protect civil rights and liberties by litigating "overbroad national security and counter-terrorism policies."
Bend the Arc: A Jewish Partnership for Justice	Jewish organization advocating against "racial injustice or economic inequality." Aims to "shape the Jewish social movement."
Black Alliance for Just Immigration	Works to "end the racism, criminalization, and economic disenfranchisement of Black immigrants, refugees, and African American communities" in New York, Oakland, Atlanta, Minneapolis, Miami, Boston, and Washington, D.C.
Blueprint North Carolina	Lobbies to address "racial injustice," closing the wealth gap, and "the privatization of public resources for private financial gain" in North Carolina.

Brennan Center for Justice	Fights to "strengthen democracy" by "modernizing American elections," "ensur[ing] a fair and accurate census," and "eliminat[ing] the Electoral College."
Brookings Institution	Provides politicians with "quality research, policy recommendations, and analysis on a full range of public policy issues."
Campaign for America's Future	Bills itself as a "strategy center for the progressive movement" and encourages Democrats to pursue progressive legislation.
Campaign for Better Health Care	Illinois-based organization with the goal of "provid[ing] a central statewide grassroots health care organization in support of the Affordable Care Act."
Campaign for Youth Justice	Aims to "end the practice of prosecuting, sentencing and incarcerating youth (under 18) in the adult criminal justice system" and instead offer "research-based developmentally appropriate rehabilitative programs and services" for those who would otherwise be tried in "the adult criminal justice system."
Campus Progress	Serves as the "youth engagement arm of the Center for American Progress" with the goal of pushing "bold, progressive ideas" and "strong leadership and concerted action" that would "change the country."
Casa De Maryland	Maryland-based "Latino and immigration advocacy-and-assistance organization" that provides their constituents with "health assistance, medical interpretations, English classes, financial literacy classes, vocational training, social services, leadership development, legal services, and employment placement for low-income families" for immigrants predominantly of Latino descent. Also provides legal services for legal and illegal immigrants.
Catalist	Progressive database used for "civic engagement purposes," such as "build[ing] membership, target[ing] persuasive messaging, engag[ing] activists, driv[ing] an issue agenda, and register[ing] or mobiliz[ing] voters."

Catholics for Choice	Aims to "dismantle religiously-based obstructions to abortion care, contraceptive access and comprehensive health care" and challenge the "vocal, well-financed and powerful Roman Catholic hierarchy, which presents itself as the sole moral arbiter on matters where sexuality and reproduction intersect with religion and faith."
Catholics in Alliance for the Common Good	Advocates for the Catholic viewpoint that "promotes the necessary conditions for a culture of life that reverences the dignity of the human person over greed, materialism and the politics of division."
Center for American Progress	Fights to "change the country" with "bold, progressive ideas, as well as strong leadership and concerted action." Aims to change the public dialogue on key issues by "challeng[ing] the media to cover the issues that truly matter" and "aggressively" perusing "extensive communications and outreach effort[s]."
Center for Community Change	Advocates for "low-income people," including "people of color, immigrants, and women" to transform the country so "our economy" is "just, equitable, and inclusive." Places a large emphasis on "fairness in the distribution of wealth and on checking corporate power."
Center for Constitutional Rights	Pushes for "social justice" by focusing on "civil liberties and human rights litigation and activism." Utilizes the judiciary "to promote its activists' work."
Center for Economic and Policy Research	Advocates for economic policies like a two-percent tax increase for Social Security, a higher minimum wage, and the Affordable Care Act.
Center for International Policy	Pushes the idea that the planet's "biggest threats" include "corruption, inequality and climate change." Advocates for ""cooperation, transparency and accountability in global relations."
Center for Reproductive Rights	Promotes abortion and "reproductive rights" as a "fundamental right" protected by the law.

Center for Responsible Lending	Fights for "those who may be marginalized or underserved by the existing financial marketplace" by advocating for "a fair, inclusive financial marketplace that creates opportunities for all credit-worthy borrowers, regardless of their income." Its emphasis is on women, minorities, rural Americans and "low-wealth families and communities."
Center for Social Inclusion	Aims to "advance racial equity" and help "communities most impacted by structural racism." Jointed The Center for Racial Justice Innovation to form the organization Race Forward.
Center on Budget and Policy Priorities	Analyzes state and federal budgets to "reduce poverty and inequality and to restore fiscal responsibility in equitable and effective ways" as a means of "help[ing] low-income people."
Center on Wisconsin Strategy	Located at the University of Wisconsin-Madison. Promotes "a more equitable, sustainable, and democratic society" by advocating for "decent wages," "environmental protections," and a "sustainable economy."
Citizens for Responsibility and Ethics in Washington	Aims to "expose ethics violations and corruption by government officials and institutions and to reduce the role of money in politics." Utilizes Freedom of Information Act requests and congressional ethics complaints as part of its watchdog function.
Coalition for an International Criminal Court	Lobbied for an International Criminal Court, where "war crimes, crimes against humanity, and genocide" are prosecuted. Aims to create a "more peaceful world" by providing justice for "grave crimes."
Color of Change	Lobbies businesses and corporations to "create a more humane and less hostile world for Black people in America." Works to "end practices and systems that unfairly hold Black people back" and instead work on "solutions" that move Black people forward.
Common Cause	Promotes a "innovative, pragmatic, and comprehensive pro-democracy agenda" that includes government accountability and "equal rights" and "opportunity" for all Americans.

Constitution Project	Bipartisan group that aims to protect civil liberties and roll back the "expansive presidential authority" following September 11.
Defenders of Wildlife Action Fund	Promotes "innovative solutions" and "conservative efforts" to protect wildlife and their habitats.
Democracy Alliance	Raises funds from Democratic donors "to promote progressive ideas, impact media coverage, develop new leadership, create sophisticated civic engagement strategies, and engage young people and communities of color."
Democracy 21	Advocates for campaign-finance reform, specifically "a new public financing system for presidential and congressional races to empower citizens by providing multiple public funds to match their small contributions." Its goal is to eliminate "secret money" in all federal elections.
Democracy Now!	Hour-long cable news show that "combines news reporting, interviews, investigative journalism and political commentary, with a focus on peace activism linked to environmental justice and social justice." Appears on taxpayer-funded networks, like NPR, PBS, and college radio stations.
Demos	Aims for a "a democracy and economy rooted in racial equity." Utilizes "policy research," "litigation," and "partnerships with grassroots organizations" to advance its cause.
Drum Major Institute for Public Policy	Looks to "identify peaceful solutions to the triple evils of racism, poverty and violence" by carrying out Dr. Martin Luther King Jr.'s "work and vision of radical nonviolence."
Earthjustice	Pursues environmental litigation "to combat climate change" as a means of "protect[ing] people's health...preserv[ing] magnificent places and wildlife...[and] advance clean energy."
Economic Policy Institute	Advocates for the economic needs of "low- and middle-income workers" through research and reports focused on "the economic impact of policies and proposals." Places a high emphasis on the "pro-union viewpoint on public policy issues."

Electronic Privacy Information Center	Fights to "protect privacy, freedom of expression, and democratic values" as well as "consumer privacy" on the internet. Aims to influence the "national debate over the future of privacy."
Ella Baker Center for Human Rights	Organizes low-income black and brown people to fight against "prisons, policing, and punishment-based approaches" and instead "shift resources away from prisons and punishment" to "public safety" nets including "having a living wage job, healthy food, and affordable childcare, health care, and housing."
EMILY's List	PAC dedicated to "elect[ing] Democratic female candidates in favor of abortion rights to office."
Energy Action Coalition	Youth organization fighting "to mitigate climate change and create a just, clean energy future and resilient, thriving communities for all."
Equal Justice USA	Works to make changes in the criminal justice system, including a "campaign to end the death penalty, an advocacy network for trauma victims, and a program to secure expanded victim services like training and funding for victims' rights groups." Focuses on working with "evangelical voters to gain support for the death penalty's elimination on religious and moral grounds."
Fair Immigration Reform Movement	Advocates for immigration reforms including "full citizenship benefits" for illegal aliens and "community-based alternatives" to detaining those in the United States illegally.
Faithful America	Utilizes "rapid-response digital campaigns" to "challenge" the "twisted definition of religious freedom" that "the religious right" uses "to serve a hateful political agenda" of "Christian nationalism and white supremacy." Promotes "a more free and just society."
Families USA	Aims to achieve "high-quality, affordable health care and improved health for all" and "played a leading role on virtually every major piece of health care legislation," including Obamacare, Children's Health Insurance Program, Medicaid expansion, and the Medicare Part D plan.

Feminist Majority	Promotes "women's equality, reproductive health, and non-violence" while identifying and training young women to "encourage future leadership for the feminist movement in the United States." Lobbies for issues like the Equal Rights Amendment, appealing the Hyde Amendment, and "safe, effective, affordable, and accessible contraception."
Four Freedoms Fund	Focuses on "immigrant rights" and working on "immigration reform, civic engagement, immigrant integration and protection of civil liberties and human rights" on the "local, state and national level."
Free Exchange on Campus	Coalition of a dozen organizations working to "protect the free exchange of speech and ideas on campus" without "political or ideological interference." Takes aim at particular conservative organizations, including the David Horowitz Freedom Center.
Free Press	Works to change media landscape to "transform society" to "a just society," which includes "equitable access to technology, diverse and independent ownership of media platforms" and "saving Net Neutrality, achieving affordable internet access for all, uplifting the voices of people of color in the media, challenging old and new media gatekeepers to serve the public interest, ending unwarranted surveillance, defending press freedom and reimagining local journalism."
Funding Exchange	Former "national network of social justice foundations" made up of wealthy advocates that wanted to "involv[e] community activists in grantmaking decisions." Prioritized providing "seed" money to "grassroots groups and social movements that other philanthropies considered too new, untested, or controversial." Dissolved following the 2018 election.

Gamaliel Foundation	International faith-based organization located in the United States, South Africa, and the U.K. that "draws on Biblical scripture, Christ's life and teaching, the Torah, the Qu'ran, Catholic social teaching, the founding principles of American democracy, the U.S. civil rights movement, and other sources" to "create equal opportunity, shared abundance, and stronger, more prosperous communities." Focuses on "social justice campaigns" with an emphasis on immigration rights, health care, jobs, education, transportation, and economic development.
Gisha: Center for the Legal Protection of Freedom of Movement	Israeli organization dedicated to "protect[ing] the freedom of movement of Palestinians, especially Gaza residents." Advocates for "awareness and sensitivity for human rights in the occupied Palestinian territories" through public relations efforts while also "represent[ing] individuals and organisations in Israeli administrative proceedings and courts."
Global Centre for the Responsibility to Protect	Works to "halt the mass atrocity crimes of genocide, war crimes, ethnic cleansing and crimes against humanity" and utilizes the United Nations' Responsibility to Protect campaign.
Global Exchange	Advocates for "social, economic and environmental justice around the world" with an emphasis on the need to "transform the global economy from profit-centered to people-centered, from currency to community."
Grantmakers Without Borders	Provides international grants to "private foundations, grantmaking public charities, individual donors with a significant commitment to philanthropy, and philanthropic support organizations" that are focused on "social justice and environmental sustainability."
Green for All	Fights for "solutions to poverty and pollution" as a means of providing better jobs and health to "low-income families and people of color."
Health Care for America Now	Originally started to support the passage of Obamacare. Now it focuses on "defending the law from opposition attacks and advocating for the law before Congress and state regulatory agencies."

Human Rights Campaign	Advocates for pro-LGBTQ legislation where "lesbian, gay, bisexual, transgender and queer people are ensured equality and embraced as full members of society at home, at work and in every community." Most known for advancing "same-sex marriage, anti-discrimination and hate crime legislation, and HIV/AIDS advocacy."
Human Rights First	Promotes "human rights" as a "vital national interest." Advocates for reforms, including closing Guantanamo Bay, repealing President Trump's Muslim ban, and releasing illegal aliens from detention facilities.
Human Rights Watch	Exposes "abuses" taking place around the world and lobbies "governments, armed groups and businesses" to "change or enforce their laws, policies and practices."
Immigrant Defense Project	Advocates for ending the "mass criminalization, detention and deportation" of illegal aliens.
Immigrant Legal Resource Center	Group of attorneys working "to improve immigration law and policy, expand the capacity of legal service providers, and advance immigrant rights" through media relations and "civic engagement."
Immigration Workers Citizenship Project	Encourages immigrants to go through the naturalization process by "providing free naturalization services."
Immigration Advocates Network	Provides pro bono legal immigration services "to bridge the digital divide, launch new campaigns, and bring the tools of justice to hard to reach communities."
Immigration Policy Center	Works to change Americans' perceptions and actions toward immigrants and the immigration system through "cutting-edge lawsuits that hold the government accountable for unlawful conduct and restrictive interpretations and implementation of the law."
Independent Media Center	Website used for journalists and media organizations to directly publish "non-corporate coverage" of events.
Institute for America's Future	Former progressive news site that provided "news, opinion and policy analysis."

Institute for New Economic Thinking	Works to "repair" a so-called "broken economy" while "creat[ing] a more equal, prosperous, and just society." Promotes "new economic thinking" by finding "support" from "influencers, policymakers, and the engaged public."
Institute for Policy Studies	"Multi-issue think tank" whose "policy and research" has been utilized with the goal of "building a more equitable, ecologically sustainable, and peaceful society."
Institute for Public Accuracy	Conducts research and media relations for progressive organizations so "voices [that] are commonly excluded or drowned out by government or corporate-backed institutions" are heard.
Institute for Women's Policy Research	Works to remove "barriers" and create "economic equity for all women." Places an emphasis on eliminated the "gender gap."
International Crisis Group	Aims to "prevent wars and shape policies that will build a more peaceful world." Utilizes "expert field research, analysis and engagement with policymakers across the world" to advance its cause.
J Street	Advocates for a "two-state solution to the Israeli-Palestinian conflict is essential to Israel's survival as the national home of the Jewish people and as a vibrant democracy." Believes Israel is the "Jewish homeland" and that Palestinians have "the right" to establish "a sovereign state of their own."
Jewish Funds for Justice	Claims to be the "broad foundation of a Jewish social change movement" based on "justice and equality for all." Later merged with Jewish Funds for Justice to become Bend the Arc.
Justice at Stake	Former group that "advocated for an end to judicial elections, and for stricter regulations regarding campaign finance for state-level judicial races" with the goal of "help[ing] Americans keep courts fair and impartial."
LatinoJustice PRLDEF	Challenges laws "to secure transformative, equitable and accessible justice" with the hope of "changing discriminatory practices via advocacy and litigation."

Lawyers Committee for Civil Rights Under Law	Works to challenge the "inequalities confronting African Americans and other racial and ethnic minorities" through litigation.
Leadership Conference on Civil and Human Rights	Coalition of two hundred human and civil rights organizations that advocate for a "more open and just society" through lobbying and "legislative advocacy."
League of United Latin American Citizens	Utilizes "community-based programs" to push for "the economic condition, educational attainment, political influence, housing, health and civil rights of Hispanic Americans."
League of Women Voters	Aims to "defend democracy" while "empowering voters." Focuses on "registering voters, providing voter information, and advocating for voting rights" and pushing various progressive viewpoints, like "abortion rights" and "universal health care."
League of Young Voters	Former subset of the League of Women Voters aimed at voters ages eighteen to thirty-four. Originally established to prevent President George W. Bush's reelection.
Machsom Watch	Israeli women that "monitor and document the conduct of soldiers and policemen at checkpoints in the West Bank" while helping "Palestinians crossing through [Israeli Defense Forces] checkpoints." Advocates for "Palestinians' freedom of movement within the occupied territories."
MADRE	Works to "address issues of economic and environmental justice, women's health and gender-based, and peace building" at the "international, regional, national, and local levels."
Malcolm X Grassroots Movement	Aims to "defend the human rights" of "Afrikans" while working to undo the "collective institutions of white-supremacy, patriarchy and capitalism" that have harmed "Afrikans." Advocates for reparations, as well as the release of political prisoners and prisoners of war.
Massachusetts Immigrant and Refugee Advocacy Coalition	Coalition of "multi-ethnic" organizations that advocates for "the rights and integration of immigrants and refugees." Provides "information and policy analysis for policy-makers, advocates, immigrant communities and the media" on immigration-related issues.

Media Fund	Funding for "independent media" that "abide[s] by the National Union of Journalists' code of conduct, are not reliant on corporate advertising, the state or billionaires for funding and are vetted and agreed upon democratically."
Media Matters for America	Serves as a "media watchdog for scrutinizing right-leaning media outlets" that was founded in response to the conservative watchdog organization Media Research Center.
Mercy Corps	Aims to "eliminate suffering, poverty and oppression" by "connect[ing] people to the resources and opportunities they need to build strong, stable livelihoods that can withstand future challenges."
Mexican American Legal Defense and Education Fund	Latino civil rights organization that takes up "legal-aid cases" surrounding education and immigration.
Midwest Academy	Works with progressive organizations to train activists as part of a commitment "to advancing the struggle for social, economic, and racial justice."
Migration Policy Institute	Offers "pragmatic and thoughtful responses" to "large-scale migration." Also "provides analysis, development, and evaluation of migration and refugee policies at local, national, and international levels."
Missourians Organizing for Reform and Empowerment	Works to "challenge capitalism and corporate power in St. Louis" on behalf of "low- to moderate-income people." Aims to "transform the current system" in hopes of a "more just, sustainable world."
MoveOn	Pushes for "social justice and political progress" through "digital organizing." Organizers "were the first" to utilize the internet to campaign by conducting "virtual phone banks, to crowdsource TV ad production, and to take online organizing offline, using the internet to mobilize activists to knock on doors and attend events."

Ms. Foundation for Women	Advocates for issues impacting women, predominantly "women of color and low-income women who are living in poverty." Aims to change "national and statewide policy change[s]" relating to "Economic Justice, Reproductive Justice and Safety."
Muslim Advocates	Works to ensure Muslim Americans receive "expert representation in the courts, the policy making process, and in the public dialogue" so all are "free from discrimination."
NARAL	Aims to expand "reproductive freedom," which includes "fighting for access to abortion care, birth control, paid parental leave, and protections from pregnancy discrimination."
NAACP	Fights for "civil rights and social justice" and "work[s] to ensure the political, educational, social, and economic equality of rights of all persons and to eliminate racial hatred and racial discrimination."
The Nation Institute	Advocates for an "independent press" while "advancing social justice and civil rights." Utilizes fellowships at *The Nation* magazine to "support groundbreaking investigative journalism."
National Abortion Federation	Union of abortionists that work to "unite, represent, serve, and support abortion providers in delivering patient-centered, evidence-based care." Members include Planned Parenthood affiliates, as well as private and nonprofit clinics, physicians' offices and hospitals.
National Coalition to Abolish the Death Penalty	Aims to end the death penalty in the United States and, ultimately, the world.
National Committee on Responsive Philanthropy	Progressive watchdog group that "monitors charitable spending in the United States." Encourages "foundations to do more for those who are marginalized, underserved and disenfranchised."
National Committee for Voting Integrity	Works to achieve elections that are "fair, reliable, secure, accessible, transparent, accurate, [and] accountable" and have the ability to be audited.

National Council for Research on Women	Produces "feminist research" and looks at the issues of "Identity, Economic Well-Being and Thriving Environments" through a "gender lens."
National Council of La Raza	Advocates for immigration reform, which includes a "path to citizenship for illegal immigrations, and reduced deportations." Partners with other organizations to help with "civic engagement, civil rights and immigration, education, workforce and the economy, health, and housing." Changed its name to UnidosUS.
National Council of Women's Organizations	Coalition of hundreds of women's organizations that "work for women's equal participation in the economic, social and political life of our country and the world."
National Immigration Forum	Pro-immigrant group that "advocates for more immigration, more refugees and more funding to foreign nations."
National Immigration Law Center	Advocates "for racial, economic and social justice for low-income immigrant" through litigation and advocacy.
National Lawyers Guild	Considers itself America's "oldest and largest progressive bar association" that works to change "the structure of our political and economic system. Places an emphasis on "valuing human rights and the rights of ecosystems over property interests."
National Organization for Women	Works to advance "feminist ideals" so a "societal change" will take place. Aims to "eliminate discrimination, and achieve and protect the equal rights of all women and girls in all aspects of social, political, and economic life."
National Partnership for Women and Families	Fights for "equality for all women" which includes "standing strong for women's health, reproductive rights and economic justice." Currently focused on "paid family and medical leave" as well as "equal pay" and "access to contraception and abortion care" while removing "the stigma associated with abortion."

National Priorities Project	Breaks down federal budget and spending so "ordinary folks" understand how "fiscal issues" impact every American. Places an emphasis on "taxes, the national debt, and government transparency," and "spending for the military, education, health care, and other social programs."
National Security Archive Fund	Utilizes Freedom of Information Act (FOIA) requests to have government documents declassified as a means of "expanding public access to government information, global advocate of open government, and indexer and publisher of former secrets."
National Women's Law Center	Aims to achieve "gender justice" in every branch of government. Places an emphasis on "childcare and early learning, education and Title IX, health care and reproductive rights, courts and judges, LGBTQ equality, military, poverty and economic security, racial and ethnic justice, tax and budget, and workplace justice."
Natural Resources Defense Council	Works to "protect the planet's wildlife and wild places and to ensure a safe and healthy environment for all living things." Utilizes "lawyers, scientists, and policy experts" to help write environmental legislation and laws.
New America Foundation	Aims to drive public policy utilizing research and technology. Utilizes "expertise in researching, reporting and analysis with new areas of coding, data science, and human-centered design" to push for "a society that promotes economic opportunity for all."
NewsCorpWatch	Media Matters project aimed at negatively portraying "News Corporation, the parent company of Fox News."
Pacifica Foundation	Conglomerate of progressive radio networks with the goal of providing public information that is "not commonly brought together in the same medium."
Peace and Security Funders Group	Works to bring together funders that seek to "build a more peaceful, just, and equitable world." Emphasizes "philanthropy that's focused on peace and security issues."

Peace Development Fund	Advocates for "social justice and peace" though private funding. Places an emphasis on "presence of equitable relationships among people, nations and the environment."
People for the American Way	Vows to "fight right-wing extremism" while implementing an equitable and justice society. Known for its "Right Wing Watch" website that features people opposing conservative takes on a number of social issues.
People Improving Communities Through Organizing	Utilizes "people of faith" to push a progressive agenda, including "universal health care, public education, affordable housing, and immigration reform."
Physicians for Social Responsibility	Health care professionals that "advocate for climate solutions and a nuclear weapons-free world." Advances its cause by producing literature about "the threats of nuclear proliferation, climate change, and environmental toxins" and testifying in front of Congress on environmental issues.
Ploughshares Fund	Aims to "prevent the spread and use of nuclear weapons, and to prevent conflicts that could lead to their use." Private funders pool resources together to provide grants to advance their cause.
Presidential Climate Action Project	Presses the president to take executive action on climate change without needing approval from Congress with the goal of "produc[ing] policy and program recommendations that are sufficiently bold to expedite America's transition to a clean energy economy, while leading the international effort to reach an agreement on reducing greenhouse gas emission."
Prison Moratorium Project	Works to eliminate "all prisons," which would result in the "freeing [of] all inmates." Advocates for investments in health care, education, jobs, and housing as a means of preventing crime.

Progressive Change Campaign Committee	Places an emphasis on "economic populist priorities like expanding Social Security, Medicare For All, a Green New Deal, student debt cancellation, and Wall Street reform." Pushes those ideas through grassroots efforts at the "local, state and federal levels," including funding "for progressive candidates and committees."
Progressive States Network	Advocates for progressive policies and changes on the state level. Utilizes research to inform state legislators on a number of issues, including economic development, education, and health and medicine.
Project Vote	Aims to diversify the American electorate to they "accurately represent the diversity of this nation's citizenry." Fights "list maintenance procedures" so that "eligible voters" are not removed from the rolls.
ProPublica	Media outlet that serves as watchdog with the goal of "expos[ing] abuses of power and betrayals of the public trust by government, business, and other institutions." Utilizes investigative journalism to advance its goal.
Proteus Fund	Provides funding to "foundations, advocates and individual donors" that work "to advance democracy, human rights and peace."
Psychologists for Social Responsibility	Utilizes "psychological knowledge, research, and practice" to "advance peace and social justice." Places an emphasis on "address[ing] economic, racial, and gender-based injustices and other forms of oppression."
Public Citizen	Advocates for "corporate responsibility and strong government regulation," especially relating to transportation, health care, and nuclear power by lobbying Congress, providing research on key issues and pursuing litigation against the government.
Public Justice Center	Originally advocated for an "anti-poverty and anti-discrimination" society, but has since focused on "advancing race equity and anti-racism" through the legal system.
Res Publica Foundation	Magazine publication focused on the "French model of republicanism and on the dialogue between civilizations and nations in the age of globalization."

Roosevelt Institute	Works to change the "imbalance between private actors and the public" by "transforming corporations, restructuring markets, reviving democratic institutions, and reimagining the role of government."
Sentencing Project	Works to promote "racial, ethic, economic, and gender justice" to "minimize" the number of Americans that are incarcerated.
Sojourners	Monthly magazine that looks at society and public policy issues through a Christian social justice lens.
Southern Poverty Law Center	Utilizes "civil rights and public interest legislation" to challenge "white supremacy groups" in court. Known for its "classification and listings of hate groups…and extremists."
State Voices	Coalition of state groups that work to "break down barriers to civic participation and to bring underrepresented and marginalized populations——and their issues——to the center of public discourse." Shares voting data and voter behavior between state organizations.
Think Progress	Former progressive news site that focused on "original reporting." It was a project of the Center for American Progress Action Fund.
Thunder Road Group	Political consulting group that "combines the roles of strategic planning, polling, opposition research, covert operations, and public relations."
Tides Foundation and Tides Center	Aims to create "shared prosperity and social justice" by providing "nonprofits and social enterprises with affordable workspace and administrative services, supporting dynamic communities."
U.S. Public Interest Research Group	Group of nonprofit organizations in the United States and Canada "that employ grassroots organizing and direct advocacy" on consumer rights issues.
Universal Health Care Action Network	Advocated for universal health care from 1992 until February 2021.
Urban Institute	Provides lawmakers with research to "expand opportunities for all, reduce hardship among the most vulnerable, and strengthen the effectiveness of the public sector."

USAction	Former coalition of advocacy groups that pushed the progressive agenda. Merged with TrueMajorityACTION in 2007.
Voter Participation Center	Focuses on registering voters that it claims make up "The New American Majority," including "young people, people of color, and unmarried women."
Voto Latino	Works to "creat[e] a more robust and inclusive democracy" by "educating and empowering a new generation of Latinx voters." Also encourages political involvement through get out the vote campaigns.
We Are America Alliance	Coalition of pro-immigrant organizations dedicated to "comprehensive immigration reform and immigrations' civic participation." Works to "coordinate, collaborate, and gain technical assistance and economies of scale…to build political power in their regions."
Working Families Party	Alternative third party that occasionally utilizes the Democratic Party primaries to advance its candidates. Sometimes "referred to as the Tea Party of the Left."
World Organization Against Torture	Aims to end "arbitrary detention, torture, summary and extrajudicial executions, forced disappearances and other forms of violence" with "the goal of eradicating torture and fostering respect of human rights for all."
Young Women's Christian Association	Advocates for "eliminat[ing] racism, empower[ing] women, stand[ing] up for social justice, help[ing] families, and strengthen[ing] communities."

The Open Society University Network

FOUNDING INSTITUTIONS

- Bard College (United States)
- Central European University (Austria)

COLLEGES AND UNIVERSITIES

- Al-Quds University/Al-Quds Bard College of Arts and Sciences (Palestine)
- American University of Beirut (Lebanon)
- American University in Bulgaria
- American University of Central Asia (Kyrgyzstan)
- Arizona State University (United States)
- Ashesi University (Ghana)
- Bard College at Simon's Rock (United States)
- Bard College Berlin (Germany)
- Bard Early Colleges (United States)
- Birkbeck: University of London (United Kingdom)
- Bocconi University (Italy)
- BRAC University (Bangladesh)
- European Humanities University (Lithuania)
- European University Institute (Florence)
- Graduate Institute of International and Development Studies (Geneva)
- Hertie School (Berlin)

- London School of Economics (United Kingdom)
- National Sun Yat-sen University (Taiwan)
- National University of Political Studies and Public Administration (Romania)
- Sciences Po in Paris (France)
- SOAS University of London (United Kingdom)
- Tuskegee University (United States)
- Universidad de los Andes (Colombia)
- University of the Witwatersrand (South Africa)

RESEARCH AND EDUCATIONAL INSTITUTIONS

- Bard Prison Initiative (United States)
- Black Mountains College (United Kingdom)
- Carnegie Council for Ethics in International Affairs (United States)
- Chatham House (United Kingdom)
- Haitian Education and Leadership Program (Haiti)
- Institute for New Economic Thinking (United States and United Kingdom)
- Institute for Philosophy and Social Theory, University of Belgrade (Serbia)
- Institut für die Wissenschaften vom Menschen (Austria)
- Parami Institute (Myanmar)
- Picker Center for Executive Education, Columbia University (United States)
- Princeton Global History Lab (United States)
- Rift Valley Institute (Kenya)
- The Talloires Network of Engaged Universities (United States)
- University of California, Berkeley Human Rights Center (United States)
- University of Connecticut Human Rights Institute (United States)

About the Author

Photo by Daniel Perrucci

Matt Palumbo is the author of *Dumb and Dumber: How Cuomo and de Blasio Ruined New York*, *Debunk This!: Shattering Liberal Lies*, and *Spygate*.